WITHDRAWN

PHOENIX

PHOENIX

BRADFORD LUCKINGHAM

THE HISTORY OF A
SOUTHWESTERN METROPOLIS

THE UNIVERSITY OF ARIZONA PRESS
TUCSON

THE UNIVERSITY OF ARIZONA PRESS

This book was set in 9.5/12 Linotron 202 Century Schoolbook.
Manufactured in the United States of America

93   92   91   90   89   5   4   3   2   1

♾ This book is printed on acid-free, archival-quality paper.

Library of Congress Cataloging-in-Publication Data

Luckingham, Bradford.
    Phoenix : the history of a southwestern metropolis / Bradford
  Luckingham.
        p.   cm.
    Bibliography: p.
    Includes index.
    Cloth ISBN 0-8165-1087-3 (alk. paper)
    Paper ISBN 0-8165-1116-0 (alk. paper)
    1. Phoenix (Ariz.)–History.   2. Phoenix (Ariz.)–Politics and
government.   3. Phoenix (Ariz.)–Economic conditions.   I. Title.
F819.P57L83   1989
979.1′73–dc 19   88-26171
                                                          CIP

TO BARBARA

CONTENTS

ILLUSTRATIONS AND TABLES

Maps, Charts, and Photographs

Tables

PHOENIX

1 PHOENIX AND THE URBAN EXPERIENCE

Arizona is one of the most urban states in the nation. Despite its image as a state of farms, ranches, and isolated mines, nearly 80 percent of its population lived in its two major metropolitan areas, Phoenix and Tucson, by the 1980s. The booming Phoenix metroplex, with nearly 60 percent of Arizona's population, represented the reality of the twentieth-century American West. A false image held by too many outsiders pictured Phoenix as "an overgrown, old-age home or a western town with board sidewalks and dirt streets," but it was the bustling, prosperous ninth largest city in the nation by the 1980s.

Phoenix also illustrated the "oasis civilization" in the American West that has dominated much of the history of the trans-Mississippi area since the nineteenth century. An oasis or urban civilization, led by Phoenix, prevailed in the Southwest—a region defined as including Arizona, New Mexico, and the western projection of Texas. The metropolitan hubs of Phoenix, Tucson, Albuquerque, and El Paso represented the urban reality, not the rural image, of the region. The centers of life in a land of wide-open spaces, especially since World War II, they helped transform the old Southwest into the new Southwest, one of the fastest-growing regions in the nation.[1]

As on other urban frontiers, the founders of Phoenix were developers and boosters. The desert did not deter them as they went about irrigating their land and building their town. The name of the town, Phoenix, represented life rising anew from the remains of the past. The Hohokam Indians may have disappeared from the Salt River Valley in central Arizona by 1400, but the new pioneers of the 1860s were determined to create a future in the area. They expanded the Hohokam irrigation system and contributed to the blooming of the desert and the rise of Phoenix. Nearly two hundred miles of canals opened up thousands of acres of arable land to cultivation. An adequate water supply, a long growing season, and plenty of sunshine, combined with hard work, served to increase production, which in turn created the need for new markets and the desire for a railroad connection to the outside. As one promoter declared in 1872, "When the railroad steams through our country, the Salt River Valley will be the garden of the Pacific Slope, and Phoenix the most important inland town." He also predicted the central Arizona oasis would become the capital of the territory.[2]

The importance of the coming of the railroads to Phoenix and the Southwest cannot be overestimated. As on other frontiers, railroads encouraged urbanization. Leaders in Phoenix, as elsewhere, aware of the close relationship between transportation and urban growth, supported the presence of railroads. With the arrival of the Maricopa and Phoenix in 1887 and the Santa Fe, Prescott, and Phoenix in 1895, the city enjoyed the use of two transcontinental outlets. The railroad outlets afforded more access to national markets and prompted the movement of more people and capital from other regions.

In the meantime, the growing importance of Phoenix was recognized by the legislature when it removed the capital from Prescott to the central Arizona hub in 1889. The coming of the railroad and the acquisition of the capital, along with agricultural and commercial progress, pleased local promoters and outside investors, and they boosted Phoenix as "the future metropolis of the territory." Like citizens of other urban frontiers, Phoenicians worked diligently to secure the capital for their city, realizing that it would bring additional power, prestige, and prosperity. Most important, as the county seat and the territorial capital, Phoenix exuded an aura of stability and permanence that boosters hoped would attract more residents and businesses.[3]

Railroad contact with the outside world, including transcontinental routes operated by the Southern Pacific and the Atchison, Topeka and Santa Fe railroads, provided the Arizona capital with links to the national economy and helped it expand as a trade and distribution center for a productive hinterland of farming, ranching, and mining communities. Not only did it serve as a vital business center, a role common to urban centers in other regions; it also served as a good place to live. Like other towns of the West, Phoenix experienced the "business of sin," but by the turn of the century it had creditably survived its youth and had achieved recognition as a center of civilization in the region. Boosters worked hard to develop Phoenix into a desirable place for those looking for amenities as well as opportunities. The amenities included the climate, and the sun culture was promoted endlessly. Phoenix became a haven for health seekers as well as a prime location for tourist resorts; it became known for its hospitals as well as its hotels.

In this respect, it resembled Los Angeles. Phoenix, in fact, stands as another example of the impact of amenities on regional growth. Following the arrival of the railroad, doctors around the country started sending patients to the urban Southwest for the winter. Phoenix became an "ideal spot" for the health seeker and the seasonal visitor. Observers noted the benefits of "perpetual sunshine"; many of those who came to the desert center for their health recovered sufficiently to lead productive lives, and some made outstanding contributions to the development of the region. Affluent, healthy tourists also were given every encouragement to visit the city, and they had the services of the Hotel Adams and other modern hotels to meet their needs.[4]

Opportunities in the Southwest included farming, ranching, and mining, but many people came to the region to share in the progress of growing communities. In Phoenix those who found success became effective leaders and boosters of the desert hub. As members of the local business and civic elite who were willing to combine private interests with community interests, they often directed, with growth and development in mind, the economic, political, and cultural lives of Phoenix. Dwight B. Heard and other developers illustrated the indispensable role of the human element in urban manifest destiny. He and his wife, Maie, benefited the growing city in many ways and gained in many ways from it.[5]

Local leaders often led the way in the struggle to gain advantages useful to regional as well as urban development. In the urban Southwest, however, unusual problems confronted boosters. Most important, progress resulting from growth was doomed unless they solved the water problem. Following the severe drought in the late 1890s, Phoenix leaders and central Arizona farming interests decided that a water storage system was the answer to the area's problem. Joining together, they formed the Salt River Valley Water Users' Association; and that organization, taking advantage of the National Reclamation Act of 1902, supported the federal government in the construction of Roosevelt Dam, completed in 1911. This and similar endeavors brought vital stability to the water supply, allowed irrigation control, and assured agricultural growth in the valley. And as the Salt River Valley prospered, so did Phoenix. The area became the leading agricultural producer in the Southwest.

The success of the Roosevelt Dam system illustrated the importance of water to the development of Phoenix and the Southwest. Since the beginning, the desert town had depended on adjacent river flows and deep underground wells for local sustenance, but the Salt River was unreliable and underground sources were uncertain. The water management system created by Roosevelt Dam allowed boosters to promote Phoenix and the Salt River Valley area as being even more promising than before.

The nation's first major reclamation project also demonstrated the vital contribution of the federal government to the growth of Phoenix and the Salt River Valley. Federal money and federal expertise proved indispensable in seeing the Roosevelt Dam project through to completion. But it took more than the cooperation of Washington to realize the successful urbanization of the desert. As on other frontiers, the progress of the Arizona hub depended on the quality of the people who lived in and promoted it. Phoenix's leaders spent considerable time both at home and in Washington lobbying in behalf of their goals. Phoenix developers realized "you cannot dream your town into a city; you must build and boost it into one," an attitude that could make the difference between urban success and urban failure. To neglect to boost growth and development of the city and the surrounding area was to risk decline and defeat in the urban sweepstakes.

Phoenicians drew on other regions for many of their ideas and institutions, hoping to re-create in their new home what they considered to be the best of the old home. At the same time, they were faced with a different environment where past experiences failed to provide answers to new problems. They became deeply involved in the development of what historians call the hydraulic West. Their daily existence depended upon the management of water, and to assure the growth of their desert city they sought the support of modern technology and the federal government. Boosters and water projects helped assure the growth of an oasis civilization in central Arizona with Phoenix as the hub.[6]

Urban leaders in Phoenix and the Southwest secured advantages especially useful to desert development, such as water projects, and at times set the pace for their counterparts elsewhere in the country. They were, for example, quick to accept the motor vehicle as a primary mode of transportation. In Phoenix the use of the auto and the bus sent the streetcar into a decline from which it never recovered. Reliance on the automobile, the bus, and the truck contributed to increased residential and business dispersion. As the concept of decentralization took hold, low-density patterns of settlement and suburban modes of living joined the amenities that provided the good life promoted by Phoenix boosters.

The city enthusiastically adopted the motor vehicle culture that developed in the West during the 1920s. In that decade, as in the past, Phoenix continued to serve as a principal junction point in the transportation structure of the Southwest. It was a vital link connecting the cities of the region not only with each other but also with national and international highway, rail, and air service networks. With its increasing importance as a transportation hub, Phoenix became more attractive to potential residents and business investors. As a business and transportation center, the Arizona capital served as a conduit between the region and the outside world, as a collector of exports from the surrounding area, and as a distributor of imports from around and beyond the nation.

In addition to providing economic functions, Phoenix served as a transmitter of civilization to its hinterland, and urban promoters helped to benefit the region by encouraging and supporting the establishment of schools, colleges, churches, libraries, museums, theaters, and other agents of civilization. Exhibiting an urban consciousness similar to that present elsewhere in the country, Phoenix leaders helped to refine the Southwest by making their city a social and cultural enrichment center.[7]

The urban centers of the Southwest influenced the social structure of the region. As the oasis cities developed, they became

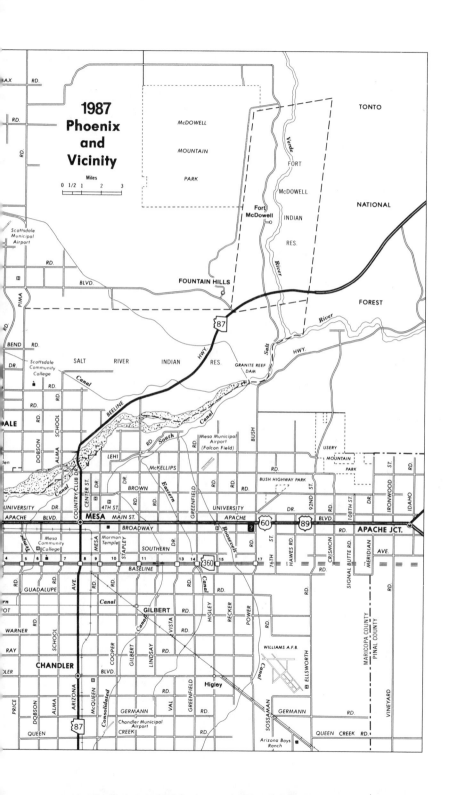

increasingly attractive to Anglo (white people of non-Hispanic descent) elements; and as the Anglos assumed power, they utilized Mexicans as an underclass to help them realize their goals, including economic growth. Having achieved a dominant position in each community, the Anglos acquired more wealth, influence, and prestige; and from these positions of strength, they dictated the terms of the ethnic arrangement, which invariably found the majority of the Mexicans and Mexican Americans living on the wrong side of the tracks. For the majority of Hispanics, as well as the less numerous blacks and Indians, upward mobility proved elusive and poverty remained a problem. Anglo residents especially dominated economic, political, and social life in Phoenix. Unlike El Paso, Albuquerque, and Tucson, Phoenix from its founding was run by Anglos for Anglos.[8]

By 1930 Phoenix was well established as the leading city in Arizona and the second largest urban center in the Southwest. As one booster put it, "Phoenix is truly the capital of Arizona, the hub of new developments. As Phoenix goes, so goes Arizona." During the Great Depression, the four major cities of the Southwest suffered less than their counterparts elsewhere, though problems emerged. During the 1930s, Phoenix especially experienced an influx of people in search of a future. To meet local demands for help, New Deal programs devised in Washington provided welcome relief and gave impetus to recovery. As was the case elsewhere in the urban West, during the 1930s a strong relationship developed between the federal government and Phoenix as the people of the city and the valley turned to Washington for aid and received it.[9]

After 1940 Phoenix and other cities of the West continued to benefit greatly from close relations with the nation's capital as the federal government poured large amounts of money into the communities, helping to make them major military and high-technology centers. During World War II they became the homes of important military bases and defense plants. Local promotional organizations, such as the Phoenix Chamber of Commerce, worked closely with Arizona representatives in Washington to secure these valuable assets. Inducements materialized as every form of cooperation was extended. Competing cities also offered inducements, but fine flying weather and the government's program to locate military bases and defense plants inland to protect them from possible attacks helped Phoenix. As in the past, federal funds and projects stimulated the local economy, and a significant amount of growth and development was due to them; in fact, their role in creating the boom in Phoenix during and after World War II can hardly be overestimated.[10]

During the Cold War, military installations such as Luke and Williams Air Force bases continued to serve as part of the national defense effort, and former war plants looked not only to military but also to civilian markets. A multiplier effect took hold, and as more manufacturers moved to the area, they attracted others. Predominant were light and clean industries, especially electronics firms, which flourished in the low-humidity climate so necessary to their success. Electronics plants used little water and produced high-value, low-weight products that could be easily shipped overland. By 1955 manufacturing had become Phoenix's number one source of income, with farming and tourism in second and third places.

In the postwar years, Phoenix achieved economic diversification, and the Valley of the Sun emerged as the metropolitan center for commerce and industry in the Southwest. Phoenix surpassed El Paso and moved to the top of the urban hierarchy in the Southwest during the 1950s, and it secured its hold on that position during the next twenty years as manufacturing remained the most dynamic growth sector. It also remained the service center of the Southwest, with that sector providing most of the jobs. Phoenix leaders encouraged federal investment and private enterprise by offering a favorable business climate and an attractive quality of life. Other cities in the region could not keep up with the Arizona capital. As an El Paso influential put it in 1978, "We want to be like Phoenix, but we don't have the kind of business leadership we need."[11]

Phoenix not only represented the new Southwest; it also represented the modern urban center in America. Though it was seen as the "anticity" by critics, particularly those from the older urban America, admirers called the sprawling, multicentered metropolis the urban form of the future. The popularity of the new form attracted hordes of newcomers to Phoenix; the "anticity" became part of the lure. To some, rapidly growing Phoenix appeared to be on the cutting edge of a new urban America. Modern Americans, declared an observer, "desired not a unified metropolis but a fragmented one"; thus they "opted for the dissolution of the city and, with the aid of the automobile, created the dispersed and fragmented metropolitan world of the late twentieth century."[12]

Phoenix celebrated its reputation as a growth machine. Characteristically, Phoenix officials and promoters offered the good life of employment and play, and the hope of development and progress. Business initiative, sunny days, and modern technology prevailed in the popular desert hub. Especially appealing were new attractions such as the miracle of air conditioning. As in other Sunbelt cities, the mass production of air conditioners in the 1950s and the consequent "age of refrigeration" attracted not only manufacturers but also more tourists and residents. No longer was the hot weather a barrier; modern technology continued to tame the desert Southwest.

Phoenix boosters, practicing the art of the possible and adopting new assets to attract more people and more business, felt they could philosophically and technologically control the environment rather than let it control them. They had overcome the problems of citymaking in the desert in the past, and they would continue to do so. In the 1980s, for example, they were busy promoting the Rio Salado Project to turn the Salt River into a water wonderland of streams and lakes, and create a magnet of attention in the Valley of the Sun. Along with parks and waterways in the Salt River bed, the plan called for new business and residential development along the banks. The seventeen-mile stretch of improvements, declared a developer, "will be the biggest and best reclamation project in the country. I'm talking about a project bigger than Mission Bay in San Diego or Paseo del Rio in San Antonio." Critics expressed environmental and financial concern, but project supporters insisted that upon completion it would help give character and identity to the Phoenix area.

As the winning combination of opportunities and amenities continued to attract newcomers, Phoenix boomed. Economic enterprise and the Phoenix lifestyle drew thousands of people to the area. Economic growth was the primary goal of Phoenix promoters, and evidence of urban maturity gave support to that goal. Boosters, anxious to create a proper image, worked hard to make the Arizona capital politically acceptable and socially and culturally appealing. Though not always successful, they nevertheless considered such goals worthwhile. Acting in behalf of their city and themselves, they supported the presence of civilization's amenities as well as economic growth and development. Schools, churches, libraries, universities, theaters, museums, and symphonies all became part of the package. Traditionally, Phoenix had served as a frontier of opportunities and amenities; and as it moved historically from town to city to sprawling multicentered metropolis, it served as a premier example of the progress and problems existing in the new urban America.[13]

Certainly not all shared in the prosperous rise of the modern metropolis of the Southwest. An *Arizona Republic* survey in 1981 declared that the twenty most powerful people in the state of Arizona were Anglos from Phoenix. At the same time, more members of minority groups, many of them business and professional people, moved into the middle class. The positive effect of such dynamic forces as the G.I. Bill, the civil rights movement, and the growth of the economy made it possible for individual minority group members to benefit from new educational and employment opportunities; but progress for Hispanics, blacks, and other minority groups as groups proved to be slow. For the majority of them, occupational mobility continued to be limited, and low economic status remained a familiar condition in many Phoenix neighborhoods. Some progress was made, however, when Phoenix ended at-large voting in 1982. Since 1983, the year in which Terry Goddard was elected mayor and eight City Council members were elected from districts, the city has been more sensitive to minority representation and neighborhood power. Minority groups, as well as other previously neglected elements of the growing population, have enjoyed unprecedented access to city government.[14]

Metropolitan Phoenix emerged a leader during the rise of the Sunbelt and became one of the fastest growing among the nation's fifty largest metropolitan areas. Despite its problems, many of them shared by other major cities of the new urban America, the lure of the Southwest metropolis could not be denied. Critics, however, saw the area as an urban complex in trouble. They pointed to growth as the crucial problem, and they intended to make sure that it persisted as the vital issue. In their view, the Valley of the Sun in 1987 was at a crossroad, and nothing less than the good life was at stake.

2 THE EMERGENT YEARS, 1867-1889

From about A.D. 300 to A.D. 1400 a people known as the Hohokam, the modern Pima word meaning "those who have disappeared," occupied the Salt River Valley in central Arizona, the present site of metropolitan Phoenix. The Hohokam Indians were agriculturalists who built canals and diverted water from the Salt River to irrigate their fields. They settled in villages, cultivated crops, and lived in harmony with the desert environment. The Salt River provided a year-round water supply, and this invaluable resource, along with the rich soil and semitropical climate of the area, allowed the Hohokam farmers to flourish. For unknown reasons, around 1400 the Hohokam occupation of the Salt River Valley ended. Explanations for their failure to survive include a great drought, a gigantic earthquake, a decimating disease, marauding invaders, declining soil fertility due to alkalinity, and excessive irrigation that caused a higher water table and waterlogging of agricultural land. The disappearance of the Hohokam remains a mystery, but the archaeology of their canal and village civilization is still present.[1]

Although other Indian tribes lived around the Salt River Valley, it remained unoccupied for several centuries following the departure of the Hohokam. While the Spanish explored much of the

Southwest and developed Santa Fe, Paso del Norte, Albuquerque, Tucson, and other towns, the future site of Phoenix was left undisturbed. Even after the United States acquired the area in 1848, following the Mexican War, few Americans expressed an interest in the Salt River Valley. Gold seekers rushing to strikes in California and Arizona in the 1850s and 1860s also avoided the place. Thus, by the end of the Civil War the location of Phoenix, by 1980 the ninth largest city in the United States, continued to contain only the canal remnants and residential ruins of the ancient Hohokam.[2]

In September 1865, the United States Army established Camp McDowell to protect the residents of Prescott, Wickenburg, and other central Arizona mining settlements from hostile Indians. The soldiers stationed at the remote post, located twenty miles northeast of the Salt River Valley, had difficulty raising their own food and feed for their horses. The residents of the mining communities experienced the same problem. The high cost of bringing in foodstuffs from California or Mexico compounded their predicament. To meet the needs of the military and civilian population of the region, the Salt River Valley agricultural settlement of Phoenix in Yavapai County emerged.

John Y. T. Smith, a former Union Army officer, harvested wild hay for Camp McDowell along the Salt River in early 1866; but it was John William (Jack) Swilling, a former Confederate soldier and deserter, Union Army freighter and scout, Arizona prospector, farmer, and speculator, who promoted the first modern irrigation system in the Salt River Valley. No one made an effort toward restoring the agricultural splendor of the Hohokam until Swilling made his appearance. Afflicted with alcohol- and drug-related problems, he later died a pauper in a Yuma jail while awaiting trial for highway robbery. Nevertheless, more than anyone else, Swilling deserves to be called the father of Phoenix.

While passing through the Salt River Valley in November 1867, Swilling noticed the ruins of the Hohokam irrigation system and sensed the agricultural possibilities of the area. In the mining settlement of Wickenburg, fifty miles northwest of the Salt River Valley, he received enough financial backing from a group of local supporters to organize the Swilling Irrigating and Canal Company. After securing supplies and hiring sixteen workers, most of whom were unemployed miners, the perceptive Swilling in December 1867 moved his business enterprise to the Salt River Valley, where he began to supervise the cultivation of the rich soil. Homestead-

John W. (Jack) Swilling, the "Father of Phoenix," c. 1870. Salt River Project.

ing land north of the Salt River, he and his companions cleaned out old irrigation ditches and constructed new ones, planted crops, and negotiated supply contracts with Camp McDowell officials and local interests in Wickenburg and other nearby central Arizona mining towns and camps.

Aware that the company was revitalizing the land of an ancient agricultural people, Swilling or one of his fellow pioneers called the settlement Phoenix, after the mythical bird that rose from its own ashes; it seemed an appropriate symbol of life rising anew from the remains of the past. It was hoped that the Phoenix community would build upon the ruins of the ancient Hohokam civilization. Most accounts give Swilling credit for naming the settlement Phoenix, but others insist that Darrell Duppa should be given the honor. Both men were present at the time and both were familiar with the classics. The Englishman Duppa, a world traveler lured to the Arizona frontier by the mining boom of the early 1860s, eventually became a stockholder in the Swilling Irrigating and Canal Company, moving with it to the Salt River Valley in December 1867. A man of eccentric habits and impressive personality, he divided his time between farming and prospecting. A local newspaper later described him as "a man of fine education, a voracious reader and a delightful conversationalist." Others called him a "foolhardy drunk."[3]

Early in 1868 a visitor to the Phoenix settlement observed that it contained "about fifty persons who have displayed great energy in the construction of their irrigation ditches and the clearing of their land. The settlement, though young, has every evidence of prosperity." Irrigated farms yielded abundant crops of corn, barley, and wheat. More canals and ditches came into being, and more settlers migrated to the Salt River Valley. The Hohokam example had inspired new irrigators to rediscover the agricultural potential of the area, and their success attracted others. The soldiers at Camp McDowell and groups of friendly Pima and Maricopa Indians protected the growing Phoenix settlement from hostile Apaches. By 1870 the population of the irrigated area had increased to 235 inhabitants, and cultivated lands had expanded to more than 1,500 acres.[4]

By 1870, the need for a permanent townsite in the Salt River Valley was voiced. With a growing population and increased agricultural production, community leaders called for a business center for the exchange of goods and services. Swilling suggested a site near a flour mill his friend William B. Hellings planned to build. Located near Thirtieth Street, between Roosevelt and Van Buren streets, the site promised to benefit Swilling, Hellings, and their supporters. James B. McKinnie and Cromwell A. Carpenter, leaders of a rival group, wanted the townsite located near Van Buren and Sixteenth Street, where they owned a saloon. Other local individuals wanted the selection of a site advantageous to them.

Finally, on October 20, 1870, John T. Alsap, a Yavapai County representative to the Territorial Legislature and a recent arrival in the Salt River Valley from Prescott, presided over a meeting of 130 interested citizens. Alsap proposed a location "on land yet unappropriated" that he preferred, but those present chose to elect a committee to recommend a townsite. On October 26, committee members John Moore, Martin P. Griffin, and Darrell Duppa recommended that the 320-acre site proposed by Alsap be accepted, and Duppa suggested that the new town be named Phoenix. The citizens approved the location and the name, and unofficially celebrated the birth of the future capital of Arizona.

Swilling may have been disappointed in the site selection, but Alsap's choice proved to be a good one. The site, which lies today in downtown Phoenix in the rectangle bounded by Van Buren on the north, Harrison (now the railroad tracks) on the south, Seventh Street, and Seventh Avenue, offered several advantages. Located on high ground more than a mile north of the Salt River, it seemed safe from floods. No Hohokam ruins cluttered the site, and it was relatively free of desert growth. Most important, it lay in the geographical center of the 40-mile-long, 15-mile-wide, 450,000-acre Salt River Valley.[5]

Although not a member of the townsite selection committee, Alsap wielded a great deal of influence in the community. A veteran of many frontiers, he had experience as a miner, a farmer, a doctor, and a lawyer before moving to Arizona from California in 1863. After settling in Prescott, he was elected to the Council (Senate) of the Territorial Legislature by Yavapai County citizens and was chosen president of that body in 1868. A year later he moved to the Salt River Valley, where he practiced law, engaged in farming, served as an officer of the Phoenix Ditch Company, and became an active civic promoter. A prominent politician and ardent booster, Alsap linked his future with that of the infant desert town.

Following the selection of the Phoenix townsite, citizens organized the Salt River Valley Town Association to secure and develop it. They elected Alsap, James Murphy, and Joseph C. Perry as the first commissioners of the organization, and directed them to supervise the surveying of the townsite and the public sale of lots.

To do the survey, the commissioners hired William A. Hancock, a local storekeeper and secretary of the Salt River Valley Town Association. A California Volunteer during the Civil War and a survivor of Apache campaigns in Arizona, Hancock promoted the townsite at every opportunity. Along with others, he hoped to benefit from the new town. He not only surveyed the townsite but also constructed the first building on it, to house his store, not long after the land was opened for settlement in December 1870.[6]

The first sale of lots proved moderately successful. Buyers, convinced that Phoenix was not a "paper town," purchased more than sixty lots for prices ranging from $20 to $140. When Hancock completed further surveying, more lots were put up for sale. As town lots continued to be sold, new Maricopa County Probate Judge John T. Alsap, acting as a trustee for the inhabitants of Phoenix, went to the nearest land office, at Prescott, and applied for a federal patent for the land at $1.25 per acre, as required by law, so that clear title to the townsite could be assured. It took time because of bureaucratic delays, but a formal patent costing $400 for the 320-acre parcel was issued in April 1874, and Alsap was finally able to give official deeds to those holding lots within the Phoenix townsite.[7]

Meanwhile, by 1871 Phoenix boosters had succeeded in making the town the seat of the new Maricopa County. Originally located in Yavapai County, the Phoenix townsite from its inception faced opposition from Prescott leaders, who feared the competition of another urban center. Seeing Phoenix as a potential threat, and determined to keep Prescott the county seat, they did everything in their power to delay the legal formation of the new Salt River Valley town. In their view, Prescott had already suffered enough loss. When Arizona officially became a United States territory in February 1863, the new community of Prescott was selected as the capital. Tucson, a larger town in southern Arizona, was ignored because of its Confederate orientation and a large Mexican population. In 1867, Prescott, a Union stronghold made up of Anglos, lost the territorial capital to Tucson, where it remained for ten years. After losing the capital, Prescott boosters were understandably reluctant to encourage the establishment of Phoenix, a possible competitor that might eventually attempt to change the political structure of Yavapai County.

At the same time, Phoenix promoters worked to bring about the creation of a new county, with the hope of making their town the county seat. During the 1871 legislative session, Councilman Alsap introduced a bill forging a new county out of the southern portion of Yavapai County. Using his influence in the legislature, he pushed the bill through that body; and on February 14, 1871, Governor Anson P. K. Safford announced the birth of Maricopa County. He also named Phoenix the county seat, subject to voter approval in a May 1 election, and appointed temporary county officials.

Alsap and other Phoenix promoters knew the importance of a town's being selected as a county seat. It brought to a community the advantage of more power, prosperity, and prestige. During the rapid settlement of the West in the nineteenth century, county seat battles frequently occurred. In many cases they emerged between sites struggling for survival. To become the seat of a newly created county meant recognition for a town and a future for its inhabitants; defeat often meant obscurity and the end of a dream. A key to victory in such contests was the intensity of the booster spirit exhibited by the participants. To neglect to boost your community sufficiently could result in the loss of the prize and defeat. Two rivals in the Salt River Valley competed with Phoenix for the designation as county seat before the election in May 1871.[8]

One rival was Mill City, the site of William B. Hellings' mill in the old Swilling settlement, and the other was George E. Mowry's ranch, located near the present intersection of Van Buren and Sixteenth streets. Both areas had previously lost in the competition to be named the official townsite, but their supporters were now determined to see their choice elected the official county seat. Old rivalries from the townsite struggle resurfaced. As on other urban frontiers, the contest was intense, and even violent at times. The *Arizona Miner*, a Prescott newspaper, reported, "The county seat question is causing some little discussion and perhaps some hard feeling between citizens of the Salt River Valley." Perhaps "old mother Yavapai should have given her first born some written instructions for new beginners, judging from the dissensions and jealousies now existing there."

When Jack Swilling and his Mill City friends heard that Phoenix supporters were bribing and intimidating Mexicans, and using Papago Indians (Tohono O'odham), posing as Mexicans, to vote their way in the county seat election, they retaliated by acting in a similar fashion. Their efforts fell short, and Phoenix emerged the winner with 212 votes; Mill City received 150, and 64 went to

Mowry's ranch. How much fraud actually occurred is unknown, but observers claimed that it was inconsequential and did not change the known wishes of a majority of the voters. There were protests, but no serious investigation of the election ever took place. As a Phoenix resident declared in a letter to the *Miner*: "We have had a very spirited election, and the feeling about the county seat aroused considerable animosity, but since it is over, everybody seems disposed to settle quietly down to their work."[9]

Hancock's townsite plan contained ninety-eight blocks, all separated by wide streets and alleys. Some of the principal arteries measured one hundred feet in width, unusual for the urban frontier. Streets running east-west were named for presidents and north-south streets for Indian tribes, with the exception of Center (Central Avenue). In 1893, local officials would replace the Indian street names with numbered streets and avenues. Washington Street served as the major thoroughfare and Center the main cross street. Near their intersection, two blocks were set aside for public buildings. Hancock's plan reflected the traditional American grid pattern. Both practical and profitable, that pattern, based on the Philadelphia model, had proved to be a success in town after town as pioneers settled the American West.[10]

Phoenix in the 1870s was not a boom town. During the early years it experienced slow growth and nothing spectacular happened. The lack of activity and the dearth of news in the community bothered local correspondents, but they attributed the absence of excitement to the amount of diligent labor required to earn a livelihood farming in the Salt River Valley. As one Phoenix reporter declared to the *Miner* in February 1871, "We have not had any earthquakes, hurricanes, or other physical phenomena that I could chronicle; neither have we had any weddings, balls, parties, or other amusements or gatherings of the people, to which the ladies come out with their Sunday finery, and the gentlemen with their 'store clothes.'" Not a very interesting scene, he lamented. "We are in fact, a very sober, industrious people, and we have been, at least the greater part of us, hard at work putting in our crops and taking care of them."[11]

When not busy constructing houses and canals and cultivating crops, local farmers visited the shops, stores, saloons, and other business establishments being located along Washington Street, near the public squares reserved by the Salt River Valley Town Association for official town and county buildings. The Association also donated lots for a public school, a Protestant church, and a Masonic lodge. An entire block was given to William Bichard and Company as a site for a flour mill. Other townsite construction projects were encouraged, cottonwood trees were planted along the streets, and soon Phoenix began to take on a more substantial look.

An ice factory producing a thousand pounds a day and a deluxe hotel with a canal-fed swimming pool appeared; the largest building in town was a brewery. Such enterprises were much appreciated in a community where temperatures often soared to 110 degrees in the summer. Water for Phoenix was drawn from the Salt River Valley Canal, dug in 1868 and otherwise known as the "Swilling ditch" or the "town ditch." The water circulated in smaller ditches along both sides of the principal streets. Occasionally used for washing, swimming, and trash dumping, the open ditches posed health problems. Unsanitary wells also were utilized during the decade.[12]

In the 1870s, the town experienced economic problems. The national depression of 1873 caused many mining operations, military posts, and government-supervised Indian reservations in Arizona to reduce expenses, including cuts in lucrative supply contracts; and farmers and merchants in the Salt River Valley felt the impact. Development in Phoenix came to a halt. The optimism of the early years declined and the future looked bleak, but by 1876 the agricultural and business economy of the area had improved. Promotion efforts and development projects resumed, and the population increased. The valley's rich soil, temperate climate, and water supply remained valuable assets, and agricultural production rates rose considerably in the later 1870s. Observers called the Salt River Valley the "Garden of the Territory" and the "Grain Emporium of Arizona."

Hohokam canal patterns continued to be followed by the irrigators, and thousands of additional acres of arable land were brought into cultivation. Along with the Salt River Valley Canal, the major waterways included the Maricopa Canal, completed in 1870, and the Grand Canal, completed in 1878. Farmers also benefited from timely national legislation. The Desert Land Act of 1877 encouraged the settlement of the Phoenix area by increasing the amount of land allowable under the Homestead Act of 1862 from 160 acres to 640 acres.

Following the depression years, Phoenix businessmen moved to meet new demands made upon them by the growing population.

They provided not only the goods necessary for daily living in the valley and the territory, but also specialty items shipped in from New York and San Francisco. As the decade progressed, Phoenix merchants offered customers "almost every conceivable article . . . from the finest cimbric needle to the latest improved agricultural machine." As on other urban frontiers, experienced Jewish merchants with business connections in New York and San Francisco led the way.[13]

By the end of the decade, Phoenix functioned as the service station of central Arizona. If not a boom town, it was a vital place. The *Salt River Herald*, founded in 1878 and the first newspaper in Phoenix, noted, "The growth of the town has not been feverish nor of mushroom order, but it has steadily and heartily improved." In 1878, the town contained the best and often the only business and professional services in the area. Among the many specialists in Phoenix were merchants and bankers, shopkeepers and saloon-keepers, doctors and lawyers, blacksmiths and carpenters, voice teachers and dance instructors. The business district concentrated around the intersection of Washington and First streets. Most of the major commercial and service establishments were located along Washington, and many of the merchants and professionals lived near their places of work. The more affluent were beginning to move to residences north along Center Street (Central Avenue) above Adams.

Phoenix promoters knew that the success of their town depended to a large extent on what the *Herald* called "the advance of the improvements of the surrounding country." They worked to benefit Phoenix by helping to develop the hinterland. Large freight teams representing Phoenix contracting firms carried commercial and agricultural products to Arizona's mining camps, military posts, and Indian agencies. Phoenix leaders, in order to facilitate trade with the outlying centers, actively promoted the development of a network of roads in the territory. And when it was announced that the transcontinental Southern Pacific Railroad planned to pass through southern Arizona before the end of the 1870s, local boosters responded by leading the drive to raise funds for the construction of a freight wagon and stagecoach road from Phoenix to Maricopa, a proposed depot site to be located on the main line thirty miles to the south.

Phoenix boosters welcomed the change in the town's appearance as it began to look more "American." As late as 1878, adobe buildings predominated in Phoenix; but the opening of a fired brick factory in that year, and the completion of the Southern Pacific main line to Maricopa in 1879, making lumber more available and affordable, caused brick and wood structures rapidly to replace adobe in popularity. "Numerous buildings are going up all over town," observed the *Herald*. "Most of them are brick, some wooden and very few adobe." By 1880, the changing physical appearance of Phoenix gave it an aura of stability and permanence appreciated by many residents, and it was beginning to remind them of the towns they had left behind in the older America.[14]

From its founding, Phoenix served as the dominant urban center in the Salt River Valley, and over the years its success inspired the promotion of nearby towns. During the 1870s, two desert settlements appeared to the east of Phoenix. Seven miles away, on the south side of the Salt River, a young man from Tucson, Charles Trumbull Hayden, started a store and a ferry service in 1871. Known at first as Hayden's Ferry, the site was given the name Tempe by Hayden, who had a classical education and had read about the Vale of Tempe in Greece. Canals and ditches of the ancient Hohokam were reconstructed and the area was brought under agricultural irrigation. In 1874, Hayden opened a flour mill. From this beginning, the farming community of Tempe grew slowly and posed no threat to Phoenix. In 1878, eight miles upriver from Tempe, Mormons from Utah and Idaho established the small agricultural settlement of Mesa City. Expert farmers, the Mormons soon had former Hohokam canals and ditches operating, and successful crop yields encouraged them to develop their town. Because of its rather particular religious orientation and its distance from Phoenix, Mesa City remained "a community apart, a clannish theocracy" for several decades. Later called Mesa, the town incorporated in 1883; Tempe incorporated in 1894.[15]

During the 1870s, citizens often complained about the inability of the Salt River Valley Town Association to keep up with the problems of growth. The organization was not a legal body. Neither federal nor territorial laws recognized its existence. For income it depended upon the sale of lots and contributions. Problems became evident in the early years, but town commissioners lacked sufficient funds to do anything substantial to correct them. They provided for the upkeep of streets and ditches with money received from the sale of lots, but more improvements were needed. County government, seated in Phoenix, delivered a number of services benefiting the community, including law enforcement and welfare programs for the unfortunate, but town problems continued to attract attention. In 1878, citizens began to call for incorporation, seeing it as the answer to their dilemma. As the *Herald* put it in August of that year, "Phoenix is now of sufficient size and importance to justify an incorporation. To be sure, it would increase the taxes slightly, but the benefits that would be derived would be worth many times the amount they paid."

The *Herald* insisted that "there should be hands, careful hands, to train up Phoenix 'in the way it should go,' to care for its streets, its squares, and the town property generally." The paper listed several "projects and privileges" that would result from incorporation and, it declared, "The town is here to stay and the more beautiful and attractive we can make it, the more will it be chosen as a place of residence and therefore the more will its business be increased." True booster talk, and few local leaders opposed incorporation. They greatly appreciated anything that contributed to the town's stability and permanence, and increased its ability to attract desirable newcomers and capital investment. Incorporation meant official recognition for Phoenix. It meant the enactment of ordinances to eliminate all sorts of nuisances. It meant more control over "half-naked Indians who disgrace our streets, bringing a blush to the cheeks of our mothers, sisters, and wives," and more control over "opium dens and brothels, which are corrupting our youth, reducing to lunacy our manhood, and degrading our community." It meant more protection for citizens and companies alike that were interested in the development of public works, such as water systems, in Phoenix.

The movement for incorporation gained strength, and by December 1880 a petition was circulating. Opponents had little chance. C. A. Luke, a local promoter speaking for those who favored the change, noted that taxes would be nominal. The petition stated that any act incorporating the town of Phoenix would limit the power of officials to tax the property of citizens to 0.50 percent of assessed valuation. It also provided for a budget in which expenses could not exceed revenues. For Phoenix to go into debt for improvements beyond its usual budget, at least 70 percent of the voters would have to approve. Luke reminded critics that town commissioners lacked the funds to adequately care for Phoenix. "They act at present by assumption and contrivance," he asserted, and asked, "Why should the citizens of this town continue to impose such arduous duties upon any one of their fellow men?" Incorporation would not only make Phoenix government "as economical a one as possible," it would encourage all property owners to contribute their fair share to its support through taxation.

A large number of town property owners signed the petition for incorporation, and in January 1881 Maricopa County representative Albert C. Baker of Phoenix presented it to the Eleventh Legislative Assembly, convened in Prescott. Both houses of that body approved the request, and the passage of the "Phoenix Charter Bill," signed by Governor John C. Fremont on February 25, 1881, enabled the town to incorporate. In the first municipal election, on May 3, the citizens elected John T. Alsap as mayor; T. W. Brown, John Burger, W. T. Smith, and J. M. Cotton as councilmen; M. W. Kales as treasurer; and Henry Garfias as marshal.[16]

Alsap, a leading force in the development of Phoenix in the 1870s, was like many urban promoters on the American frontier in that he combined private interests with community interests. Since his arrival in Phoenix in 1869, Alsap had been deeply involved in the economic, social, cultural, and political life of the town. Leaders like Alsap had faith in themselves and in their towns, and their booster spirit often reflected the success or failure of a new settlement in the American West. In Phoenix, Alsap and others established a multifunctional hub for the farming, mining, and military interests of the Salt River Valley and central Arizona. In the census of 1880, Phoenix recorded a population of 1,708, but obstacles to potential progress remained, notably the absence of a suitable railroad connection to the outside world. Yet incorporation had inspired confidence in the future of the young town—a bright future, according to observers—that would surely include a railroad and perhaps even a transfer of the territorial capital from Prescott to Phoenix.[17]

On May 9, 1881, Mayor Alsap informed the City Council, "There is no money in the treasury and there is no indebtedness." To create a financial base for Phoenix, the Council followed Alsap's advice and established reasonable property and license taxes. It also enacted a series of ordinances designed to protect the city and its population, including one that prohibited the deposit of filth on the streets and sidewalks or in the canals and ditches. Others concerned issues ranging from the distribution of water to the impoundment of stray animals. The first mayor and Council members tried to set conservative goals and practice economy

John T. Alsap, first Mayor of Phoenix, c. 1880. Salt River Project.

in administration, and for the most part they were honest and conscientious. Despite their attitudes and actions, however, critics appeared who claimed that the city was overgoverned. They complained especially about property and license taxes, but no movement for disincorporation ever succeeded.

At the same time, citizens complained that city government did not pay enough attention to the condition of Phoenix streets and ditches. During the dry season, critics called for more use of the sprinkling cart to settle the dust on city streets; and during the winter season, rains came and flooded the streets, turning them into mud bogs hazardous to people and horses. Sidewalks and crosswalks helped, but complaints to city officials continued; at one point, a walkway made of overturned beer bottles was installed to help keep pedestrians out of the dust and mud. Also irritating to Phoenicians was the practice of filling in holes or ruts in the streets with horse dung. Even more upsetting was the conduct of citizens who, despite an ordinance against it, insisted on dumping horse dung and other filth into the city ditches. On hot days, the smell from the streets and ditches could be sickening. Observers warned that the lack of good sanitation in Phoenix posed a dangerous public health problem. From time to time, city officials directed the chain gang made up of city prisoners to clean the streets and ditches, but their success was limited.[18]

City government in Phoenix, as in other cities on the urban frontier, tended to respond best to problems only after a severe crisis. In 1883, two smallpox epidemics erupted, and finally a permanent public health officer was hired. It took several disastrous fires in 1885 and 1886 before a fire-fighting force emerged in Phoenix. After a $100,000 blaze destroyed or damaged fourteen buildings on Washington Street in August 1886, a special election was called and voters approved a $10,000 bond issue to provide city volunteers with proper equipment, including fire engines. Soon the Pioneer Hose Company No. 1, made up of prominent Anglo citizens, led the Phoenix Volunteer Fire Department in meeting the conflagration problem. The Yucatec Hose Company No. 2, made up of Spanish-speaking residents, also participated. Fortunately, calamities did not have to happen before the city took action in other areas of community concern in the 1880s. During the decade, contracts and franchises were awarded to private companies to provide water and gas works, electric lights, a streetcar line, and a telephone system.[19]

In 1885 a change in the city charter divided Phoenix into four wards, each represented by a councilman. The mayor, marshal, and treasurer continued to be elected at large, but councilmen now felt as responsible for the welfare of the neighborhoods that elected them as they did for the entire city. Partisan politics became more evident, and a patronage system quickly evolved. While councilmen kept an eye on their neighborhoods, few of them were accused of corruption, but incidents of "honest graft" occurred. For example, in 1883 Councilman J. M. Cotton, appointed as a committee of one to secure a place for the city's prisoners, was observed receiving rent for the use of his property as a jail. Such activity was not unusual. A number of Phoenix businessmen serving as city councilmen during the decade were paid city funds for contractual work done for the city. In this way businessmen-politicians gained financially from city projects, but they believed that Phoenix gained from their work.

Phoenix promoters worked hard during the 1880s to secure the construction of a county courthouse and a city hall on the two public squares reserved for them. Since 1870, city and county governments had lacked adequate space to function properly. Local leaders realized that two impressive public buildings made of brick would serve several purposes. Both would enhance the "American" appearance of Phoenix, as well as contribute to its economic stability and political stature. Still, some shortsighted private interests, feeling the squares were too valuable for governmental or recreational use, insisted on subdividing them for business blocks, and their persistent opposition helped delay the construction of the two buildings. Despite their objections, in 1883 Maricopa County supervisors finally ordered the erection of a $25,000 courthouse on its reserved site fronting West Washington Street, and in 1887 Phoenix voters approved $15,000 in improvement bonds for the construction of a city hall on its reserved site fronting East Washington Street. Both buildings increased the governmental role of downtown, and the city hall tower, the tallest structure in Phoenix, quickly became an object of local pride.[20]

During the 1880s the Salt River Valley became known as the "most fertile and productive in the territory." Since the 1860s the irrigation system had expanded and contributed to the blooming of the once barren desert and the rise of Phoenix. Miles of waterways, including the Salt River Valley, Maricopa, and Grand canals, enabled the "new Hohokam" to open up thousands of acres of arable land to agricultural cultivation. Farmers experimented with a variety of crops, from grains to citrus, and stockmen tried cattle feeding and sheepherding. Local boosters called Phoenix the "Garden City of Arizona" and contended that the valley offered as much potential as any place in California.

In the 1870s and the early 1880s, most of the irrigation canals utilized by Jack Swilling and other Salt River Valley pioneers were built upon the existing Hohokam system or extensions of it; but the remarkable Arizona Canal, completed in June 1885, was a striking departure. Wider and longer than earlier canals, it measured fifty-eight feet across at the top, thirty-six feet across at the bottom, and five feet deep, and ran forty-one miles through land not previously irrigated by the Hohokam or their successors. From a point thirty miles northeast of Phoenix on the Salt River, the canal ran through the upper valley north and northwest of the city to a point on New River. A bold undertaking, it lay above all the other canals, and promoters expected it to open eighty thousand acres to cultivation. It was also unique in that it required more outside capital to complete than any other project up to that time in Phoenix or the Salt River Valley. Local promoters could not afford to build it on their own, so for the first time (but certainly not the last) they sought help from talented experts and wealthy investors elsewhere.[21]

In December 1882, a group of local promoters led by land developer Clark A. Churchill incorporated the Arizona Canal Company. In April 1883, Churchill placed William J. Murphy under contract to develop the entire project. Murphy, a former Union Army officer and veteran of the Civil War from Illinois, had worked as a construction contractor for the Santa Fe Railroad as it moved westward across northern Arizona into California. After completing that job, he came to Phoenix in May 1883 to start work on the Arizona Canal. When a lack of funds threatened to end the project, Murphy, who had agreed to build it on speculation, led the way in seeking capital from outside investors. He sold Arizona Canal Company bonds to money men in San Francisco, Chicago, New York, Boston, and other financial centers. He even sold bonds in London and Edinburgh. Despite the efforts of Murphy and other promoters, accumulating the financing necessary to complete the canal proved difficult, but enough was secured to keep the project from failing. Money obtained from investors was kept in the newly formed Valley Bank of Phoenix. Organized in April 1884 by Murphy's friend and fellow developer William Christy, a former Union Army officer, Iowa banker, and Prescott health seeker, the bank also provided liberal loans to preferred customers, such as Murphy and the Arizona Canal Company.[22]

The Arizona Canal and its support system were completed in June 1885. The *Arizona Gazette*, a Phoenix newspaper, called it "a grand improvement," noting, "It will furnish water to reclaim lands which have been an unproductive desert of no value for any purpose. It will be of incalculable benefit to this valley and the whole territory." Murphy, Christy, Churchill, and other investors benefited not only from its construction but also from their acquisition of large amounts of property near the canal. Led by Murphy, in June 1887 they formed the Arizona Improvement Company, a water and land development corporation. It soon conducted an aggressive promotion campaign, attracting to the Salt River Valley many new farmers who settled on lands watered by the Arizona Canal; even citrus and fruit growers from southern California arrived to enjoy the advantages of "a modern irrigation system in the agricultural capital of the Southwest." The company also created Grand Avenue, a one-hundred-foot-wide thoroughfare that began at the intersection of Seventh Avenue and Van Buren in the northwest corner of the city of Phoenix and angled across sections of land to the northwest for eighteen miles. Along its path, the company surveyed, and boosted on land it owned, the townsites of Alhambra, Glendale, and Peoria.[23]

Increased agricultural production in the Salt River Valley helped create the need for new markets and the desire for a railroad link to the outside world. In the late 1870s, the Southern Pacific Railroad built its transcontinental route across the Arizona Territory, but the nearest it came to Phoenix was Maricopa, a depot settlement thirty miles to the south. To help relieve the Phoenix community's isolation from the railroad, boosters built a freight wagon and stagecoach road from Maricopa to the city in 1879, but over the years it did not adequately serve the needs of the population. Under the best conditions, it took freight teams two days, and stages six hours, to make the trip. A railroad, promoters declared, linking Phoenix and the Salt River Valley to the Southern Pacific main line would surely help propel the "Garden City of Arizona" into a new era. They knew the importance of securing a railroad connection. As on other urban frontiers, it was a key to success. Observers predicted that this essential ingredient for growth and prosperity would help make Phoenix "the most populous city in the Arizona of the future."

Before the railroad dream could be realized, enough capital had to be acquired to finance its construction. Several attempts to achieve this goal ended in failure, but in June 1886 a group of local promoters organized the Maricopa and Phoenix Railroad Company. Financed by Chicago and San Francisco investors, including the Pacific Improvement Company, a development firm closely allied with the Southern Pacific Railroad, the Maricopa and Phoenix started to lay track in October 1886. Although the Southern Pacific did not directly control the Maricopa and Phoenix, it did control the Pacific Improvement Company, and that firm possessed 51 percent of the stock of the new railroad; thus Southern Pacific officials were assured that their wishes would always be considered.

The cooperation and support of the Southern Pacific assured the success of the Maricopa and Phoenix line. Once construction started, thanks in part to the pressure of Phoenix representatives and other friends of the new railroad, it benefited from $200,000 in subsidies, in the form of Maricopa County railroad bonds authorized by the Territorial Legislature. In addition, Phoenix donated two blocks in the southeast corner of the city for a depot site. Bureaucratic problems, especially those involving permission to pass through the Gila River Indian reservation, along with adverse weather conditions and difficulty in bridging the Gila and Salt rivers, caused delays in construction. On June 19, 1887, the branch line reached Tempe.[24]

In Tempe, local boosters declared that the sound of the locomotive whistle "now excited our long deferred anticipation." The town now had "a connection with the great outside world by bands of iron up to her very front doors." Tempe agriculturalists were elated to be able to ship their produce over the new railroad, and merchants welcomed a rise in business. On July 3, before a large crowd in Phoenix, William A. Hancock drove the last spike. Hancock, the pioneer who had surveyed the Phoenix townsite seventeen years earlier, noted the importance of the event and quickly joined in the rousing celebration. The Phoenix Brass Band played late into the night while happy citizens enjoyed appropriate refreshments. On July 4, the dream of a railroad for the Salt River Valley urban center was finally realized when the first scheduled train arrived. On that occasion, Phoenicians watched a colorful parade and listened to patriotic speeches, but for many of them it was the presence of the railroad that made Independence Day of 1887 truly a memorable occasion.

Like the Arizona Canal, the Maricopa and Phoenix Railroad proved to be a valuable asset in the development of the city and the Salt River Valley. Each day inbound passenger cars brought new residents and visitors, and freight cars brought loads of merchandise to be distributed in Phoenix or its hinterland of farming, ranching, and mining communities. Outbound traffic was mainly agricultural, and it reflected the area's reputation as the "Garden of the Territory." Salt River Valley farmers, including F. M. Fowler, owner of the largest agricultural operation in Arizona, regularly used the railroad to ship grain, citrus, fruit, and livestock throughout the country.[25]

Progress in agriculture and transportation helped Phoenix increase its population to 3,152 by 1890. The growth of the city, the *Gazette* noted at the time, "has been the result of real and substantial causes, without fictitious booms." While the population doubled during the 1880s, the business district expanded to meet new needs. Washington Street remained the principal thoroughfare throughout the decade, but social and commercial activity expanded beyond it to Adams, Jefferson, and Madison streets. A wide range of goods and services could be found in this busy area. In the southeast corner of Phoenix, near the railroad tracks and depot, new mills, factories, and warehouses appeared. Stockyards located to the east of the new industrial development. A variety of residential neighborhoods filled in parts of the incorporated city and its peripheral suburbs. The more affluent citizens continued to build homes north along Central Avenue. More than ever, the architecture of the homes and businesses of residents reflected the city's "American" heritage. "Phoenix. . . . It is thoroughly American and its citizens are live and go-ahead people full of push and enterprise," a local booster declared. "The streets are broad and regularly laid out, business blocks of brick, while most of the recently constructed dwellings are of the same material."[26]

Although home building to the north of the business district continued during the decade, residential development east and west of downtown became more evident after the Phoenix Street Railway Company began operating a mule-drawn line along the length of Washington Street in November 1887. This popular new mode of transportation encouraged the opening of additions to the Phoenix townsite at both ends of Washington Street. The additions were owned by former Californian M. E. Collins and former New Yorker Moses H. Sherman, holders of the Phoenix Street Railway Company franchise. As on other urban frontiers, in Phoenix street railway development and real estate promotion were closely connected.

Backed by investors in California and the East, and local friends such as banker William Christy, Collins and Sherman were street

Washington Street east from First Avenue, c. 1880s. The Herb and Dorothy McLaughlin Photographic Collection.

railway developers and real estate promoters, and they and their financial supporters profited substantially from the sale of property at both ends of the Washington Street trolley tracks. After 1887, Collins and Sherman were responsible for a number of additions to the original townsite, most of them 160-acre residential subdivisions connected to their expanding horse-drawn street railway lines; and by 1890 streetcar-structured growth patterns in the urban sector were clearly evident. By that year Sherman had bought out Collins, and for many years thereafter his trolley system greatly accelerated city and suburban development by extending its lines to various residential, recreational, and governmental sites in the Phoenix area west, east, and north of Washington Street.[27]

To provide goods and services to the growing population of Phoenix and its hinterland, an increasing number of local people worked at occupations other than farming. Some groups were particularly city-oriented. Jews, for example, continued to engage in business and banking. Many of them had lived in California or other parts of the American West before migrating to the desert center and, like their coreligionists on other urban frontiers, the

Jewish pioneers made their mark in Phoenix. In the 1880s, with goods imported from New York, San Francisco, and Los Angeles, the stores of Charles Goldman and Hyman Goldberg evolved into major Phoenix attractions. Martin W. Kales and Emil Ganz operated the First National Bank. Ganz also founded the Bank Exchange Hotel and served two terms as mayor of Phoenix.

Civic-minded, the Jews played an active role in the political and fraternal life of the community during the decade; many of them joined the Phoenix Volunteer Fire Department and organizations such as the Masons and the Odd Fellows. Although no synagogue existed in Phoenix during the 1880s, Jews held religious celebrations and services in private homes and halls. Unlike Jews in many older American cities, in Phoenix they lived in residences located throughout the community, and overt discrimination against them because of their religion was rare.[28]

Overt discrimination against non-Anglo minority groups, however, continued in Phoenix. Critics often blamed them for the crime, vice, and other problems in the city. At a mass meeting of citizens in Phoenix in September 1881, a banner read: "Removal or Death for the Apache." During the decade, while the Apache wars went on elsewhere in the territory, local Indians were regarded with hostility and contempt. Peaceful Pima and Maricopa Indians continued to visit the city, but the dominant white population failed to appreciate them. "Lounging about the streets are a great many Indians," noted an observer in 1888. Critics were especially upset over the tendency of the natives to hang around the city hall plaza, the railroad depot, and other local landmarks. Not welcome in Phoenix, and the object of much verbal and physical abuse, the "naked savages" also were the target of restrictive legislation in May 1881, when a city ordinance was passed making it illegal for Indians to appear on city streets "without sufficient clothing to cover the person," or to be in the city after dark unless employed by a Phoenix resident.[29]

The railroad brought more Anglos than ever before to Phoenix during the 1880s, and as a result the Mexican population grew proportionally smaller. Most Mexican men continued to work as laborers and field hands, and many women worked as domestics. A few Mexicans, notably Marshal Henry Garfias, served the city in an official capacity or as businessmen catering to the Mexican population, but as a group Mexicans exerted even less authority or influence than they had in the past in the primarily Anglo community. Local leaders proudly agreed with an observer in 1888 when he called Phoenix "a progressive American city" without the "sleepy semi-Mexican features of the more ancient towns of the Southwest." Often shut out of the larger community, Mexicans created their own social and cultural life centered around family activities at home and religious services at St. Mary's Catholic Church. Patterns of discrimination and segregation, along with a sense of ethnic identity and cultural awareness, encouraged the development of the Phoenix Mexican community.[30]

There were few blacks in Phoenix in the 1880s, but a number of Chinese, many of them victims of prejudice in California and exploited as Southern Pacific railroad workers in Arizona, settled in the city during the decade. Ambitious and diligent, some members of this small minority group operated laundries, grocery stores, vegetable stands, and restaurants. Phoenix residents and newspapers, no doubt influenced by the "Yellow Peril" publicity emanating from San Francisco and Los Angeles, resented the Chinese for engaging in businesses that competed with enterprises run by white Americans; in February 1886, for example, the *Gazette* deplored the "Chinese monopoly."

Especially disturbing to critics were the opium dens opened by the Chinese. Periodic raids against opium joints caused numerous Chinamen to spend time in the Phoenix jail. Most of the two hundred Chinese in the city by 1890 were honest, industrious individuals, and prejudice against them was mild compared with that in California, but it existed. In part they lived in the area bounded by Madison, Jefferson, First, and Second streets to escape the larger society. The concentrated Chinese community in Phoenix, much like Chinatowns in other frontier cities, served as a place of refuge in an alien world where members could be among their own kind, speak a familiar language, and live a Chinese life as much as possible.[31]

The dominant Anglo community continued to develop Anglo institutions. Methodist, Presbyterian, Baptist, and Episcopalian churches served as Anglo social centers as well as places of religious service. In addition, the three public schools in Phoenix by 1890 acted as multifunctional gathering places for Anglo children and adults. Fraternal lodges and cultural organizations also offered a sense of common identity and a feeling of fellowship to many Anglos who had severed traditional ties in migrating to Phoenix. They were important links to the past, reminders to members of similar associations they had belonged to or wanted to belong to in the older America they had left behind. In addition, Anglo newspapers operated as cultural conservators by promoting "Anglo-Americanism" at every opportunity; at the same time, they never hesitated to make derogatory remarks about racial minority group members, often convincing them to seek refuge in their own neighborhoods and institutions.

Anglo people "from elsewhere" dominated the desert center, and they tried to re-create what they considered to be the best of the past in their new environment, hoping to refine it in the process. Affluent men and women made a special effort to furnish their homes with eastern furniture and to wear eastern clothes. In Phoenix, Anglo gentlemen wore fine suits and hats, and gentlewomen wore gloves, even in hot weather. As one Phoenix woman later put it regarding her mother, who had lived in the city during the 1880s: "My mother, being from the East, always prided herself on keeping up with things. And many people made a very big effort when they came West. Women were well-dressed and they were very style conscious because they didn't want to feel isolated just because they lived in the West." The East, not the West, was considered the proper model.[32]

As the valley and the city developed, promoters began to organize a campaign to remove the territorial capital from Prescott to Phoenix. They realized the value of the Arizona Canal and the Maricopa and Phoenix Railroad to growth and progress, and they were certain that a plum such as the Arizona capital would add considerably to the city's prosperity and prestige, and increase its ability to attract desirable newcomers and capital investment. In 1877, the capital had been moved back to Prescott from Tucson, much to the dissatisfaction of southern Arizona residents. During the next several sessions of the Arizona Legislature, which met every two years, the subject of the capital location was debated, but Prescott managed to retain it despite the opposition of Tucson and Phoenix.

In the 1885 session, Phoenix received the Arizona Insane Asylum with an appropriation of $100,000, and Tucson received the University of Arizona with an appropriation of $25,000, but both institutions were considered by promoters to be less prestigious and less valuable than the territorial capital. In Phoenix, the asylum was constructed at Van Buren and Twenty-fourth streets, and in the eyes of many city boosters it became a liability rather than

A bird's eye view of Phoenix in 1890 (from map by C. J. Dyer). The Herb and Dorothy McLaughlin Photographic Collection.

an asset. In Tucson, indignant citizens complained that the city acquired the territorial university instead of the capital; some of them would even have preferred the more profitable territorial asylum rather than the university.[33]

By the 1889 session, Phoenix promoters viewed the city as "the future metropolis of the Territory," and they were anxious to make it the capital. At this time, even Tucson boosters began pushing Phoenix for the honor. The central Arizona hub offered a number of advantages. Its location in the middle of the territory made it a convenient compromise site between Prescott in the north and Tucson in the south. The winter weather was much better in Phoenix. The Territorial Legislature met in January and, according to one report, a legislator recently "had his ears frozen going from the depot to the hotel in Prescott." A Prescott defender retorted that it was better for Arizona "to have one or two of her legislators frozen to death or drowned in slush occasionally, as they only have to be at the Capital two months every other year, than to have all her other territorial officials baked and sizzled, melted and stewed nine months of the year with the intolerable heat of the Salt River Valley."[34]

In Prescott territorial legislators met in inadequate and uncomfortable facilities; Phoenix promoters offered them the use of an impressive new city hall with plenty of space to house the territorial government until a capitol building could be constructed. Better hotels and restaurants were available in Phoenix, along with other amenities and services. Phoenix business and professional interests, many of which expected to profit from the relocation of the capital, did everything possible to make the city attractive to legislators. They went after the capital in the same way they went after the Arizona Canal and the Maricopa and Phoenix Railroad. During the decade, in fact, Phoenix had acquired a "reputation for acquisitiveness" in the territory. At this time, of course, Prescott was especially upset at "hungry, greedy Phoenix" for "selfishly reaching after the earth and the balance of the universe." Local promoters were not discouraged, however, by reports accusing them of wanting "the sun to rise and set in Phoenix." As the *Herald* asserted in December 1888, "The report that Phoenix wants the penitentiary, the university, the capital, the San Carlos Indian Reservation and the Colorado River to run through her backyard and an overland railroad on her principal sidewalks, may be a figurative expression for the energetic way in which Phoenix does business."[35]

Prescott defenders accused Maricopa County representatives of arranging political deals with delegates from other parts of the territory in exchange for their votes on the capital removal bill, and they condemned Phoenix boosters for buying the support of stubborn legislators with funds from a "boodle sack" of $10,000 raised in Phoenix for the purpose of acquiring the capital. As on other frontiers, it was not unusual for urban promoters in Arizona to smooth the way with inducements to obtain support from decision makers. Both Tucson and Prescott had been accused of influencing delegates in this manner in the past. Local boosters had to be competitive; for example, in September 1888, Phoenix streetcar and real estate developer Moses H. Sherman put it this way to an associate: "You see, Phoenix wants the capital, and the whole crowd is working to this end. It may take a little money, and if it does, we fellows are ready to put up some."[36]

Despite the critics, on January 23, 1889, the House passed the bill, thirteen votes to ten, and two days later the Council passed it nine to two. Governor C. Meyer Zulich, known to favor Phoenix, signed the bill into law as soon as it reached his desk. Both houses quickly agreed to adjourn on January 28 and reconvene on February 7 in the new capital of Phoenix. Prescott leaders were furious over this sudden departure, but the city had lost its last fight. Rather than take the stage over rough roads for nearly 130 miles, legislators boarded a special Santa Fe train provided for them by Phoenix promoters and enjoyed a pleasurable trip to Los Angeles. From there they rode the Southern Pacific to Phoenix, where they joined in a celebration welcoming their arrival. All the expenses of the removal, including the 1,140-mile train trip, were paid from a fund raised by Phoenix citizens. Legislators liked the new location; three weeks after they arrived, they expressed their appreciation by passing a bill authorizing the reimbursement of Phoenix citizens for the costs of removal.[37]

Banker William Christy, merchant Charles Goldman, realtors Clark A. Churchill and J. W. Evans, hotel owners A. D. Lemon and W. T. Smith, lawyer-businessman Jerry Millay, streetcar developer Moses H. Sherman, and other local promoters knew the advantages of a city's being a capital city. Being the territorial capital gave Phoenix instant prestige, and it increased business, a result considered by some to be more significant than prestige. As the *Herald* put it on January 29: "Today Phoenix is not only the capital of Arizona but it is her commercial metropolis, a matter that is of more importance."

Time and again, Phoenix boosters supported public and private projects that would stimulate the economic growth and development of the city and the Salt River Valley, and they usually considered long-term as well as short-term benefits. For example, they were committed to making Phoenix the permanent political center of Arizona. This meant the city needed a permanent capitol building, something neither Tucson nor Prescott had constructed. Phoenix leaders began searching for a capitol building site soon after the legislature relocated, in order to ensure that the "capital on wheels" would remain in Phoenix for all time.[38]

Several Phoenix real estate promoters offered to donate a capitol building site, knowing that it would help them sell property they owned in the vicinity. M. E. Collins and Moses H. Sherman, the developers of the Phoenix Street Railway Company, owned 160 acres of land west of Washington Street, and in June 1889 they outbid the others. They had subdivided their property and called it the Capitol Addition to Phoenix. Not only did they donate a ten-acre site for the capitol at the heart of their property, but they also agreed to extend old streets and open up new ones to the Seventeenth Avenue location, landscape the capitol grounds, create a capitol park, and extend streetcar service along Washington Street to the new capitol building. They also gave each of the three members of the site selection committee several lots of land adjacent to the ten acres they donated for the capitol building, and they named a street in the Capitol Addition after each of them.[39]

The selection of Phoenix as the permanent capital of the territory and future state of Arizona crowned a decade of prosperous advancement for the city. In the year following the capital removal, Phoenix reported $488,000 in new building projects. By 1890 some boosters were even calling Phoenix "the Denver of the Southwest," for as one of them declared, "The wonderful growth and progress of the 'Queen City of the Plains' is to be more than duplicated in the garden belt of Arizona." Still, whatever high hopes local leaders had for their city, they realized that a great deal of effort would have to be expended before Phoenix could seriously remind anyone of Denver, a city of 107,000 in 1890. They were aware, however, that the population of the Colorado city had almost tripled from 36,000 in 1880, and envisioned a similar growth rate for Phoenix. Certainly they felt it quite possible for the desert hub to become the metropolis of Arizona.[40]

3 ARIZONA CAPITAL, 1890-1913

By 1890, three thousand people lived in Phoenix. Growth was slow but steady, and the Salt River Valley center offered an impressive array of urban goods, services, and amenities. By 1890 it was the seat of Maricopa County and the territorial capital, and boosters had dreams of its becoming a railroad as well as a business hub. By 1913, when they celebrated Phoenix's growing reputation as a progressive city, promoters had secured a second transcontinental railroad connection, solved the water problem, and retained a leadership role in the economic, political, social, and cultural development of Arizona and the Southwest. Problems accompanied progress, but the many opportunities and amenities available in the desert center remained attractive and alluring.

Becoming the metropolis of Arizona and the second largest city in the Southwest behind El Paso seemed possible, but this would depend in large measure on better rail connections. Dissatisfied with a single branch railroad into the city and valley, Phoenix promoters worked to increase transportation links to the outside world. The Maricopa and Phoenix Railroad served as an important outlet to the Southern Pacific transcontinental line, and boosters noted time and again that the city owed much of its prosperity to the M&P, but it was felt an additional line would provide the com-

petition necessary to gain fairer rates and better service. A railroad
north from Phoenix, connecting it to the east-west transcontinental line of the Atchison, Topeka and Santa Fe Railroad extending
across northern Arizona from Albuquerque to California, would
result in enormous benefits to the city and the surrounding area.[1]

The Southern Pacific, a beneficiary of the Maricopa and Phoenix
monopoly in the city and the Salt River Valley, feared the competition and opposed another railroad, but one was vigorously promoted both within and outside of the area. Finally, with sufficient
inducements, including money and land, the Santa Fe, Prescott
and Phoenix Railroad was incorporated in May 1891. To encourage
the building of the line, in March 1891 the Territorial Legislature
had passed a twenty-year tax exemption bill for new railroads that
commenced construction within six months of the legislation. Promoters of the SFP&P, led by Prescott mining magnate Frank M.
Murphy and Phoenix entrepreneur William J. Murphy, backed by
Chicago and Detroit investors, and supported by Santa Fe Railroad
officials, received from the city of Phoenix right-of-way privileges
and a depot site at Jackson Street and First Avenue. Construction
of the line began in October 1891, but mountainous terrain, along
with financial woes brought on by the national depression of 1893,
made the project a long and difficult task. The SFP&P entered
Phoenix from the northwest on February 28, 1895, connecting the
central Arizona hub with Prescott and the northern Arizona town
of Ash Fork on the east-west transcontinental line of the AT&SF.
In Phoenix, citizens held a two-day festival to celebrate the event
and what it signified for the future of the city.

The new railroad benefited Phoenix and the Salt River Valley
in many ways. It provided an outlet to a second transcontinental line and competition for Southern Pacific interests. It afforded
more access to midwestern and eastern markets, and it encouraged
the movement of more people and capital from those areas into
Phoenix and the valley. The SFP&P also extended branches from
its trunk line into the mining and timber regions of central and
eastern Arizona, thus making Phoenix a more convenient shipping
and supply center for the mining and lumber industries. Cattle
from northern Arizona could easily be brought to the valley to feed
and fatten.[2]

Many boosters hoped the arrival of the SFP&P would mean "a
big boom for Phoenix." In December 1891, a local paper stated,
"Phoenix is destined to be a great railroad center," but the new

Territorial capitol building, c. 1900. The Herb and Dorothy Mc-Laughlin Photographic Collection.

north-south line did not usher in a period of overwhelming prosperity. The completion of the SFP&P in February 1895 marked an easing of the national depression in Phoenix and the Salt River Valley, but a boom did not occur, for which some residents were grateful. As the *Republican* declared on the eve of the train's arrival: "Many are disappointed that the expected boom, the era of chaotic prosperity, has not set in." City lots and farm property "have not doubled or tripled or quadrupled in value as so many confidently and unreasonably hoped." The "hubbub which was assured is beautifully absent," noted the paper, "for which those who are interested in the permanent future of Phoenix rather than in her unstable present are unduly thankful." At the same time, "There is a great deal of quiet and healthful prosperity in Phoenix which would not have been here but for the new road."[3]

In the years following the arrival of the SFP&P, several local corporations and both the Southern Pacific and the Santa Fe constructed lines running from Phoenix to nearby towns and to outlying areas. By serving as a transportation hub, the city stimulated farming, mining, livestock raising, and other regional pursuits, and regional interests were encouraged to look to Phoenix for vital goods and services. Of special importance, in December 1903 the AT&SF announced the building of a branch line from a point on the SFP&P five miles north of Wickenburg, west to Parker on the Colorado River, and then into California to hook up with the Santa Fe main line to Los Angeles. The branch line, incorporated by the Santa Fe as the Arizona and California Railway, was completed in June 1910. Known as the Parker cutoff, this route provided Phoenicians with a shorter trip to the west coast, and it opened up new areas of land to human settlement and resource exploitation. In this way, as in other railroad centers of the Southwest, new routes into and out of Phoenix benefited the city and its surrounding areas.[4]

More railroad connections helped Phoenix progress, but the problem of too much or too little water in the Salt River Valley continued to plague residents. The area had survived the devastating floods of the early 1890s, and late in the decade a severe drought hit the valley, forcing thousands of acres out of cultivation. Many farmers and city dwellers, feeling defeated, moved away. Those who remained recognized that progress resulting from growth was doomed unless they solved the water problem. After much debate they decided that a water storage system was the only answer. The idea was not new. For years local leaders had supported the need for a controlled water supply to overcome periodic floods and droughts, but not enough private capital to harness the erratic Salt River could be raised. Because of this failure to accumulate sufficient funds, Phoenix promoters contended the federal government should undertake this job. Once completed, it was declared, a water storage system would bring "an era of good times such as no region of the West has ever known."

Droughts had parched the American West during the 1890s, causing an irrigation movement to mobilize throughout the region, including the Salt River Valley. The National Irrigation Congress convened in Phoenix in December 1896, and local leaders met Frederick Newell, Arthur P. Davis, and other Washington influentials. During the drought, city and valley residents formed committees to investigate conditions and to seek a more dependable supply of water. In April 1900, at a mass meeting in Phoenix, the Board of Trade recommended providing $1,500 to the Department of the Interior to finance surveys of the area. This offer was referred to Secretary of the Interior Ethan A. Hitchcock by Benjamin A. Fowler, who represented Phoenix and valley interests. Acceptance

of the proposal led to the arrival of government experts in central
Arizona to observe and report their findings to Washington. Local
initiative also inspired Fowler and George H. Maxwell to spend
considerable time in the nation's capital lobbying in favor of federal
reclamation legislation. Their friendship with Hitchcock, Newell,
Davis, and other government officials proved to be beneficial to
their cause.[5]

Fowler's leadership at both the local and the national level was
especially effective. A native of Massachusetts and a graduate of
Yale University, he had been a businessman in New York and Chicago before moving to the Salt River Valley for his health. Owner
of four hundred acres in Glendale, he knew from experience the
impact of the drought, and he became an active supporter of water
storage. He served as a delegate to the National Irrigation Association. Valley residents elected him to the Arizona Territorial
Legislature, and his fellow farmers elected him president of the
Arizona Agriculture Association. He also served as president of
the Phoenix Board of Trade. Newell, the first director of the United
States Reclamation Service, remarking on his relationship with
Fowler, declared that he had never met "a man of more persistent
effort and tireless energy, combined with patience and tact."[6]

Fowler, Maxwell, and other Salt River Valley promoters lobbied
diligently in Washington to secure passage of the reclamation
bill sponsored by Nevada Congressman Francis G. Newlands. The
original draft of the bill concerned only public land; but since most
of the land in the Salt River Valley was privately owned, Fowler
and Maxwell, with the help of their friend President Theodore
Roosevelt, convinced Congress to amend the bill to include lands
in private ownership. The Newlands Act, passed in June 1902,
provided federal money for reclamation projects in the arid West.

In February 1903 area farmers, led by Fowler, Maxwell, and
Judge Joseph H. Kibbey, joined together and formed the Salt River
Valley Water Users' Association. This organization, taking advantage of the Newlands Act, supported the construction of a water
storage system for the valley. With the endorsement of most residents, in June 1904 it negotiated a contract promising to repay the
federal government the cost of building Roosevelt Dam, a reservoir
project to be located in the mountains about sixty-five miles northeast of Phoenix at the confluence of the Salt River and Tonto Creek.
The Association's articles of incorporation, drawn up by Judge
Kibbey, pledged the lands (over 200,000 acres) of the members as

Benjamin A. Fowler, promoter of Roosevelt Dam and first president of the Salt River Valley Water Users' Association, c. 1905. Salt River Project.

collateral to guarantee repayment of the federal construction loan. Fowler, repeatedly elected president of the Association, continued to exercise strong leadership in the efforts to bring harmony to the undertaking.[7]

Judge Kibbey also contributed in many ways to the success

of the Association. A lawyer from Indiana who had migrated to
Phoenix in 1888, he developed a special interest in irrigation law.
A year later he was appointed to the Territorial Supreme Court,
and as chief justice in 1892 he enhanced his reputation as a water
expert when he rendered a decision in the case of *Wormser* v. *Salt
River Valley Canal Company*, which established the principle that
in Arizona water belongs to the land and is not a commodity
that can be bought and sold apart from the land. Kibbey also made
it clear that early water users had priority over latecomers.

The Kibbey decision on the rights of water appropriation for
irrigation in the Salt River Valley would be reaffirmed by Chief
Justice Edward Kent in his 1910 decision in the case of *Hurley* v.
Abbott. The Kent Decree, as it became known, relieved the federal
government of any potential embarrassment in the distribution of
water from its Salt River project, for it confirmed a preestablished
system of water distribution rights based on the principle of prior
appropriation. And since one of the duties of the SRVWUA was
to supervise the distribution of project water, that organization
supported the Kent Decree because it brought more law and order
to the system.[8]

An "ideal spot for a dam and a reservoir" had been found
as early as 1889 by local promoters William M. Breckinridge,
James H. McClintock, and John R. Norton. Government officials
agreed that the location, just below the junction of the Salt River
and Tonto Creek, was "a perfect site." As Arthur P. Davis, a United
States Geological Survey engineer put it in 1897: "It would probably be impossible to find anywhere in the arid region a storage
project in which all conditions are as favorable as for this one." The
"capacity of the reservoir, in proportion to the dimensions of the
dam, is enormous." In a 1902 report, Davis reiterated his positive
view of the site, declaring that upon it "the most permanent and
secure form of high dam that is known to engineering science can
be constructed."

Officials in Washington, wanting a successful project to initiate the new reclamation program, were impressed. In February
1904, the federal government secured property rights and rights-
of-way enabling construction of the project, and in August, Secretary of the Interior Hitchcock signed the formal contract with
the SRVWUA to make it official. A road (later called the Apache
Trail) was cut from Phoenix via Tempe and Mesa to the dam site,

and construction began in September 1906. The project, then the largest masonry dam in the world, was completed in February 1911. It created what was then the largest artificial lake in the world, 25 miles long and 2 miles wide, covering more than 16,000 acres.

In the meantime, supporting facilities, designed to direct the precious water into the canal network serving the valley, were completed. The construction of the Granite Reef diversion dam was finished in May 1908, and by that time the federal government had purchased the north side and the south side canals from private interests. These additions to the water storage and water delivery system were costly, but were considered essential by the federal government and the SRVWUA. The multipurpose project provided hydroelectric power as well as water. In addition, government experts introduced the latest techniques in scientific husbandry to valley farmers, and they were increasingly utilized.

The building of Roosevelt Dam and its support system brought vital stability to the water supply, allowed irrigation control, and assured agricultural growth in the valley, and as it prospered, so did Phoenix. It was truly a significant day for the city and the Salt River Valley when the dam was dedicated on March 18, 1911, by former President Theodore Roosevelt, who predicted a "glorious future" for the central Arizona oasis, destined in his view to become "one of the richest agricultural areas in the world."[9]

Once construction on Roosevelt Dam started, local boosters and outside investors, including federal government spokesmen, began to promote the Phoenix area as being more promising than ever. The nation's first reclamation project, it was declared, would bring careful water management to the region, and the Phoenix Board of Trade inaugurated a "Tell the World About It" advertising campaign. Also, the Southern Pacific and the Santa Fe railroads published numerous accounts detailing the "marvelous future" awaiting newcomers to the busy city and the rich, irrigated Salt River Valley. For example, in August 1908 the Santa Fe devoted a special issue of its magazine, *The Earth*, to the attractions of Phoenix and the valley, and distributed it to over eighty thousand people. As a result of this publicity, farmers flocked to the area as construction of the water storage system progressed. At the end of the drought period in 1905, a report noted that cultivated land in the Salt River Valley had dropped to 96,863 acres, down from 127,512 acres in 1896. In 1909, cultivated land totaled 126,717 acres and agricultural productivity was indicating a return to more prosperous times.[10]

Growth had been slow but steady in Phoenix, with the population reaching 3,152 in 1890 and 5,544 in 1900. By 1910, the desert hub contained a population of 11,134, an increase of over 100 percent since 1900. Maricopa County in 1910 had a population of 34,485, up from 20,457 in 1900 and 9,998 in 1890. For both the county and the city, growth was the only acceptable course. "A nation which does not expand is marked for decay," declared the *Gazette*. The "same idea has been expressed with regard to cities and towns. Those which do not progress go backward—there is no standing still. It must be either grow or dry rot." The paper warned, "When opportunities for expansion present themselves they must be taken advantage of at once or the opportunities may not come again." Most Phoenicians agreed with the *Gazette*, and they supported growth.

Investors from elsewhere also promoted the view that Phoenix and the Salt River Valley should continue to develop, especially once the potential of the area became widely known. As Marshall Field, a wealthy Chicago investor in the SFP&P, put it during a visit to the Arizona capital in February 1894, "I am delighted with the country, and with Phoenix; both are far above expectations. I have just been writing to a friend in Chicago that this is the best country I have so far struck in the west." He went on to say, "You certainly have a great future here. Your country has not been half-advertised and as soon as its opportunities are better known in the east, to this valley will come a rush that will speedily fill your vacant areas." Field invested his own money in Phoenix; for example, in 1896 he gave at least $25,000 to former Chicago businessman and current Phoenix health seeker John C. Adams to help him construct a hotel.[11]

In the 1890s, local business and civic leaders supported efforts to provide the trappings of a modern city, for it was important that a desirable image be projected. With the advent of the SFP&P and its Santa Fe system connections, new settlers and investors from the Midwest, East, and California arrived, making it necessary to provide for their needs. By the end of the decade, the city offered a wide range of urban goods, services, and amenities; "in Phoenix can be found the usual conveniences of Eastern cities," noted an observer.[12]

Shaded walkways were appreciated by Phoenicians in the 1890s. The Herb and Dorothy McLaughlin Photographic Collection.

Downtown Phoenix, c. 1900. The Herb and Dorothy McLaughlin Photographic Collection.

Phoenix streetcars and Maricopa County Court House in the 1890s.
The Herb and Dorothy McLaughlin Photographic Collection.

During the 1900s, brick buildings, some of them three and
four stories tall, lined Washington Street from Third Street to
Third Avenue, and the business core extended north and south
of Washington Street between Second Street and Second Avenue.
The decade also witnessed continued business development along
Central Avenue between Van Buren and Jefferson streets. At the
same time, industries, warehouses, lumberyards, and slaughter-
houses tended to locate near the SFP&P and the M&P railroad
depots along Jackson Street in the southern part of the city.
South Phoenix also contained the poorer residential neighborhoods, while the more affluent housing areas continued to emerge
in the northern part of the city.[13]

Streetcar suburbs north of Washington Street became more apparent following the electrification of Sherman's trolley system in
September 1893. His streetcars not only promoted his own real
estate investments but also served as an attraction for other suburban subdividers interested in developing the north side. They
paid Sherman subsidies to route his streetcars through their property, thus making their real estate developments more valuable

and more attractive to buyers. For example, the Indian School line, completed in 1900, ran through north side subdivisions owned by Phoenix land developers Lloyd B. Christy, Dwight B. Heard, and William E. Thomas. Sherman also contributed to the city's physical expansion and his own financial welfare by extending his trolley system to local landmarks such as the territorial capitol building, the Indian School, the territorial fairgrounds, and Phoenix Park, later named Eastlake Park, to which his streetcar made regular runs, to the delight of countless residents and visitors.[14]

Automobiles also spurred suburban growth. After the first cars arrived in the city in the summer of 1900, prominent Phoenicians began purchasing them and loving them. No longer restricted to walking or riding streetcars, those who could afford an automobile were able to privatize the commuting experience by driving to and from work according to their own schedule. The automobile provided even more mobility than the streetcar, and suburban infilling increased. Members of the Phoenix elite, however, continued to reside along North Central Avenue, the most prestigious address in the city, and in elegant neighborhoods like Los Olivos the latest automobile models could be seen on display. Many of these people worked together as businessmen and professionals, and they played together at the select Arizona Club, the Phoenix Country Club, and Iron Springs, an exclusive summer resort located in the mountains near Prescott.

After the introduction of Henry Ford's inexpensive, mass-produced Model T in 1908, more Phoenix residents could afford to buy a car, and by 1913 the city contained ten automobile dealers. More automobiles meant more residential dispersion and commercial decentralization. A symbol of modernity throughout America, but especially in the oasis cities of the Southwest, where the climate and topography allowed effective use of motor vehicles, the automobile was among the amenities that allowed Phoenicians to reject the more traditional city structure and pursue the good life being offered as a result of incipient sprawl. Annexation proceeded apace, and by 1913 the city encompassed 3.2 square miles, up from 0.5 in 1870. By 1913, the city limits extended on the west to Twenty-third Avenue between Van Buren and Harrison, on the east to Sixteenth Street between Van Buren and Harrison, on the north to McDowell between Twelfth Street and Seventh Avenue, and on the south to Yavapai between Seventh Avenue and Central.[15]

More suburbs and automobiles increased the demand for roads.

Automobiles on display in Phoenix, 1905. The Herb and Dorothy Mc-Laughlin Photographic Collection.

As early as November 1903, an automobile club was organized in Phoenix to secure decent roads for the city and the Salt River Valley, but it proved to be unsuccessful. In December 1907, the Maricopa County Automobile Association was formed to promote better roads and better rules for drivers. It encouraged the Territorial Legislature to pass bills creating a road system to connect Phoenix with all the county seats and other important towns in Arizona. Prompted by the behavior of reckless drivers, in 1910 the Association stepped up its campaign for city ordinances to regulate traffic. By that year, there were 382 licensed automobiles in Phoenix, and traffic problems were causing alarm. In June 1910, the first motorcycle policeman appeared in the city, and the enforcement of speed limits of twelve miles per hour in the central business district and fifteen miles per hour in the suburbs improved.

Dusty streets in dry weather and muddy streets in wet weather also posed problems for automobile drivers. In November 1910,

Mayor Lloyd B. Christy organized the Phoenix Citizens' Street Paving Association to consider solutions. A special investigative committee, led by Dwight B. Heard, visited El Paso, Los Angeles, and other cities to gather street paving data. Experts were brought in to inspect and advise. The City Council approved the committee's plans, and property owners adjacent to the streets to be paved agreed to pay assessments.

In January 1912, nineteen blocks of the business core, mainly Washington Street and Central Avenue, were paved. In February, the paving of all additional streets between Van Buren, Jackson, Fourth Street, and Fourth Avenue commenced, and by March 1913 paving to cover all the streets in the area of the original townsite was authorized. Other roads in the city remained dusty and muddy, depending on the weather, but would be paved in the future as the automobile became more and more popular.

The car also inspired the construction of the Central Avenue bridge for vehicular traffic across the Salt River. Conceived in February 1908, the project was promoted by Dwight B. Heard and other Phoenix leaders who had large landholdings south of the waterway. Noting that Roosevelt Dam was becoming a reality, and once again citing the goal of a "Greater Phoenix," they declared that a Central Avenue bridge would stimulate the development of thousands of acres on the south side. The Central Avenue bridge was completed in March 1911, in time for the automobile caravan to pass over it en route to the Roosevelt Dam dedication ceremony.[16]

During the period promoters used the drawing power of the climate to attract health seekers and tourists to the desert oasis. Those "chasing the cure" were told that Phoenix was "the healthiest city in the known world," and winter tourists were invited to come and enjoy "Phoenix, the favored; Phoenix, the balmy; Phoenix, the sun-kissed." Critics complained that services needed to be improved considerably before the city could seriously call itself a health resort, but advertisements and testimonials praising the place had their effect. The result was the arrival of more people, and to meet their needs new facilities appeared; St. Joseph's Hospital, for instance, was founded in March 1895, and in December 1896 the elegant Hotel Adams opened.

St. Joseph's Hospital, founded by the Sisters of Mercy, moved to a larger building in 1900, and by 1912 it had expanded to meet the needs of additional patients. Physicians in the East had proclaimed time and again that "the one cure for lung trouble is desert air," and an influx of patients with various respiratory problems resulted in Phoenix and the valley becoming a "lungers' mecca" by the turn of the century. The area, noted local authorities, "is a natural sanatorium." The "climatic desideratum in pulmonary diseases is a mild and dry climate. Southern California has a mild climate, but it is not dry. Colorado has a dry climate, but it is not mild. The Salt River Valley has a climate at once mild and dry." Dr. E. Payne Palmer, a respected Phoenix physician, had himself been sent to the central Arizona city "to experience the curative effects of sunshine and climate for his incipient tuberculosis." The writings of Palmer and others inspired many health seekers to move to the area, and more health facilities were built. In December 1907, the Episcopal Church opened St. Luke's Home for tubercular patients. Experiencing demands similar to those placed on St. Joseph's Hospital, it also had expanded by 1912.[17]

For affluent health seekers, the Desert Inn Sanatorium provided the best accommodations. Located on "100 acres of beautiful grounds" six miles east of Phoenix, it claimed to be "especially suited to benefit incipient bronchial and pulmonary cases, and convalescents for la grippe, pneumonia, and other extremely debilitating diseases." A number of wealthy afflicted bought or rented homes. For example, Whitelaw Reid, owner and editor of the *New York Times*, suffered from respiratory problems and, taking the advice of medical advisers, he spent several winters in Phoenix. Renting a three-story mansion built by local physician Roland Rosson, Reid enjoyed his visits, invested in the area, and invited his well-to-do friends from throughout the nation to follow his example and visit and invest in Phoenix and the Salt River Valley.

Tent camps appeared throughout the valley, and some of them housed indigent health seekers. A 1903 ordinance prohibiting the erection of tents within the municipal limits forced many health seekers to live beyond the city in poor desert settlements such as Sunnyslope, where they endured a life of rejection, isolation, and destitution. For many of them, the desert proved to be a death warrant rather than a cure. In short, the sick poor existed as best they could, often without food, clothing, or care.[18]

In and about Phoenix, Christianna G. Gilchrist carried on her benevolent work among the indigent as supervisor of the Associated Charities, a local cooperative society sponsored by churches, lodges, businesses, and other organizations. From the time of its inception in November 1904, the Associated Charities gave much of its aid to poor health seekers. In a letter to New York reformer Jacob Riis in January 1907, Gilchrist wrote that from December to April the population of Phoenix increased by one-fourth, and 90 percent of the newcomers were tuberculars, most of them hoping to find work to pay their expenses. Since few employers were hiring the disabled, hundreds of sick poor became dependent on the Associated Charities and other Phoenix benevolent organizations.

Although its contributors included a good many Phoenicians, the Associated Charities experienced budget problems. Noting that over three hundred persons had been helped during the winter of 1907–08, Gilchrist lamented the "great draft on charity in Phoenix." Nevertheless, she worked diligently to overcome the problem, and she was appreciated. "The people have come to know her as a patient, faithful worker of the Lord and give without stint," observed the *Gazette*. Gilchrist, born in Indiana in 1862, and a graduate of Hanover College, had taught school in Colorado before moving to Phoenix in 1899 for health reasons. Active in the Women's Christian Temperance Union and the Presbyterian Missionary Society, she spent many years as supervisor of the Associated Charities. Through example she inspired many Phoenix men and women to devote time and money to the problems of poor health seekers and others in need of assistance.

The contributions of concerned individuals and groups helped, but generally local leaders considered health seekers who lacked income a burden and did not welcome them. Those with few or no funds were often discouraged from coming or staying. For example, the literature sent out by the Phoenix and Salt River Valley Immigration Commission stated, "While presenting every attraction to the health seekers, the valley and its cities and towns do not offer an asylum for indigent people who wish to regain health. . . . Persons coming for health reasons should arrive with sufficient money to pay all living expenses for at least one year." Those who failed to follow this advice and arrived in Phoenix with few or no funds risked being returned by public officials to their last place of residence.[19]

At the same time, affluent, healthy tourists were given every encouragement to visit Phoenix and the Salt River Valley, and they were provided with the services of several large, modern hotels equipped to meet their needs. The Ingleside Inn, an eight hundred-acre development located nine miles northeast of Phoenix, was the best of the pre-1912 resorts. Unlike the health seekers' retreats, the Ingleside Inn declared in bold print that it was "not a sanatorium and could not receive as guests any persons suffering from communicable diseases." This attitude, unfortunately for health seekers, would become more and more evident in the desert center. As the sick arrived in increasing numbers, they heightened the fears of some healthy Phoenicians who felt threatened by them. They felt that the Phoenix area was becoming an "unsafe place for well people."

Meanwhile, by 1913 it was estimated that as many as three thousand winter tourists were visiting the valley. Resort facilities could accommodate only a small percentage of them, so most tourists stayed in downtown hotels. The Hotel Adams, for example, enjoyed a reputation as one of the largest and finest in the Southwest. Located at the corner of Central Avenue and Adams Street, the four-story structure contained 150 well-furnished rooms, exterior verandas on each floor, an enormous dining room, and a roof garden for dancing and sightseeing. Constructed by John C. Adams, a transplanted Chicago investor and health seeker, the hotel became the meeting place for the prominent and "the showplace of Phoenix." A terrible fire consumed the Adams in May 1910, but it was quickly rebuilt and remained as popular as ever.[20]

First-class department stores as well as hotels began to appear in Phoenix in the 1890s. Unlike the smaller general stores of the past, these impressive structures required substantial capital to operate. As in the past, Jewish merchants were in the forefront. The New York Store, founded in September 1895 by Sam Korrick, was soon followed by Nathan and Isaac Diamond's Boston Store, and Baron Goldwater opened a branch of the Prescott-based M. Goldwater and Brothers. All three stores developed into the leading retail outlets in the city. Martin W. Kales, Emil Ganz, Charles Goldman, and Simon Oberfelder remained leading bankers in the city. While Jewish merchants and bankers prospered in Phoenix, not all were engaged in such large business and financial enterprises as the New York Store or the National Bank of Arizona. By 1910 most Jews in the city belonged to the middle-class world of shopkeepers and tradesmen.

Jews continued to be active in the public life of Phoenix. Emil Ganz served as mayor of the city at the turn of the century, and several Jews sat on the City Council during the period. They contributed to the development of St. Joseph's Hospital, the YMCA, and other Phoenix institutions, and they joined the Masons, the

Odd Fellows, and other local fraternal orders. Overt discrimination against Jews continued to be the exception rather than the rule; the Goldwaters, Goldbergs, Ganzes, and Oberfelders belonged to the Phoenix Country Club, the Arizona Club, and other prestigious organizations. No synagogue existed in Phoenix until 1922, but private services and celebrations abounded.[21]

The bias against Native Americans in the city continued into the 1890s, despite the creation of the Phoenix Indian School. Reservation Indians remained unwelcome in Phoenix, as ordinances regulating their behavior in the city indicated, but federal money was always appreciated. In October 1890, Commissioner of Indian Affairs Thomas J. Morgan informed local leaders of the federal government's desire to "civilize" central Arizona's natives by educating them in a boarding school to be established in Phoenix if the city donated a suitable eighty-acre site. Phoenix leaders, supported by most of the population, pledged their utmost cooperation. One booster noted that a school for four hundred children should attract over $100,000 per year in federal funds; another declared that it would be worth more to Phoenix than "ten Capitols, Universities or Normal Schools." Not only would the federal government inject $100,000 or more into the Phoenix economy annually, but the school would provide "cheap and efficient labor" for local employers. Phoenix and Salt River Valley business and agricultural interests were urged to take advantage of this opportunity and guarantee an acceptable school site as soon as possible.

A few critics objected. Charles D. Poston, a Phoenix resident and a former Arizona superintendent of Indian affairs, charged that the school would "increase the number of Indian drunkards and prostitutes now infesting the town by day and night." Commissioner Morgan retorted that past experience with Indian schools failed to substantiate that charge. In December, Secretary of the Interior John W. Noble, impressed with the enthusiasm of local promoters, requested a congressional appropriation to open a school for Indians in Phoenix.

In April 1891, the federal government purchased 160 acres of improved land from Frank C. Hatch. Located east of Central Avenue and just south of the Grand Canal, the land cost $9,000. Because of the expanded acreage, the government agreed to provide two-thirds of the purchase price, with local citizens donating the remaining $3,000. The land was choice, with ample room for a school farm. At the time, the desired site was located three miles north of the city, but Moses Sherman promised to quickly construct a streetcar line to the new institution.

In September 1891, the Phoenix Indian School started classes in the West End House, a converted hotel located at the corner of Washington Street and Seventh Avenue. The initial class consisted of thirty-one Pima and ten Maricopa boys. In April 1892, the students were transferred to the first completed building at the Central Avenue site, a large two-story structure designed to accommodate 125 students. From the beginning, the school stressed agricultural and vocational training. The value of manual labor and the English language was emphasized. Strict discipline was utilized to inculcate American ways; otherwise, officials asserted, the Indian students might be tempted to "drop back into their old filthy ways." At the school, life was severely regulated, and for practical experience the "outing" system sent students into Phoenix and the Salt River Valley to work for private employers. For example, local farmers requested Indian males to help harvest their crops, and local matrons requested Indian females to serve as family domestics.

During the 1890s, the Phoenix Indian School expanded. By the turn of the century, the institution maintained fifteen major buildings and enrolled over seven hundred students. It was the largest Indian school in the United States with the exception of Carlisle. The ethnocentric *Gazette*, reflecting the attitude of the white population, noted that "here hundreds of boys and girls were annually transferred from the native condition of indolence and uselessness into civilized and useful members of society." As long as they kept their proper place in society, the Indian students were tolerated and exploited. The "outing" system, for example, provided inexpensive labor for local employers. As one observer put it, "The hiring of Indian youth is not looked upon by the people of this valley from a philanthropic standpoint. It is simply a matter of business."

As the institution expanded, federal expenditures continued to boost the local economy and contribute to the welfare of many local citizens. Promoters of tourism in Phoenix and the valley also capitalized on the school. It became a tourist attraction, and no parade or celebration in the city was complete without the appearance of the Phoenix Indian School Band. Such festive occasions usually had more "wild Indians" in war paint and traditional dress representing the past, and this pleased many tourists; but the

Phoenix Indian School band, c. 1905. The Herb and Dorothy Mc-Laughlin Photographic Collection.

well-dressed, well-disciplined Indian band contrasted nicely life in the "new Arizona" with the "Indian problem" of recent history.[22]

Few Indians resided in Phoenix, but other non-Anglo minorities lived in distinct residential areas located south of Washington Street. By 1910, Mexicans concentrated in an area of poor housing south of the tracks between Seventh Avenue and Seventh Street. Mexicans, noted a Phoenix promotion pamphlet, "make excellent day laborers." Inexpensive and efficient, the majority of the Mexicans were farm workers who were especially valuable to growers in the Salt River Valley. Many of them had been driven out of rural Mexico during the unpopular reign of Porfirio Díaz. In Mexico, they had received wages of ten cents per day; in Phoenix, they received fifty cents per day. In Phoenix, Mexican field hands were often arrested for being drunk and disorderly. Anglos always seemed to be given less time in jail than the Mexicans after being arrested for committing the same offense.

Finding acceptance in the Anglo-dominated community difficult to obtain, most Mexicans created their own communal life. St. Mary's Catholic Church remained a vital institution, and Mexican voluntary associations such as the Alianza Hispano-Americana emerged to provide members with a sense of security and sociability. Unlike Tucson, Phoenix did not contain a Mexican elite whose families dated back to earlier periods and who often mingled with Tucson's Anglo elite. In the Arizona capital, a few Mexican leaders continued to serve the Mexican population, but for most Mexicans upward mobility proved elusive and poverty remained the norm.[23]

While the 1,100 Mexicans residing in Phoenix in 1910 made up 10 percent of the total population, the 110 Chinese represented only 1 percent. Chinatown, however, remained a lively place. Contained within Jackson, Jefferson, and First and Third streets, Chinatown in 1910 was the most tightly knit ethnic community in the city. Like other racial minority groups, the Chinese were encouraged by the white population to seek refuge in their own neighborhood. As the *Arizona Republican*, a Phoenix newspaper, observed in June 1890, "The wily Mongolians should be kept in as small an area as possible." That pronouncement reflected an attitude that still prevailed in 1910.

During the period, the Chinese continued to operate laundries, grocery stores, vegetable stands, and restaurants; by 1910 the three largest restaurants in Phoenix were controlled by Chinese. The restaurants were often visited by whites, but other Chinese businesses catered mainly to Chinese, Mexican, and black customers. The raiding of Chinese opium dens also persisted. In March 1911, for example, the Phoenix police raided Chinatown looking for narcotics. "Four opium dens were discovered, all in full blast, and packed to the doors with hop-smoking Chinks."

In September 1911, while visiting the city, the famous black leader Booker T. Washington interviewed the unofficial leader of Chinatown, Ong Dick, known as "China Dick" and, derisively, as "Yellow Dick"—but mostly as "Mayor Dick" because of his exalted position in the Chinese community. "Mayor Dick" served as "the supreme authority in Chinatown," Washington stated, and he "seemed to have a pretty clear understanding of American customs and manners." The black leader asked the Chinese leader how he came to be called "Mayor," and Dick responded: "Well, you see, I am here thirty years. I know American custom. When Chinaboy get in trouble he come to see me. When policeman get in trouble with Chinaboy, both come to me. I know how to make it all right. So the newspapers say I am Mayor of Chinatown. Yes."

Dick also told Washington that the Chinese population in Phoenix was gradually decreasing. He explained, "Every Chinaman must some time go back to China. He is never more than a sojourner in America. If he does not go back alive, he goes back in his coffin." Reflecting on his conversation with Dick, Washington was especially impressed with the extent to which "the Chinaman is an alien in this country. I doubt whether any other portion of the population remains so thoroughly foreign as is true of the Chinaman." During the period, of course, the development of anti-Chinese sentiment and anti-Chinese immigration legislation at the national level did not encourage them to settle in Phoenix or in Arizona in large numbers.[24]

When Washington visited Phoenix in September 1911, nearly four hundred blacks lived in the city. Most of the males worked as field hands, common laborers, or in unskilled service jobs, but many owned small businesses; women usually worked as domestics. With limited funds and limited opportunities, members of the black community concentrated around the Second Baptist Church and the Frederick Douglass Elementary School, both segregated institutions located on the block bounded by Jefferson, Madison, Fifth, and Sixth streets. This south Phoenix neighborhood also contained Block 41, the unofficial headquarters of prostitution in the city, and as Geoffrey Mawn has noted, "While there appeared to be no direct participatory connection to blacks to prostitution, whites certainly considered the neighborhood 'less desirable' and thus opened it to black settlement without notice or protest."

In white neighborhoods, however, attitude problems and race restrictions precluded the entry of blacks; indeed, even cemeteries in Phoenix were segregated. Black institutional life centered in the churches: the African Methodist Episcopal Church, South, at Second and Jefferson streets, and the Second Baptist Church (Colored), at Fifth and Jefferson streets. Black fraternal lodges also served as focal points in the black community, especially the Colored Masons, the Colored Odd Fellows, and the Colored Knights of Pythias.

A number of black business establishments had emerged by 1910 to serve neighborhood residents and visitors. When John Lewis, black owner of the Fashion Barber Shop, opened a "hotel for colored people" on Seventh and Jefferson streets in July 1912, he declared that in Phoenix "all the better class of hotels and rooming houses cater exclusively to white people. There are a few cheap places where a colored man can find accommodations, but there are many colored men who do not care to patronize such places, both because the accommodations are poor and because of the low class of humanity often met there." The local press dutifully mentioned the business and social life of the black community in the city. It noted lectures delivered to the Colored Forum, concerts given by the Colored Band and the Colored Glee Club, and games played by the Colored Cubs, a Phoenix baseball team, but at times the press emphasized what it considered to be the negative side of black life in the city. The Afro-American Club, for example, was in June 1912 called a "moral sink," a "vehicle for the exercise of license and debauchery," a "lawless nigger club," and a "disgrace to the city of Phoenix."[25]

Black leaders resisted second-class citizenship in Phoenix, but to no avail. School segregation, for example, did not prevail without a protest. In March 1909, the Territorial Legislature passed a proposal allowing Arizona school districts, when they deemed it advisable, to segregate students of African ancestry from students of other racial backgrounds. Few white Arizonans opposed the measure, but one who did was Governor Joseph H. Kibbey, who promptly vetoed it. Kibbey had already served as chief justice of the Arizona Supreme Court and as a prominent Phoenix lawyer and leader of the Salt River Valley Water Users' Association when he was appointed governor of Arizona Territory in 1905 by President Theodore Roosevelt. Kibbey opposed the segregation proposal on economic and moral grounds: "It would be unfair that pupils of the African race should be given accommodations and facilities for a common school education, less effective, less complete, less convenient or less pleasant so far as the accessories of the school and its operations are concerned than those accorded pupils of the white race in the same school district; and the bill in terms contemplates nothing less." The Territorial Legislature reacted by overriding Governor Kibbey's veto, and school segregation became legal on March 17, 1909.

Few districts in Arizona adopted school segregation, but Phoenix did. In April 1910, the Phoenix School Board, supported by the majority of the white population in the city, adopted a segregation policy. In protest, the blacks hired Kibbey, once again in private practice in Phoenix, to initiate injunction proceedings against the school board to prevent the segregation of white and black students. The injunction suit on behalf of black plaintiff Samuel F. Bayless, who contended that segregation imposed an unfair burden on his children, against defendants L. D. Dameron, Sims Ely, and W. G. Tolleson, all board members, asked that the board be enjoined from segregating black children from those of other races and requiring them to attend a school for black children. Kibbey argued that separate could never be equal. To provide "separate but equal" facilities was "impracticable," but "if it is not done, this law is unjust and unfair, and justified by no just consideration whatever." In July, the injunction suit was set for trial in December; in the meantime, the construction of what would become Frederick Douglass Elementary School for "colored children" on Madison Street between Fifth and Sixth streets, in the midst of the predominant black neighborhood in Phoenix, proceeded.

In August 1910, District Attorney George Bullard contended that black citizens favored a separate school for their children. He stated that a group of black parents indicated to him that their children did not receive an "even break" with white students in integrated schools, and that in segregated schools they would not "suffer from ostracism." Reacting quickly and strongly to Bullard's comments, black leader William P. Crump denied that a basis of black support for segregated schools existed. Noting that 98 percent of the blacks he knew in Phoenix bitterly resented the policy, Crump declared the following:

> We do not oppose it from any desire for social equality, for that is foreign to our thoughts. We fight it because it is a step backward; because there are not enough colored children here to enable them to establish a fully equipped school; because it is an injustice to take the money of all the taxpayers to establish ward schools and then force the colored children to walk two miles to school while their property is taxed to provide ward schools for all other children; because from the organization of the territory to the present time the children of all classes of its cosmopolitan citizenship have gone to school together and there has been no friction or trouble of any kind, and as a result there is not a community in America where the relations of the black and white are more amicable and peaceful than in Phoenix.

Crump, operator of a successful fruit and produce business, had arrived in Phoenix in 1897 from West Virginia. After securing employment as a waiter at the Ford Hotel, he sent for his family. By 1902, he was a prosperous commission merchant selling Salt River Valley fruits and vegetables throughout the West. Crump, a community leader, and his family resented Jim Crow restrictions in hotels, theaters, restaurants, and other gathering places in Phoenix. Segregation made the Crump family angry, his daughter Emily later recalled. "We felt it deeply, that we were treated so differently." Rather than send Emily and her sister Elizabeth to the "colored school," Crump enrolled them in St. Mary's Catholic Church School, where they were among the first of their race to graduate in 1916.

The idea of school segregation infuriated Crump, and when he called on the black population to protest "this unnecessary and uncalled for outrage," white Phoenix reacted. "The Negroes who protest against the segregation law are doing their race a great injury," asserted the *Arizona Democrat*, a local newspaper. It stated, "The colored people in Arizona are nicely treated," and suggested that "they conduct themselves in such a manner that this kindly feeling will continue." The "people of Arizona are in favor of this segregation of the races in our public schools and they propose to have such segregation; and protests will only result in making the demand for it persistent."

In September 1910, sixteen black children enrolled at Douglass School to study under black principal J. T. Williams and black teacher Lucy B. Craig; by December fifty-four had enrolled. In that month, the trial of *Bayless* v. *Dameron et al.* unfolded and Kibbey presented his case. At this time, Bayless had two daughters, six and ten years old, who prior to segregation had walked five blocks to school. After Douglass School opened, the girls were forced to walk two miles and to cross the tracks of both the Southern Pacific and the SFP&P, an act that imperiled life and limb. Kibbey argued that to impose this unequal and dangerous situation on the black students was unfair. Kibbey also called upon Crump, the black businessman who had once taught school in West Virginia, and he testified that ungraded schools were not as good as graded ones. On the other side, Phoenix Superintendent of Schools John D. Loper declared that black schools were equal to white schools.

Judge Edward Kent commented that he could not understand why "Africans" would want to attend white schools when they would be happier "with their own." He also believed the Territorial Legislature had the power to segregate on the basis of race where "equal facilities for each are afforded." Kent agreed with the *Republican* assessment that the black students were actually better off than the whites in their new school building, and he felt they would especially benefit from close attention in small classes. Kent agreed with Kibbey that unjust discrimination did exist in the distances and dangers the children had to overcome, and he exempted black students in the first four grades from attending Douglass School.

District Attorney Bullard appealed Kent's decision regarding the exemption in January 1911, but the case did not reach final settlement until after Arizona became a state in February 1912. The Arizona Supreme Court, after citing the "separate but equal" doctrine enunciated in the 1896 United States Supreme Court case of *Plessy* v. *Ferguson*, confirmed the constitutionality of the segregation law. As for the distances traveled and the dangers encountered by black students that led Judge Kent to exempt the first four grades from attending Douglass School, the Arizona justices concluded that they furnished "no substantial ground of complaint." The case was dismissed, and under the segregation law Douglass School continued to provide classes for all black elementary school students in the public system; at the same time, the majority of black students in Phoenix in 1912 lived in the area east, south, and west of Douglass School and probably would have attended the institution without the law. For the few black students who managed to reach the secondary level of public education, Phoenix Union High School offered its "colored room." [26]

When Booker T. Washington arrived in Phoenix on September 22, 1911, to participate in "The Great Emancipation Jubilee," he was greeted mainly "by his own people," who escorted him from the SFP&P depot to Eastlake Park at Sixteenth Street and Jefferson. Following a reception hosted by members of the Second Baptist Church, Washington delivered a speech in which he rejected social equality for blacks but insisted they receive equal protection of the law. He also stressed to blacks the importance of work and the dignity of labor.

Washington delivered several speeches on the same themes during his three-day stay in the city, and they were well received by whites as well as blacks. His moderate views did not threaten whites, and he inspired blacks. Following a special service in his honor at the Second Baptist Church on Sunday morning, he attended a concert at Eastlake Park featuring the music of the

Colored Band, the Mexican Band, and the Indian School Band. Shortly after Washington left Phoenix on September 24, local black leaders formed the International Council to foster better understanding between blacks and "all other peoples." Members of the organization hoped "to help develop the resources of Arizona, and to assist in making a greater Phoenix."[27]

Racial relations in Phoenix reflected on the local level much of what was occurring in urban America during the earlier years of the twentieth century. Although the period is often called the Progressive era in American history, black Americans could argue that for them progress failed to develop. At the same time, reform movements erupted throughout the United States during the Progressive period as citizens participated in crusades they felt would help make their cities better places in which to live. In Phoenix, for example, the structure of municipal government changed from the mayor-council system to a commission-city manager system in 1913.

As Phoenix more than doubled in size between 1900 and 1910, the management of city government became more complex and difficult. Progressive reform on the national level influenced politics in Arizona and Phoenix. Urban America was undergoing a transformation, and it introduced structural changes in the desert city. The Civic Federation, organized in September 1908, was designed to "promote unselfishly anything that will benefit and uplift Phoenix." In April 1911, the Commercial Club's plan for a "Greater Phoenix" predicted that the city would be for Arizona what Los Angeles was for southern California. Sufficiently boosted and rightly governed, it proclaimed, "Phoenix cannot fail to become the big city between LA and El Paso."

Boosterism was rampant in the city, but good government seemed elusive. There was little graft or corruption in Phoenix, compared with larger urban centers elsewhere in the nation, but increasingly proponents of the commission form of city government argued that it was more efficient and progressive than the mayor-council system existing in the Arizona capital. Convinced that more modern methods would prove more successful in running fast-growing Phoenix, reformers secured reports on good city government from the National Municipal League, and charter change became their principal goal. After a few false starts, a nonpartisan Charter Committee of One Hundred, composed of the city's most prominent men, was organized in January 1913 to discuss the issue. When Phoenix women, having acquired the vote in November 1912, complained about being excluded from the committee and being left out of the charter formation process, twenty-five were added, making it the Charter Committee of One Hundred and Twenty-Five.

Charter reform received widespread support in Phoenix. Eventually the great majority of the people, the three newspapers, and the leading organizations—including the City Club, the Arizona Club, the Board of Trade, and the Merchants' and Manufacturers' Association—promoted it. It was important to Phoenix boosters that their city possess a modern, progressive image. After a number of meetings, the Charter Committee of One Hundred and Twenty-Five selected a fourteen-member subcommittee, under the leadership of Joseph H. Kibbey and made up of representative business and professional men, to draft a formal charter document. The proposed new charter provided for a commission-city manager form of government consisting of a mayor, four commissioners, and a city manager.

Except for the city manager, who was appointed by the commission, city officials were to be elected at large; thus the ward system was abolished. It was felt that the ward system unnecessarily factionalized the city; under the new charter, elected officials would be accountable to the entire electorate, not sections of it. At the same time, advocates knew that by eliminating the ward system, they eliminated the political power of the less affluent, less numerous part of the population residing in south Phoenix. Under the old structure, the city was divided into four wards, the dividing lines being Central Avenue and Washington Street, with the northeast quadrant being ward 1 and the remaining three numbered counterclockwise. Thus, wards 3 and 4 were located in south Phoenix, while the more affluent, more populous wards 1 and 2 were located north of Washington Street. As R. L. Dyer, secretary of the Good Government League, put it at a meeting of that charter reform organization in early February 1914, "The third and fourth wards are composed of a class of people who do not meet with the high ideals of those here present." Under the new charter, elected at-large officials from the north side would replace those who had represented the less affluent, less numerous residents of the south side wards in the past. As a result, it was felt by dominant interests, the government of Phoenix would be in the hands of the "right people."

Supporters also hoped that an efficient city manager, account-able to elected officials, would help take politics out of city hall and improve the management of municipal affairs. In August 1913, the new charter was submitted to the City Council, and in October city voters, including women, favored it by a vote of 958 to 313, a three-to-one margin. The Republican majority usually ruled in Phoenix, but both Republicans and Democrats, or at least those interested enough to vote, supported the change. In December, Democratic Governor George W. P. Hunt approved the document, and reformers eagerly looked forward to the upcoming city elec-tions in March 1914.

Phoenix was one of the first dozen cities in the country to adopt the commission-city manager form of government. Considered an efficient, businesslike approach to city administration, this struc-tural reform was widespread in the smaller urban centers of the United States by the time of World War I. Unfortunately, the high expectations Phoenix had for its new charter government were quickly dashed.[28]

4 URBAN OASIS, 1914-1929

Phoenix government soon failed to live up to expectations. A period of economic boom and bust swept over the city and the valley during and after World War I, but the 1920s served the area well. By the time of the Great Crash of 1929, Phoenix was the leading city in Arizona and the second largest in the Southwest, after El Paso. During the 1920s the Arizona capital was a focal point of life in the region. A downtown construction boom and automobile-inspired suburban growth expanded the physical dimensions of the city, and new facilities—plus the beckonings of booster organizations —encouraged more tourists and health seekers to visit the sunshine center. As the city continued to offer more opportunities and amenities, its population and its potential increased considerably.

In March 1914, Phoenicians elected George U. Young as the first mayor under the commission government, and Joseph M. Cope, Peter Corpstein, Michael J. Foley, and Frank Woods as the first city commissioners. After assuming office in April, the commissioners unanimously appointed William A. Farish as the first city manager of Phoenix. An experienced irrigation engineer and government administrator, Farish had worked for both the United States Reclamation Service and the city of Phoenix. He also was a resident of the city, a requirement for the position. According to the state constitution, all city officials had to be residents of the city at the time of their election or appointment. This meant that only local residents were eligible for appointment to the office of city manager; it was not sufficient for a prospective manager to agree to move to the city subsequent to his appointment.[1]

Under the commission-city manager form of administration, Farish was given substantial power, and he used it to cut costs and reward merit. He alienated many businessmen by being too efficient in enforcing and collecting license fees; he found that in the past many of them had escaped the payment of fees by reason of favoritism or neglect. Farish also introduced competitive bidding on city projects, thus reducing the cost of construction, and he urged public ownership of private utilities that failed to offer decent service and fair rates. Farish also acquired enemies when, in making appointments and hiring workers, he denounced patronage and emphasized honest, nonpartisan professionalism in Phoenix government. Disregarding the "traditional qualification of political connections," he discharged employees and consolidated positions in the interest of proficiency and economy.

In important areas of public responsibility Farish was quick to meet the needs of the community. He added new personnel and purchased new equipment for the fire department, and he supervised the establishment of two new fire stations in the city. Under the direction of Farish, Phoenix developed a professional police department for the first time. He increased the force from fifteen to twenty-four men and women, and instituted progressive, preventive, and protective methods, including more effective police leadership and patrol patterns. In addition, Farish worked to upgrade the public sanitation and public health systems in Phoenix; for example, he repeatedly requested that the city erect a municipal sewage treatment plant, a facility completed in August 1915.[2]

Reform advocates hoped that the charter changes would guarantee businesslike government. Efficiency and economy in local administration promised to make Phoenix a progressive, modern urban center. The inclusion of a city manager and a commission in the structural change made the new charter an up-to-date document, and the city a participant in the vanguard of the national municipal reform movement. Phoenix boosters felt that giving the Arizona capital the latest in municipal innovations might benefit the entire city, and themselves as well. Unfortunately, in practice the reforms proved to be, in many instances, too progressive

Firefighters in Phoenix, 1916. The Herb and Dorothy McLaughlin Photographic Collection.

for Phoenix, and local leaders tended to ignore them. Especially bothersome to Phoenix political leaders was the powerful role given to the city manager. The competent, if not always diplomatic, Farish turned out to be the strongest and most disturbing personality in Phoenix government, and from the beginning he often found himself at odds with the mayor and the four commissioners. The independent Farish posed a problem to them, so they decided to remove him.

Farish had made numerous enemies in Phoenix because of his policies and his personality, and they rallied to support the mayor and the commissioners when they held a formal hearing to discuss the status of the city manager in February 1915. There had been complaints from former city employees as well as protests from anonymous groups regarding Farish, and under the new charter the city manager could be dismissed "for cause" by the mayor and the four commissioners. They charged Farish with incompetence, but he ably defended his actions as city manager.

Arizona Gazette editor Charles H. Akers appealed to Mayor Young and the commissioners to end the proceedings. He declared, "The people of Phoenix are sick and tired of the entire business. Not a single charge has been substantiated, and the whole thing has degenerated into as farcical an exhibition of silliness as has ever disgraced Arizona." Getting to the point of the confrontation, the *Arizona Republican* commented, "It is a matter of common knowledge that the unfriendliness of a majority of the members of the commission grew out of the city manager's resentment of their attempted interference with his duties, plainly prescribed by the charter." Commission members also failed to appreciate the city manager's "disregard of the desire of the members of the commission for the appointment of certain persons to positions and the retention of certain persons in positions, in spite of the charter provisions that such employees were to be appointed or discharged as the judgment of the city manager alone might dictate." The paper concluded, "If the city manager had been weak and yielding there would have been no charges, no hearing and no attempted removal."

Calling the city manager's defense insufficient, in March the mayor and the four commissioners unanimously adopted a formal resolution announcing that Farish "did not possess the executive and managerial ability required for the efficient conduct of the office of city manager." They removed Farish and named Robert A. Craig, a local businessman, to succeed him. The new city manager related better to Mayor Young and the commissioners. In April, Phoenix voters approved amendments to the city charter redefining the powers of city officials. Basic changes reflected a desire on the part of the elected mayor and commissioners to regain lost patronage and decision-making power from the appointed city manager. For example, according to the new amendments, in the future the major appointees to city government would be named by the commissioners rather than the city manager. Minor appointees would continue to be selected by the city manager, but must be confirmed by the mayor and commissioners. In short, the city manager's power was greatly reduced, and he became more subservient to the mayor and the commission.[3]

In addition to approving amendments to the city charter redefining the powers of city officials, the April 1915 election resulted in the repeal of a number of progressive measures, including license fee reform. Soon a return to the patronage and favoritism of the past occurred, and local government once again reached a level of mediocrity that would persist for years. As for the office of city manager, it became the choicest plum of all, with twenty-four different Phoenicians involved in thirty-one changes in the position during the thirty-five-year period following the dismissal of Farish. City managers in the Arizona capital lasted an average of thirteen months before 1949. During those years, Phoenix led the nation in the total number of city manager changes. At the same time, Phoenix had twenty-two different men involved in twenty-eight changes in the mayor's chair, five being reelected after being out of office for at least one term. Frequent change and chronic instability, rather than progressive administration, marked Phoenix government in the years following 1914; contrary to the goals of local reformers, mediocre leadership, petty factionalism, and "politics as usual" continued to reign.

Throughout the period, Phoenix government resembled a game of musical chairs. Few mayors or commissioners remained in office for more than one term, and city managers came and went with them. Critics lamented the lack of true change in Phoenix government as a result of charter revisions as they observed city hall being operated "on a political, rather than on a business basis."

During the 1920s, there emerged a few minor movements to revise the charter so that it better reflected its original intent, but to no avail. The majority of Phoenix residents felt no great need for more charter changes; as long as basic city services continued to be provided, most of them simply accepted "politics in city hall" as normal. That the city manager remained a participant in the political game did not necessarily disturb them. The famous political scientist Leonard D. White visited Phoenix in 1927, and wrote, "The managers of the Arizona city have become deeply entangled with local politics." White discussed the "relation of the manager to politics" in the city with a group of leading citizens, and they agreed without dissent that in Phoenix "the manager had always been in politics." They also agreed that "it is part of the manager's business to see to it that friendly commissioners are elected." Otherwise, the city "would, as a matter of course, change managers." When White informed the Phoenix leaders that city managers "ordinarily take no part in a campaign, even when they are the issue and their tenure of office is in the balance," they expressed "no little surprise, if not polite incomprehension."[4]

While political reform remained elusive in Phoenix, there

existed no shortage of boosterism. With the successful completion of the water and power delivery systems of the Salt River project, the city, as well as the valley, rapidly developed. By April 1915, when Lake Roosevelt contained over 1.3 million acre-feet of stored water, valley farmers cultivated 250,000 acres of alfalfa, grain, citrus, cotton, and other crops. Alfalfa remained the principal product; most of it was exported, but it also supported local cattle and sheep operations.

During America's participation in World War I, Phoenix and the valley enjoyed boom times as agricultural activity expanded to new dimensions. At this time, long-staple cotton became a crop essential to the war effort. Foreign cotton exporters were cut off from the American market, and defense contractors were forced to find new domestic supplies of long-staple cotton necessary in the production of tires and airplane fabric. The Salt River Valley proved ideal as a new source, and as market prices rose, farmers and "cotton plungers" invested in long-staple cotton, known as white gold. The Goodyear Tire and Rubber Corporation of Akron, Ohio, in order to keep its plants operating during the shortage, bought cotton from Salt River Valley growers and purchased two tracts of desert land to grow its own cotton in early 1917: eight thousand acres southeast of Phoenix, called Goodyear, and sixteen thousand acres west of Phoenix, called Litchfield. Goodyear executive Paul W. Litchfield recruited and hired experts, and both projects developed and flourished; under his direction, thousands of acres of cotton were planted, cotton gins and mills were built, and two company towns were constructed.

In 1918, cotton production replaced alfalfa growing as the leading industry in the Salt River Valley. In that year, 72,000 acres of cotton were planted, up from 7,400 in 1916, and by 1920 that amount had increased to 190,000 acres, three-fourths of the irrigated land in the valley. During these years a "cotton craze" erupted in the area as the price of cotton soared from $.28 to $1.35 per pound. Land prices also rose rapidly. According to one fascinated observer, "In January 1916, 80 acres of land near Peoria sold for $60 an acre. In January 1919, it sold in similar tracts for $500 an acre. That is an increase of 833%."[5]

In 1917, there were almost eight hundred miles of main canals served by low-cost water from the Roosevelt Dam system. In 1919, a reporter visiting the "lively, enterprising Arizona city" of Phoenix

Irrigation scene, c. 1920. The Herb and Dorothy McLaughlin Photographic Collection.

Cooling off in a Phoenix canal, 1924. The Herb and Dorothy McLaughlin Photographic Collection.

declared that he looked upon "a beautiful valley, with a great irrigation system, which has reclaimed 250,000 acres of fertile land from the desert." He called it "the agricultural center of Arizona; and one of the most productive portions of our country," noting, "Such acres with their never failing streams of water mean production, profit, and contented life." These acres in 1920 contained mostly cotton. By that year, market specialists were forecasting a price of $1.50 per pound, and the great majority of the 7,200 farmers in the Salt River Valley had given up the cultivation of other crops and joined in the cotton boom.[6]

The cotton market collapsed in the fall of 1920, causing a short-lived depression. A cotton glut occurred when foreign growers dumped enormous amounts of cotton surplus on the American market at the same time the United States was returning to lower peacetime demand. The price of long-staple cotton plummeted from $1.35 to less than $.35 per pound. Having planted every available acre in long-staple cotton and having borrowed heavily to buy and plant additional acreage, valley cotton interests faced severe losses in the sale of the 1920 crop. The "cotton bust" brought much suffering to the area. Many of the growers went bankrupt, business in general declined, and Mexican farm workers, who had been exploited for years, became destitute and their situation increasingly deplorable. Hard times continued in Phoenix and the valley during the early 1920s as a result of the depression, but lessons were learned. Cotton would remain important to the economy in the future, but more crop diversification would once again be the rule.[7]

In order to promote crop diversification, valley banks offered generous, low-interest loans to farmers wanting to produce a variety of agricultural products. Soon alfalfa and grain fields, citrus groves, and dairy herds reappeared. The abundance of alfalfa, wheat, and barley boosted cattle ranching and livestock feedlot operations to their former prominence in the local economy. Such bounty led to the emergence of the Arizona Packing Company, founded by Edward A. Tovrea; by 1928 it was "the largest and most modern equipped packing plant between Fort Worth, Texas, and the Pacific Coast." The company's stockyards and slaughterhouse, located on Tempe Road five miles east of the Phoenix business district, attracted cattle, hog, and sheep interests, and the Tovrea family made a fortune; eventually they lived in a nearby residence known as Tovrea's Castle.

Early in the decade, citrus groves reappeared in the valley, especially north of Phoenix along the Arizona Canal from Scottsdale to Glendale. By 1928, more than five hundred carloads of oranges and grapefruits were being shipped from Phoenix each year to cities throughout the country. Refrigerated railroad cars guaranteed safe shipment of fragile valley fruits and vegetables, such as cantaloupes and lettuce, and enabled valley producers to compete in distant markets. All this new agricultural activity, along with the continued planting of long- and short-staple cotton on a lesser scale, increased crop diversification in the Salt River Valley beyond pre-cotton boom levels by the end of the decade.[8]

Increased crop diversification inspired a variety of agricultural support services in Phoenix and the valley. Storage yards and warehouses, packing sheds and processing plants, located along the railroad tracks in south Phoenix, helped make the city the collecting and distributing point for "The Garden of Arizona." A half-dozen organizations, led by the Arizona Cotton Growers' Association, headquartered in Phoenix, making the city the agricultural administration and marketing center for the state. The Salt River Valley Water Users' Association, based in Phoenix, also contributed substantially to the redevelopment and expansion of agri-

Roosevelt Dam, c. 1920. The Herb and Dorothy McLaughlin Photographic Collection.

Shipping citrus out of Phoenix during the 1920s. The Herb and Dorothy McLaughlin Photographic Collection.

culture in the area. The federal government turned over control of the Salt River project to the SRVWUA in September 1917, and from that time on, the organization assumed its management and maintenance.

Early in the 1920s, in order to prevent such problems as the waterlogging of irrigated fields, the SRVWUA built additional hydroelectric power units to operate pumps to control groundwater levels, and during the decade it financed and constructed three more dams below Roosevelt Dam on the Salt River to increase the capacity of the water storage system and the supply of electric power for the valley. Mormon Flat Dam, completed in 1925, created ten-mile-long Canyon Lake; Horse Mesa Dam, completed in 1927, created seventeen-mile-long Apache Lake; and Stewart Mountain Dam, completed in 1930, created twelve-mile-long Saguaro Lake.[9]

The 1920s proved to be good years for the area. Maricopa County increased in population from 34,498 in 1910 to 89,576 in 1920 to 150,970 in 1930. The city of Phoenix recorded similar gains; its population rose from 11,134 in 1910 to 29,053 in 1920 to 48,118 in 1930. The 1920 total made the capital the largest and most important urban center in the state. Tucson became the second city of Arizona in 1920, with a population of 20,292, up from 13,193 in 1910. If the population of surrounding towns and the hinterland is included, the difference between the Phoenix and Tucson areas becomes even more pronounced, since the 1920 population of Maricopa County was 89,576, compared with 34,680 in Pima County, and the 1930 population of Maricopa County was 150,970, compared with 55,676 in Pima County.[10]

Physical expansion proceeded apace, and vertical and horizontal development in Phoenix reached unprecedented proportions. Construction work begun during the cotton boom came to a halt during the bust but soon resumed, and each year during the decade saw gains in the value of building permits. The amount increased from $1.7 million in 1921 to $3.1 million in 1925 to $5.2 million in 1929, and many new private and public buildings emerged in Phoenix, especially in the downtown area. Banks and department stores, theaters and hotels, city and county government facilities, as well as other imposing structures, appeared, many of them of the skyscraper variety.

Skyscrapers in the 1920s were considered signs of progress, and observers were impressed by the seven-story Dwight B. Heard Building, constructed in 1920, and the ten-story Luhrs Building, completed in 1924, which were the tallest structures in the city until 1928, when the sixteen-floor Hotel Westward Ho was erected. The eleven-story medical-dental Professional Building, completed in 1929, and the twelve-story Luhrs Tower, finished in 1930 and a favorite office location of lawyers, added to the Phoenix skyline by the end of the decade. The newly combined City and County Building, bounded by Washington and Jefferson and First and Second avenues, was finished in June 1929. This striking edifice, along with a new State Office Building, completed a year later near the State Capitol Building at Seventeenth Avenue and Washington Street, bolstered the image of Phoenix as a center of political life and governmental activity in Arizona.

Extensive horizontal as well as vertical growth took place in and about Phoenix during the 1920s. The most expensive, exclusive neighborhoods continued to be located along North Central Avenue, while behind them middle- and lower-class neighborhoods extended eastward and westward. As Michael Kotlanger observed, "The distance of a homesite from Central Avenue determined the value of the residence." During the decade, intensive infilling took place in many of the neighborhoods north of Van Buren between Twelfth Street and Nineteenth Avenue. Considered among the

*Northwest corner of Central Avenue and Coronado Road, c. 1920. The
Herb and Dorothy McLaughlin Photographic Collection.*

most desirable residential areas were the Las Palmas, Central, Los
Olivos, Kenilworth, Palmcroft, Encanto, and Broadmoor additions,
along with the Phoenix Country Club district, located northeast of
the city limits.[11]

Phoenix leaders urged citizens to keep the city clean and nicely
landscaped. The Chamber of Commerce prevailed upon its members to "grow grass and plant flowers" in "the city of trees." In
1926, the Valley Beautiful Committee conducted one of its "Let's
Do Away With the Desert" campaigns, pleading with residents to
"Plant the Roses Now," for the organization hoped to show that
the Phoenix area "surpassed Pasadena for quality, size, fragrance,
and variety of roses." When a member of the committee made the
suggestion that "the now neglected bed of the Salt River from Joint
Head on the east to Nineteenth Avenue on the west" be developed
"into a beautiful park for the city of Phoenix," it was rejected; as a
critic put it, no one wanted "to saddle any valley community with
monetary responsibility" for dealing with "the disgraceful condition of the riverbed."

Neighborhood cleaning and beautification projects, however,
continued to serve the city and the valley; the North Central Ave-

nue Improvement Association, for example, conducted a successful program to make their favorite thoroughfare "the State's Most Majestic Boulevard." Phoenix promoters encouraged and appreciated these efforts because they knew a spotless city helped attract residents and visitors, thus benefiting the volume of business as well as the quality of life.[12]

In 1925, Moses Sherman, who had moved to Los Angeles, sold his streetcar company to the city, which made improvements in the system. However, the population did not hesitate to accept the automobile as the principal mode of transportation in the desert center. It offered more convenience, privacy, and mobility than the trolley, and in the city and the Salt River Valley it was quickly adopted. In 1920 a local official, observing that Phoenix was becoming a "car city," declared, "The people in this town have forgotten how to walk. If they have to go two blocks they get in a machine and drive." The number of cars registered in Maricopa County rose from 646 in 1913 to 11,539 in 1920 to 53,064 in 1929, a year in which there was one car for every three people in the Phoenix area.[13]

Salt River Valley, c. 1920. The Herb and Dorothy McLaughlin Photographic Collection.

As more automobiles appeared, citizens called for better thoroughfares in the city, and the amount of pavement in Phoenix rose from seven miles in 1915 to twenty-five in 1920 to eighty-six in 1929. The automobile also facilitated movement between Phoenix and outlying points. In May 1924, the *Republican* announced, "Through the Salt River Valley, radiating from Phoenix in all directions like spokes of a great wheel, are paved roads. No farm house is over two miles from a paved road." Along with substantial improvements to Van Buren Street and Grand Avenue, respectively designated U.S. 80 and U.S. 89 in 1925, Washington Street was extended and paved to the Tempe bridge, thus creating another major artery from Phoenix to the east side of the valley.

The paved Phoenix-to-Los Angeles highway over the Colorado River bridge at Blythe, California, was completed in 1928, making available a shorter route to the Pacific coast. Earlier in the decade, the paved Phoenix-to-Miami Globe highway had opened, allowing easier access to the mining towns of eastern Arizona, and the Phoenix-to-Yuma-to-San Diego highway had been paved. City, county, state, and federal funds made the projects possible. Local organizations, such as the Maricopa County Good Roads Association and the Phoenix-based Arizona Good Roads Association, lobbied effectively; and Arizona representatives in Washington, led by Phoenician Carl T. Hayden, worked diligently to secure passage of federal highway acts affording funds in 1916 and 1921. Phoenix became the highway hub of Arizona during the 1920s; cars, trucks, and buses or "passenger stages" traveled over roads that connected the capital city with all parts of the Southwest and beyond.[14]

While motorized transportation brought greater horizontal mobility, the new Phoenix Union Station, completed in October 1923, helped to invigorate the downtown area. Business and civic leaders promoted the railroad depot for the same reason they promoted roads: it boosted the development of Phoenix. Several thousand people attended the celebration when the impressive-looking structure at Harrison Street between Fourth and Fifth avenues opened. Both the Southern Pacific and the Santa Fe railroad interests contributed to the cost of the joint-use Union Station building, and they also upgraded and improved most of their other facilities in Phoenix and the Salt River Valley. All this construction activity encouraged local leaders to continue pushing for a main line route through the city.

A.T. & S.F. trains at new Phoenix Union Station in the 1920s. The Herb and Dorothy McLaughlin Photographic Collection.

From 1913 to 1924 the banner slogan of the *Gazette* declared "Phoenix Must and Will Have a Main Line Railroad," but little happened until June 1924, when the Southern Pacific and the El Paso and Southwestern railroads consolidated operations. The Interstate Commerce Commission set as a condition for the merger the approval of a main line to be constructed through the Salt River Valley within two years; the new line was considered "beneficial and necessary for ongoing regional development." At Washington hearings Phoenix boosters, led by Mayor Louis B. Whitney, had urged the ICC to support the merger, and following the ICC decision, the Phoenix Chamber of Commerce hosted a gala luncheon for Southern Pacific officials at the Arizona Club.

The new Southern Pacific main line formed a 216-mile loop by leaving the El Paso-to-Los Angeles Southern Pacific transcontinental route at Picacho, 46 miles northwest of Tucson, and rejoining it at Wellton, 37 miles east of Yuma, after passing through Phoenix. On the morning of October 15, 1926, a crowd of ten thousand people welcomed the simultaneous arrival of two special trains from El Paso and Los Angeles, and there followed "a day of rejoicing for Phoenix." A main line had finally reached the desert center; indeed, soon four transcontinental trains were passing through the city each day.[15]

Phoenix proved to be slow in acquiring an adequate airfield. In October 1925, after two years of promotional effort by the Chamber of Commerce and other organizations, Phoenix Municipal Airfield opened on 160 acres six miles west of the city, but it remained largely undeveloped. Several private airfields were located throughout the Salt River Valley, the best one being the Phoenix Commercial Airfield at Henshaw Road on South Central Avenue; at this site in November 1927, the Aero Corporation of California operated Standard Airlines and offered scheduled flights to Tucson and Los Angeles. Unable to compete with the private airfields, in August 1929 the city sold the Phoenix Municipal Airfield to a local alfalfa farmer.

In November 1928, Scenic Airways, a corporate venture backed by Chicago and Phoenix investors, bought an airfield site two miles east of the central business district. Bounded by Twenty-fourth and Thirty-second streets, Henshaw Road, and the Southern Pacific railroad tracks, the new airfield was named Sky Harbor. Standard Airlines and several other carriers joined Scenic Airways in using the facility, and before long it offered the best service in the area, reaching into many parts of the state, the region, and the nation. On September 2, 1929, more than eight thousand people turned out to officially dedicate Phoenix Sky Harbor, a new hub of air transportation in Arizona.[16]

Transportation improvements made it easier for a variety of people to venture to the Arizona oasis. For example, Phoenix remained a popular place for health seekers during the 1920s. After it opened in October 1924, observers compared the Phoenix Sanitarium, "where health is regained through proper care, sunshine, and pure air," with the best of similar institutions around the nation. Located on North Central Avenue, it was called "the most complete of all lung disease hospitals in the West." St. Joseph's Hospital, St. Luke's Home, and a third institution, Deaconess Hospital and Home, founded in October 1911 by Methodists and renamed Good Samaritan Hospital in September 1928, enlarged their facilities during the period to meet the increase in patients. Although all three had specialized in lung ailments in the past, in the 1920s

St. Joseph's and Good Samaritan began to concentrate on offering general hospital services to the public.

For the sick poor, remote communities beyond the city limits continued to be available. Elizabeth Beatty, who lived in Sunnyslope in the early 1920s, noted that there were in the area "scattered tents and unpainted shacks, most of them floorless. In each was a sick person living alone or with other members of the family. In several cases, more than one member of the family was ill with tuberculosis." She and other members of the Friendship Circle often discussed the plight of these unfortunate victims. Members of the Friendship Circle, all Presbyterian women, began assisting in the care of the sick persons, providing them with food and clothing, and promoting the establishment of a medical mission. In turn, in December 1927 the Presbyterian Church opened the Desert Mission Sanitarium in Sunnyslope to care for the sick poor. Many Phoenix residents contributed their time and money to the effort, and a number of Phoenix doctors and dentists spent many hours treating hundreds of patients free of charge at the mission clinic.

In the 1920s, however, the emphasis moved from treating health seekers to attending to tourists. The transition was inspired by local promoters, who preferred hotels to hospitals. As local writer Goldie Weisberg observed in 1929, boosters "saw the possibilities in the place and determined to sell Phoenix to the world." They "saw the weakness of playing up the climate to the health-seekers alone, who were often just remittance men living in sanatariums." It was "too good a selling point to disregard, but they began looking about for another market." They "found it among the elderly gentlemen who like to play golf all year around, and among the ladies of all ages who like to applaud them." According to Weisberg,

It worked. Today Phoenix no longer thinks of itself as first of all a health-seeker's paradise. There is no rule against regaining one's health here, but it is not in the best taste to discuss it. Phoenix is going metropolitan. It is turning smart. The oldtimer, pushed to the wall, looks on rather bewildered and not a little hurt. Once a year, on Pioneer Day, he parades down the street and sees on either side the outside faces watching him —gaping faces from Oklahoma, amused faces from Michigan, smug faces from Kansas, bored faces from New York. No doubt he feels embarrassed.[17]

Being a health mecca was unhealthy, declared the critics, so boosters developed a promotion program to make Phoenix "the Southwest capital of tourism." The Phoenix-Arizona Club, organized in 1919, led the way. This 550-member organization advertised Phoenix as the city "where winter never comes," and it was responsible for much of the growth of tourism during the decade. In 1924, it sponsored a national advertising campaign that promoted Phoenix and the Salt River Valley as "the winter playground of the Southwest." The campaign prompted thousands of people throughout the United States to visit the area. The Southern Pacific and the Santa Fe railroads cooperated with the Phoenix-Arizona Club and contributed generously to its fund drives.

Business and civic organizations worked diligently to develop the image of "Delightful Phoenix, the Garden Spot of the Southwest." They invited weather-weary Northerners to "winter among the palms and roses" in "Phoenix, Where Summer Winters." All the publicity resulted in a progressive rise in the number of tourists, and national promotion campaigns costing several hundred thousand dollars evolved. Enticing advertisements appeared in such magazines as *Time*, *Atlantic Monthly*, *National Geographic*, *Harper's*, *Vogue*, *Better Homes and Gardens*, *American Golfer*, *Scribner's*, and *Literary Digest*. At the same time, new resort hotels and guest ranches were established in and about the city, including such luxurious places as the Westward Ho and the Arizona Biltmore.

The arrival of the main line railroad in October 1926 and the inauguration of scheduled airline service in November 1927, along with the popularity of the automobile and the appearance of better roads, encouraged more people to visit the Arizona oasis. The demand for suitable accommodations created a boom in downtown hotel construction. In 1928, both the San Carlos and the Westward Ho opened, and in order to compete with them and remain the most favored hotel in Phoenix, the Hotel Adams underwent extensive renovation and expansion.

Outside of the city, the Arizona Biltmore opened in early 1929 and joined the Ingleside Inn (1910) and the Jokake Inn (1924) as first-class resort complexes. The $2 million Arizona Biltmore, located six miles northeast of Phoenix between Squaw Peak and Camelback Mountain, was designed by Albert McArthur, a student of Frank Lloyd Wright and brother of Phoenix automobile dealers and hotel promoters Charles and Warren McArthur. The

Hotel Adams's double-decker bus provided good service to guests in 1925. The Herb and Dorothy McLaughlin Photographic Collection.

McArthur brothers, who had come to Phoenix from Chicago, and other Phoenix investors backed the Bowman-Biltmore hotel chain's six-hundred-acre development consisting of two hundred acres for the hotel and golf course, and four hundred acres to be subdivided and sold for residential use. The hotel was an instant success, and in July 1929 William Wrigley, Jr., chewing gum magnate, owner of the Chicago Cubs, and a Phoenix winter resident, invested $1.7 million in the hotel company, assuring the Arizona Biltmore's future as one of the best resort hotels in the nation. Wrigley built a mansion adjacent to the hotel; wealthy investors from throughout the country followed his example and constructed winter homes in the vicinity. Along with Wrigley, Louis Swift, Cornelius Vanderbilt, Jr., George Bartlett, and other business barons helped Phoenix attain a reputation as a fashionable place for the wealthy to winter.

By 1930, hotels, guest ranches, motor camps, and motels provided facilities for thousands of winter residents and tourists. Phoenix also became a popular convention site during the 1920s. The Chamber of Commerce, in particular, encouraged and orga-

nized meetings of state, regional, and even national groups. One
of its primary goals during the decade was to make Phoenix an
ideal convention city. The role played by booster associations such
as the Phoenix-Arizona Club and the Phoenix Chamber of Commerce was extremely important in increasing the popularity of the
city and the valley. Competition was keen between the Phoenix
area and other Southwestern resort centers to attract winter visitors, and local leaders put to work whatever assets their cities and
areas possessed. In Phoenix, they knew the value of the climate,
and they successfully sold it to the nation. In 1929, tourism produced revenues of over $10 million for the first time in the city's
history.[18]

Phoenix promoters realized that for a city to be truly inviting, it
had to be a good place to live as well as work; it had to offer cultural
and social amenities as well as economic opportunities. Schools
were deemed especially important. By 1930, educational facilities included thirty-two public primary schools, up from thirteen
in 1916. Phoenix Union High School, with an enrollment of several thousand students, remained the principal secondary school
in the city. The largest high school in the Southwest, its campus
contained a number of impressive buildings and a 10,500-seat stadium. The stadium, built in 1927, served as a site for many school
and community events.[19]

In 1920, to help meet the needs of post-secondary students in
the city, two cottages were set aside on the Phoenix Union High
School campus for use as Phoenix Junior College. Increased enrollment caused it to move in 1928 to its own campus at Seventh and
Fillmore streets; by 1930 it served nearly five hundred students.
Along with Arizona State Teacher's College in nearby Tempe,
Phoenix Junior College provided local students with higher education opportunities, but most of those eligible attended the University of Arizona in Tucson.[20]

Churches and fraternal lodges multiplied, benefiting those interested. Phoenix, declared an observer in 1930, "is a city of schools,
homes, and churches." In that year, the desert center contained
fifty-nine churches, up from twenty-nine in 1916. Representing
all religious persuasions, the churches as cultural associations
not only served the needs of their members for spiritual security,
but also served their members as social rallying points, centers
of group life. They conducted many activities that were spiritual,
educational, charitable, recreational, and reform in their purpose.

Phoenix Union High School, 1923. The Herb and Dorothy McLaughlin Photographic Collection.

And as an instrument of cultural conservation, they embodied and perpetuated in their different forms the social traditions of diverse and often conflicting groups.

Protestant and Catholic edifices had been present since pioneer days, and in 1922 the Jews erected a place of worship. Until that year, Phoenix Jews had utilized their homes or rented halls for services and celebrations, but the need for a synagogue was evident. In April 1920, the Phoenix Hebrew Center Association, led by Charles Korrick, mobilized Jewish organizations in the city, such as B'nai B'rith and the Council of Jewish Women, to raise money for a synagogue. Rabbi Dr. David L. Liknatz of Los Angeles was brought to Phoenix to oversee the construction of Temple Beth Israel at Second Street and Culver. It opened in the fall of 1922.[21]

Fraternal lodges, combining sociability and mutual aid, proved popular in Phoenix from the beginning, and by 1920 virtually every interest in the city was represented. Michael Kotlanger, in his study of Phoenix during the 1920s, called it "a city of joiners." Not only did Phoenicians belong to fraternal lodges such as the

Masons, the Odd Fellows, the Elks, and the Knights of Columbus, and civic organizations such as the Rotary, the Kiwanis, the
Lions, and the Optimists, but they joined all sorts of cultural and
social clubs. Members of the Phoenix Women's Club continued
to "widen the boundaries of cultural development" in the city,
and members of the Phoenix Country Club continued to promote
and host state, regional, and national golf tournaments. While
the Phoenix Chamber of Commerce, the Phoenix-Arizona Club,
and the Phoenix Commercial Club boosted the economic growth
of the area, the Phoenix Symphony Association, the Phoenix Little Theatre, and the Phoenix Fine Arts Association supported the
appearance of more and better concert performances, dramatic
productions, and museum displays. Nationally renowned groups,
ranging from the New York Metropolitan Grand Opera to John
Philip Sousa's Traveling Band, visited the capital city during the
decade, and starting in 1926, the Masque of the Yellow Moon, an
annual festival featuring a dramatic pageant involving thousands
of local participants, became a Phoenix tradition.[22]

The attempts of Phoenix boosters to promote the cultural and
social, as well as the economic, life of the city were often motivated
by the desire to create a proper image, one that would contribute to the city's aura of stability and permanence, and increase
its ability to attract desirable newcomers and capital investment.
Many of the promoters were transplanted Easterners, and they
wished to re-create the best of their old home in their new home.
Phoenix businessmen often became cultural agents as well as affluent entrepreneurs. Among the outstanding leaders of the Phoenix
elite, for example, was Dwight B. Heard.

A successful businessman in Chicago, Heard moved to Phoenix
in 1895, hoping the climate would help him recover his health.
Heard and his wife, Maie, were both impressed with the Arizona
capital; and he, along with some of his friends in Chicago, began
investing in the economic growth of the city and the Salt River
Valley. Maie became involved in raising the cultural tone of the
city. Heard opened his home, the finest in the city, to potential
investors from the East and Midwest, and did everything he could
to encourage their interest in the Phoenix area. His investment
company, specializing in real estate, became a leading force in the
development of the city and the valley. Heard's newspaper, the *Arizona Republican*, exerted a strong influence in politics and other
aspects of life in Phoenix and the rest of the state. Heard was an

active civic promoter and an ardent booster; he and his wife were instrumental in securing many benefits for the city, including the Heard Museum. When Dwight Heard died in March 1929, he was eulogized as "Arizona's greatest citizen."

Phoenix benefited from the Heards, and they gained in many ways from the city. With the backing of his father-in-law, Adolphus Bartlett, a wealthy Chicagoan, Heard became one of the largest landowners in the city and the valley. In 1900, the Bartlett-Heard Land and Cattle Company purchased a fertile 7,500-acre tract paralleling the Salt River south of the city, and it soon became a model farming and ranching operation. In addition to raising prize cattle, Heard grew alfalfa and cotton, and cultivated orange and grapefruit trees. At the same time, Heard and Bartlett purchased 160 acres of prime land along Central Avenue north of McDowell Road, and Heard developed it into an exclusive residential subdivision called Los Olivos. There he and Maie built Casa Blanca, their exemplary home. They planted hundreds of palm trees along four miles of roads in Los Olivos; other residential areas created by Heard included Palmcroft. A tireless developer, Heard made a fortune. With Maie he shared a concern for the community.

Heard was a driving force behind the bringing of Roosevelt Dam, the Central Avenue bridge, South Mountain Park, and other benefits to the Phoenix area. He served at various times as head of the Arizona Grain Growers' Association, the Arizona Cattlemen's Association, the Arizona Cotton Growers' Association, the Arizona Good Roads Association, and several other prominent organizations. He also devoted time to the Community Chest, St. Luke's Home, the Boy Scouts, the YMCA, Trinity Episcopal Church, the University of Arizona, and many other causes.

Heard's wife, Maie, who was especially active in cultural and social work, has been called "the single most generous philanthropist Phoenix has ever known." She donated land for the first Phoenix Women's Club building and land for the Phoenix Civic Center, upon which would be constructed in the 1950s the new Phoenix Public Library, Phoenix Little Theatre, and Phoenix Art Museum. Upon her arrival in the desert center, Maie Bartlett Heard became involved in a variety of community institutions and organizations, including the YWCA, St. Luke's Home, the Camp Fire Girls, and the Phoenix Fine Arts Association. Her major concern proved to be the Heard Museum, completed in 1929. She and

Dwight contributed the land, the building, and their magnificent collection of Indian artifacts to the new museum; unfortunately, it did not open until after Dwight's death, but with Maie's devoted support it became one of the Southwest's premier preservers and promoters of Indian art and culture.[23]

Then, as now, a great many Phoenicians ignored the development of cultural landmarks such as the Heard Museum. When the Chicago Opera, the London String Quartet, the Minneapolis Symphony, and similar groups performed in the city, the Heards and other leaders in the cultural world of Phoenix usually attended. Other residents and visitors, however, preferred to enjoy the circus or rodeo at the state fairgrounds; watch sports events and variety shows at local stadiums, gymnasiums, and auditoriums; dance away the evenings at the Riverside Ballroom; or take part in special gatherings of one of the twenty-seven state societies that existed in the city by 1930. By that year, there were seven movie theaters and two network-affiliated radio stations, KTAR and KOY. The radio, with its national perspective, helped bring average Phoenicians into the mainstream of American culture.

Regarding the influence of music on the Phoenix social scene, a local woman declared, "We are learning the new dance steps less belatedly than of yore. The radio keeps our fingers on the pulse of New York. We are making merry with all the gusto that, we take it, is the manner in Chicago, Syracuse, and points east." Moreover, noted an observer in 1929, for the "playfully inclined," Phoenix "is as choice as any city in the Union. . . . As in Des Moines, or Peoria, or Flatbush, if a man cannot golf in one place, he can golf in another; if he cannot motor in a Packard, he can motor in a Chevrolet; if he cannot dance at the Country Club, he can black bottom at the Old Hay Barn; if he dare not aspire to bridge at the club, he can ask the neighbors in after dinner."[24]

As in other cities, adequate enforcement of the prohibition laws in Phoenix during the 1920s proved to be impossible. As one chronicler of local social life stated late in the decade: "Now, though we are still distinctly a godly city in many ways—witness the fact that we do not dance on Sunday—the newest generation, and especially the prosperous young married set, has crowded the conservatives into an admission that making whoopee has its charms and that every self-respecting gentleman must have an intimate understanding of at least three kinds of cocktails, and access to the makings of a decent high-ball."[25]

Mae West in Phoenix for the opening of her new picture at the Orpheum Theatre, 1929. The Herb and Dorothy McLaughlin Photographic Collection.

Bootlegging was a flourishing business in Phoenix, and anyone from any level of society who wanted to drink could do so easily. Drugs also were available, especially marijuana. The use of marijuana had spread from some members of the Mexican community to some members of the Anglo community, and concerned citizens called for strict enforcement of local ordinances and federal laws against the use of marijuana as well as "any narcotic drug such as morphine, cocaine, heroin or opium." Two Phoenix ordinances passed in 1917 and 1918 called for fines up to $300 and/or terms of imprisonment up to six months. The 1917 ordinance stated, "The use of Cannabis Indica or Marijuana tends to cause insanity and render the user thereof a menace to the public peace and safety." The 1918 ordinance declared it "unlawful for any person other than a duly licensed druggist or physician to have, own, possess, or use any narcotic drug such as morphine, cocaine, heroin or opium or to have, own, possess, or use any pipe, lamp, syringe, or other appliance or apparatus for the preparation or use of any such drug." More "stringent measures" had to be adopted for "the suppression of the use of narcotic drugs," asserted local leaders; the 1918 ordinance would help preserve "the public peace, health, and safety."

Periodic crackdowns failed to solve the problem, although they did help to alleviate the pressure. In January 1919, for example, following a drug raid that resulted in the arrest of the "king pins of the drug ring in Phoenix," J. N. "Ping Pong" Greene and his companion, Ethel Warren, the *Republican* declared, "Phoenix has quietly become the 'dope headquarters' of the Pacific slope." The city became the federal drug law enforcement headquarters in Arizona in 1922 as reports of widespread use of "morphine, cocaine, and heroin" continued, much of it being consigned to Phoenix from Nogales and other Mexican border towns. Cooperation among city, county, and federal authorities led to more arrests, but the use of drugs remained "a steadily increasing evil" in the desert center.

Gambling and prostitution also thrived in Phoenix during the 1920s. Periodic cleanup campaigns had their effect and took their toll, but gambling and prostitution survived because "they provided a steady source of municipal revenue in the form of fines." As one editor put it, "Gamblers and prostitutes enriched the city treasury with fines." Brothels and gambling places operated throughout the city during the decade, but mostly in south Phoenix; and the operators, when not paying fines, were paying for police protection.[26]

That south Phoenix contained most of the brothels and gambling places was not unusual. It also contained the low-rent neighborhoods shunned by affluent Anglos and left to the Phoenix underclass. In 1920, the Arizona Board of Health "found housing conditions among the poorer families of Phoenix fully as bad as in the tenement districts of New York and other large centers of population." Poor and in a subservient position, the majority of the Indians, Mexicans, and blacks provided a source of cheap agricultural and domestic labor, while the Chinese ran several laundries, restaurants, and other businesses, including notorious opium dens. As local boosters continued to conduct promotional campaigns to attract new residents and visitors, affluent Anglo-Americans were clearly preferred. The ethnocentric Chamber of Commerce did not try to hide that feeling. One of its representatives recorded in a 1920 city directory: "Phoenix is a modern town of forty thousand people and the best kind of people, too. A very small percentage of Mexicans, negroes or foreigners."[27]

Throughout this period, the Phoenix Indian School, with an enrollment of 950 students by 1929, was a lucrative market for local businesses and a source of cheap labor for local employers. Students at the institution received vocational training, which they used in the employ of area business and agricultural interests. Males became competent workers and females obedient domestics. One young female graduate described her educational training at the institution as learning how "to make beds, wait on tables, and sing 'America.'" The school also served as a valuable tourist attraction and as a suitable opponent of Phoenix Union High School in the annual Thanksgiving Day football game.

> The big event of the year for the Indian school is the football game with the Phoenix High School team, which is known locally as the Thanksgiving classic. The Indians' team is formidable, its brass band at least as loud as the pale-faced band, and everybody turns out for the game. Their girls root and sing and wave pennants and yell, and quite often the Indians win the game. Then they go primitive. The grid becomes a council camp after battle and the football heroes are warrior chiefs. To the accompaniment of mad applause from the young squaws they do a war dance of victory, trampling a hundred pale-faced ghosts in the dust with each step.[28]

According to the census, 300 Indians lived in Phoenix in 1930, up from 105 in 1920, and most of them lived in low-income neighborhoods in the southern part of the city. Reservation Indians visited Phoenix to sell their goods and "lay about public places." Especially on Saturdays, a resident wrote, many of them "came struggling into town in wagons loaded with mesquite firewood, which they sell." The "women, their proportions exaggerated in billowing calico gowns and shawls of bright silk, squat on the downtown sidewalks and spread their pottery, beads, and baskets." When "the men have sold their wood and the women as much as possible of their art, they fill a gunny sack with the week's supply of bread, meat and canned foods and start back to the reservation." While the natives often attracted the attention of tourists, and pleased boosters so long as they "behaved" in Phoenix, local critics supported withholding from them such benefits as the right to vote, segregated them in theaters and other public places, and accused them of alcohol and drug abuse.[29]

Mexicans made up the largest minority group in Phoenix, increasing from 2,323 in 1920 to 7,293 (15.2 percent of the population) in 1930. During the cotton boom and bust more Mexicans settled in the barrios of south Phoenix. Rather than return to Mexico, they remained in the Arizona city, seeking any kind of available employment and living in some of the poorest neighborhoods. On the south side, most Mexicans concentrated in the area south of Washington extending from Seventh Avenue to Twenty-fourth Street. Certain sections contained better homes, but generally Mexicans could afford only substandard housing. Upward mobility proved elusive and poverty remained a problem, but a number of institutions and associations helped residents meet their needs.

Churches, for example, played an important role. Located on the site of the old church at Monroe between Third and Fourth streets, a new St. Mary's Church was dedicated in February 1915. Many Mexicans, however, grew tired of attending special masses held in the basement of the church for Spanish-speaking worshipers while Anglo Catholics attended English masses upstairs, so in the 1920s they began attending services at two new churches that became centers of Mexican community life in the city. In 1925, St. Anthony's Chapel opened on Seventh Street between Yavapai and Maricopa, and in 1928, the Sanctuario del Corazon de Maria at Ninth and Washington streets. Both churches came to serve the special needs of Mexican Catholics in Phoenix.[30]

In the post-World War I years, a national movement to "Americanize" foreign-born newcomers swept the nation. In the Southwest, this meant primarily Spanish-speaking individuals from Mexico, and in the Arizona capital the Phoenix Americanization Committee worked diligently to establish educational courses that included classes in English and civics, which were the foundation of all Americanization programs. Led by Carrie Green, a former teacher and social worker, in 1921 the committee began using a small house located on West Sherman Street in a south Phoenix Mexican neighborhood. The facility became known as Friendly House, and in it Green conducted classes in English, civics, hygiene, and home economics. Her "philosophy that guided Friendly House's programs assumed that immigrants should be loyal to the United States but should be encouraged to preserve and take pride in their native culture as well."[31]

The institution also served as an employment bureau and a relief agency. Called a "community house" in Phoenix, it fulfilled many of the functions of a traditional urban settlement house. Referred to as "the American Home in a foreign section," Friendly House moved to larger quarters directly across from the original facility on South First Avenue in 1927, where under the direction of Carrie Green it continued as a "gathering place for foreigners" and an "Americanization Center for Mexicans." Friendly House served a useful purpose throughout the decade, but basic economic and social problems facing the Mexican community in Anglo-dominated Phoenix remained unchanged.[32]

Institutions and organizations contributed to life in Chinatown during the period. The area bounded by Jefferson and Jackson, First and Third streets contained 250 Chinese in 1930, up from 130 in 1920, still less than 1 percent of the total Phoenix population. Chinatown in the 1920s remained the most tightly knit ethnic community in the city. As was true of other minority groups, a sense of ethnic identity and cultural awareness, along with patterns of discrimination and segregation, encouraged the Chinese to settle together in a community of their own within the larger community. The Chinese Temple was a center of religious activity, and a number of voluntary groups ranging from the Chinese Merchants' Association to the Chinese Masons helped provide a sense of order and stability in the enclave.

Especially successful in the restaurant, grocery, and other service businesses, some Chinese entrepreneurs gained considerable wealth and acted as leaders in the Chinese community. The Ong clan, led by Ong Dick ("China Dick, the Mayor of Chinatown"), continued to predominate in the 1920s, but others made their mark. Tang Shing, for example, arrived from China and opened a small grocery store in 1911. In 1929 his Sun Mercantile Company, offering "the most diversified line of any general jobbing-merchandising house in Arizona," moved into its new $80,000 facilities at Jackson and Third streets.

During the decade, Chinatown maintained its reputation for gambling places and opium dens. A Chinatown lottery was popular among Anglos as well as the Chinese and other racial minority groups; moreover, noted the *Gazette* in March 1926, "white residents of Phoenix" often frequented Chinatown "for the purpose of smoking opium." Periodic raids by authorities on gambling places and opium dens in Chinatown had little effect. In August 1923, for example, local police arrested five Chinese and seized "large quantities of drugs, mostly opium, worth several thousand dollars." The raid failed to end drug trafficking in Chinatown, however; the problem adversely affected its image throughout the decade and beyond. In the 1930s, however, the Japanese, although fewer in number than the Chinese, would bear the brunt of local xenophobia, a feeling so strong that it would motivate critics to attempt to drive them out of Phoenix and the Salt River Valley.[33]

The number of blacks in Phoenix increased from 1,075 in 1920 to 2,366 in 1930, slightly less than 5 percent of the total population. Most of them worked at low-income jobs, and they lived in two south Phoenix neighborhoods, one south of Madison to Buckeye Road between Seventh and Seventeenth avenues, and the other south of Washington to Buckeye between Second and Sixteenth streets. If a black could afford and wanted to live in a home in north Phoenix, restrictive covenants and real estate codes kept him out. Discriminated against and segregated from the dominant Anglo community, blacks developed their own communal life. The African Methodist Episcopal Church and the Colored Baptist Church remained centers of vitality in black Phoenix; other groups, ranging from fraternal orders to branches of the National Negro Business League, the National Association for the Advancement of Colored People, and the National Urban League, also served the black population.

Because many black groups—such as the black YMCA, the black YWCA, the black Boy Scouts, the black Camp Fire Girls, the black American Legion, the black Veterans of Foreign Wars, the black Elks, the black Masons—had few adequate facilities of their own outside of the black churches, they supported the Phoenix chapter of the Arizona Federation of Colored Women's Clubs in its fund drive to build the Phyllis Wheatley Community Center. The center opened in March 1927 at Jefferson and Fourteenth streets.[34]

Segregated from the Anglo community in restaurants, theaters, hospitals, hotels, swimming pools, buses, and other public places, blacks were viewed by white Phoenicians as second-class citizens. Eastlake Park, in a black neighborhood, served black residents; and Douglass (Booker T. Washington in 1921), Eastlake, and Ninth Avenue elementary schools, all in black neighborhoods, served black students. As for secondary schools, in 1926 the Phoenix Union Colored High School opened.

Arizona law stated that once a high school had an enrollment of twenty-five students of "African descent," a district could vote to establish "a separate Negro high school." Although the high schools for blacks and whites were to be separate, the law required that they be equal, in that "provisions in the Negro school should always be the same as those in the white school." A black critic later found it "amusing to contemplate that any one could ever believe that conditions can be provided for twenty-five children that are equal to the facilities provided for several hundred children in another plant." He noted, however, "The people who made such laws in Arizona had come from states with experience in piously making such meaningless statements into laws affecting Negroes."

In Phoenix, citizens voted to establish Arizona's first segregated high school. Successive classes, under the direction of the "colored department," moved from the "colored room" to the "colored cottage" on the Phoenix Union High School campus, to rented quarters in 1925, and finally to a campus of their own in 1926. White pressure, particularly from "some prominent Phoenix people who came from the South" and "objected strongly to Negro children attending classes with their children," helped create Phoenix Union Colored High School, but the unfortunate circumstances of blacks in the city also contributed. From the time of the "colored room," school segregation in Phoenix proved to be a humiliating and limiting experience for blacks. What little protest existed, failed to put black students back into classes with whites. It was "a 'David and Goliath' contest," asserts black educator W. A. Robinson; thus "the prospect of a school of their own such as they had known back in Oklahoma or Texas, where they came from, seemed to Negroes to be the height of reason and good fortune."[35]

Table 1. Urban Arizona, 1880–1930

City	1880	1890	1900	1910	1920	1930
Phoenix	1,708	3,152	5,544	11,134	29,053	48,118
Tucson	7,007	5,150	7,531	13,193	20,292	32,506
Prescott	1,836	1,759	3,559	5,092	5,010	5,517
Flagstaff	—	963	1,271	1,633	3,816	3,891
Yuma	—	—	—	2,914	4,237	4,892

SOURCE: U.S. Census of Population, 1880–1930.

Table 2. Urban Southwest, 1880–1930

City	1880	1890	1900	1910	1920	1930
El Paso	736	10,338	15,906	39,279	77,560	102,420
Phoenix	1,708	3,152	5,544	11,134	29,053	48,118
Tucson	7,007	5,150	7,531	13,193	20,292	32,506
Albuquerque	2,315	3,785	6,238	11,020	15,157	26,750

SOURCE: U.S. Census of Population, 1880–1930.

Blacks kept migrating to Phoenix. How many of them read the booster organization brochures describing Phoenix as the "city where diligence and industry will bring you the best of the worldly goods" is unknown, but the majority who came from Louisiana, Arkansas, Oklahoma, Texas, and other southern states looked upon Arizona and Phoenix as places "holding more opportunities for their social and economic betterment." That many of them were disappointed is a matter of record, but it could have been worse. As one black who came to Arizona in 1916 after stays in Georgia and Oklahoma later observed, "At least they didn't lynch you here, like they did back there."[36]

In 1930, El Paso remained the metropolis of the Southwest, with a population of 102,420. Phoenix, with a population of 48,118, was the second largest urban center in the region and the largest in Arizona. Local leaders felt justified in calling Phoenix "truly the capital of Arizona, the hub of new developments. The storehouse and supply house for the state. As Phoenix goes, so goes Arizona." Since 1913, it had experienced problems as well as progress, but it was clearly a winner in the race for urban supremacy in the Southwest. Promoters of the Arizona capital forecast more prosperity in the coming decade of the 1930s, but national economic distress interfered with their predictions.[37]

5 DECLINE AND RECOVERY, 1929-1940

Phoenix suffered less from the Great Depression than cities in the older, industrial America, but it did experience problems. Many people in need benefited from New Deal programs developed to respond to the economic climate of the 1930s. Most important, during the decade a strong relationship developed between the federal government and the Phoenix area that would endure. Moreover, by 1940, the towns surrounding Phoenix were well established, and they helped the capital city serve not only as the metropolis of Arizona but also as the center of the most populous metropolitan area in the Southwest.

The stock market crash in October 1929 did not seriously disrupt life in Phoenix. Phoenix newspapers, for example, gave it little attention. The great majority of local residents did not invest in the stock market, and those who did were assured the decline was only temporary. The capital city, the largest urban complex between El Paso and Los Angeles, continued to serve as the leading retail and wholesale trade center in the state and much of the Southwest; and hinterland residents, including the vast majority of farmers and miners in the region, depended on Phoenix sources to meet their needs. With a central location and transportation arteries reaching throughout the area, Phoenix served as a marketing and distributing center for a productive population.[1]

Soon after the crash, however, the state of Arizona and much of the Southwest were in trouble. Copper mining, for example, one of the area's greatest assets, experienced a decline when consumption decreased and the market became hopelessly glutted, sending copper from 18.1 cents in 1929 to 5.6 cents a pound in 1932. Between 1931 and 1933 most of Arizona's copper mines either shut down or cut back production. Arizona, the leading copper-producing state in the nation, experienced a drop in the value of mining production from $155.7 million in 1929 to $14.7 million in 1932. Farm production fell from $41.8 million to $13.8 million, and livestock production declined from $25.5 million to $14.7 million during the same period. Unemployment in the mining towns proved especially severe; indeed, the total population of the state dropped from 435,573 in 1930 to 380,000 in 1933, primarily due to the evacuation of mining towns. Many of the jobless miners who did not leave the state moved to Phoenix, looking for work or aid.[2]

In Phoenix, the economy reflected conditions in the state. A sharp drop in activity occurred in the years 1931 to 1933. Two of six banks failed, as did two of five building and loan associations. Businesses closed, jobs disappeared, wages decreased, and city construction came to a halt. At the same time, Phoenix did not suffer as badly from the Great Depression as cities in other sections of the nation. By comparison, resident unemployment in Phoenix was minimal, mortgage foreclosures and bankruptcies were few, and commercial failures were small. For the 80 percent of the work force with regular jobs during the period 1931 to 1933, life continued in a subdued 1920s fashion. By 1934 the worst was over and economic activity, by and large, had returned to the 1929 level. As Jay Edward Niebur has put it, for local individuals who remained at work "the depression was more a time of worry and concern than a time of need and travail."

The employed were grateful, and many of them placed more value on what they had than in the past. They were more cautious and conservative. They settled for less, but as one observer noted in January 1933: "Our schools go on, our movies remain open, our shops do business, our girls and boys skim about in motor-cars, marry, and have babies—our world still moves." And "if money has been scarcer than before the depression, then bread and sugar and shoes and rent have been lowered in price too." At the same time, "almost everybody has 'shortened sail,' in good nautical fashion, to meet the gale, and as it lessens it won't hurt us to find ourselves wasting less, expecting less, needing less."[3]

For the unemployed, however, the situation was quite different. Unemployment proved to be the most significant problem of the depression in the city. In 1931 and 1932 the unemployed exhausted local private and public welfare funds, and Phoenix leaders feared that they might be tempted to seek redress in "subversive" activities, including riots.

Many of those in need, attracted by the climate and looking for work or aid, had drifted into Phoenix from elsewhere. In September 1932, the Phoenix Social Service Center noted in a report, "There are constantly arriving in the Phoenix area families in broken down automobiles, or through any possible way, usually with children or sick members of the family, tragically searching for a place where the climate is milder through the winter. . . . Thinking this an agricultural area, they hope it will furnish them something to eat." These people, many of them "Okies" from the Dust Bowl and unemployed workers from the mining towns of Arizona, increased the local burden. Transients unwilling to work in return for help often were encouraged to move on to another city. Organized charities and emergency relief committees formed by concerned citizens did what they could to alleviate the distress of the needy, especially the resident jobless, but it was never enough. By October 1933, there were close to ten thousand people receiving some kind of relief in Phoenix.[4]

"Not deprecating needs elsewhere in the state, or in the United States, relief needs per capita are exceedingly great in this Valley," declared Charles Stauffer, publisher of the *Republic* and chairman of the Governor's Maricopa County Committee of the Arizona Reconstruction Finance Committee, in September 1932. The drain of local private and public relief funds and the growing ranks of the unemployed caused Phoenix leaders to overcome their reluctance to seek aid from Washington. They increasingly saw a need for federal funds to relieve a serious problem unsolvable by local agencies. By 1932, they no longer considered it "socialistic" to accept government money when it would help prevent the unemployed from subverting the social order. As Stauffer put it, "Under no circumstances must we run the risk of public rioting in Phoenix."

Although most of the employed in Phoenix appeared oblivious to the unemployed during the period 1931 to 1933, there were those who cared. Many of them engaged in the relief work conducted by at least forty-seven organizations and institutions, with the Community Chest directing most of the activity and the Social Service Center carrying most of the burden. Under President Herbert Hoover, the Reconstruction Finance Corporation and other new federal agencies provided several million dollars to help Phoenix, Maricopa County, and Arizona, but it was under President Franklin D. Roosevelt, elected in 1932, that the federal government, through New Deal programs, truly began to alleviate distress in the city, the valley, and the state. With the advent of the New Deal, federal relief projects and local welfare boards were instituted under the guidance of concerned professionals, and government responsibility for the economic betterment of the public was assumed.[5]

As in other cities across America, a strong relationship developed between the federal government and Phoenix during the New Deal years. The federal government had helped alleviate distress in Phoenix and the Salt River Valley in the past, notably in the case of the Salt River project, but the impact of Washington became more pronounced during the 1930s. When President Roosevelt took office in 1933, a spirit of optimism prevailed in Phoenix. Most residents had voted for him, and they expressed confidence in his leadership. In March 1933, a Phoenix executive reflected the local sentiment when he declared, "The psychology of depression is past and the psychology of better times is here." In the next two years, President Roosevelt's New Deal poured millions of dollars into Phoenix, Maricopa County, and Arizona. All major economic indicators pointed upward, and Phoenix became a leader in many aspects of recovery.[6]

By 1935, Phoenix business had recovered sufficiently to show considerable growth, and the federal government was Maricopa County's biggest employer and buyer, having injected more than $10 million annually into the local area by 1937. In that year more than fifty federal agencies, bureaus, or offices employed nearly six thousand residents and paid salaries totaling $6 million. The federal government supported private business establishments by spending at least $4 million for materials, equipment, and supplies. Since the emphasis was on relief by work programs, the variety of government projects led to the social improvement as well as the physical expansion of Phoenix.[7]

Downtown Phoenix, c. 1935. The Herb and Dorothy McLaughlin Photographic Collection.

Many people in need benefited from New Deal measures in the Salt River Valley, and in Phoenix the New Deal helped the city meet the problems that followed in the wake of the 1929 crash. Federal agencies bought the products of local cotton, citrus, and cattle interests. They provided jobs for the unemployed and subsistence for the jobless. They sponsored projects that led to the improvement of Phoenix streets, schools, hospitals, airports, parks, utilities, and government buildings.

Residents supported federal programs because they usually resulted in visible, positive gains. In 1940 local department store executive Barry Goldwater, reflecting on the economic picture of Phoenix during the previous decade, noted that among other changes, a factor "of extreme importance to retailing in all its branches had been huge expenditures of public money in this area. Arizona ranks near the top in per capita money received from the New Deal." Goldwater called it "sheer folly for any of our numerous branches of business to consider this money as a permanent source

of income to business. . . . If it continues, it will be at the expense
of business and is, so to speak, robbing Peter to pay Paul." Nevertheless, he declared, "The millions of dollars spent in Phoenix and
Maricopa County for the purpose of supplies, etc., have made their
mark and have had their effect upon our economic picture during
the last ten years."[8]

Although the Great Depression slowed the pace of progress, the
city continued to grow. The population of Phoenix increased by 36
percent, from 48,118 in 1930 to 65,414 in 1940. By the latter year
the desert center, having recovered rapidly from the effects of the
depression, felt secure about its future. As an observer asserted in
December 1940, "The future of Phoenix is guaranteed as a trade
center for a rich agricultural region, and a collecting and distributing point for a much greater area." He added, "People of means
come here from other parts of the country, just for the delight of
living in The Valley of the Sun."

The Salt River Valley, called "the Nile Valley of America," retained during the 1930s its status as one of the richest agricultural
sections in the world. It was known for its cotton and citrus, but
"almost anything will grow," noted an expert, because "there is
plenty of water, good soil and excellent weather." Farmers, along
with other residents of the surrounding area, found the urban center of Phoenix to be a vital place. The city, although it represented
only 35 percent of the population of Maricopa County, had cap-
tured over 70 percent of all the retail business in the county by
1939. In that same year, 1,207 retail stores and 194 wholesale establishments in the city did a total volume of over $1 billion as
Phoenix continued to be the leading retail and wholesale center for
the state. In addition, three major banks served Phoenix and its
outlying areas, thus maintaining the city's standing as the financial center of Arizona.

Phoenix had some eighty manufacturing concerns, including
flour mills, steel companies, ice factories, and packing plants. Also
based in the city were a number of air conditioner manufacturers,
and they enabled the desert oasis to claim the title of "Air Condi-
tioned Capital of the World." Early twentieth-century Phoenicians
had to settle for electric fans and other ineffective devices to combat the intense summer heat. Air-cooled commercial buildings had
existed since the 1920s, but in the 1930s several local firms developed and produced evaporative coolers for the home. The cooler
companies, operated by such air-conditioning pioneers as Paul and

Mike Johnson, Adam and Gus Goettle, and Oscar Palmer, created a thriving industry in Phoenix and eventually shipped their products all over the nation and abroad.

By the end of the decade, Phoenix led the nation in the number of home air-conditioning units installed. Local builder Del Webb stated in 1940, "Air conditioning apparatus has enabled Phoenix to meet and conquer the summer heat, long the bane of southwestern existence." Promoters, who in the past had never mentioned the hot summers in the Arizona city, now explained that air-cooling devices made it no longer necessary for people to sleep in a yard, or on a roof, or on a porch under wet sheets to keep cool during the summer. Air-conditioning made homes and offices much more livable during the long summer. It also stimulated business and increased the productivity of employees.[9]

The Phoenix urban area expanded as a result of New Deal policies in the banking and construction fields, and by 1940 residential and business construction was moving forward at the fastest pace ever, exceeding even the boom days prior to 1930. In Phoenix alone, building permit records showed that over $15 million had been spent during the decade. That figure, declared Del Webb, did not include "the subdivisions just outside the city limits and therefore shows but a fraction of the total investment." According to Webb, a major contractor in Phoenix and the Southwest, "No accurate check has been made to date in the suburban residential areas around the Valley, but authorities are convinced the volume of residential construction is at least equal to, and in all probability surpasses, that of the city."

Webb and other local business leaders were quick to take advantage of New Deal programs conducive to the continued growth of Phoenix. A former Californian, Webb started in Phoenix as a carpenter in the 1920s and parlayed hard work and good luck into a thriving construction firm in the 1930s. "Construction is no longer a private enterprise," he asserted at the end of the decade, "but rather a subsidiary of the federal government." New Deal grants and loans enabled Webb and other contractors to reap millions of dollars building large and small projects in Phoenix and the valley. Webb personally was involved in a number of profitable New Deal promotions, erecting everything from private homes and businesses to public schools and hospitals; he also was a good Democrat, a friend and supporter of President Roosevelt and his policies throughout the period.[10]

Walter Bimson, Phoenix banker and art collector, 1937. Valley National Bank of Arizona.

Another friend of Roosevelt's, Walter R. Bimson, took control of the Valley National Bank in Phoenix, the largest in Arizona, in January 1933. The experience and expertise of Bimson, a Chicagoan, proved beneficial to the city, the valley, and the state. As president of the VNB during the 1930s, Bimson enthusiastically accepted New Deal legislation and adopted liberal loan policies that shocked many conservative bankers but delighted customers.

Walter's brother, Carl, joined him at the VNB, and they both actively promoted the passage of the Federal Housing Act of 1934. Under its provisions, the VNB made close to two hundred thousand loans from 1934 to 1945, drawing people to its doors "who had never done business with banks previously."[11]

New Deal programs combined with the energetic leadership of local promoters such as Webb and the Bimson brothers, and as a result, the physical dimensions of the urban center expanded. New public and private structures, notably the Federal Building and the Phoenix Title and Trust Building, appeared downtown, and home construction in the suburban neighborhoods increased considerably. Trucks, buses, and automobiles traveled over transportation arteries improved by $1.5 million in federal funds; by 1939, for example, Phoenix contained 117 miles of paved streets. New Deal money also helped develop the attractions of Encanto Park, a 230-acre, water-laced retreat located on Thomas Road, and it brought major improvements to Sky Harbor Airport. Purchased by the city in 1935 in order to qualify it for federal funding, in the next five years the facility was improved with the more than $350,000 Phoenix received from Washington for that project. By 1940, Sky Harbor had emerged as the principal airport in Arizona. "Deprived of ever having a seaport Phoenix very fittingly has created for itself a Sky Harbor with all the facilities for receiving the ships of the air," noted an observer, "a port through which will flow much of the important commerce that will go into the future making of Phoenix."[12]

During the 1930s water remained a requisite for survival, and New Deal reclamation projects provided more jobs, more money, and more water for the city and the valley. Structural improvements to all Salt River dams and the completion of Bartlett Dam on the Verde River in 1939 expanded the irrigation system. Bartlett, when completed, became the world's highest multiple-arch dam, capable of holding more than 180,000 acre-feet of water. It was built by the federal government, but the Salt River Valley Water Users' Association (Salt River Project) agreed to pay 80 percent of the total cost of $4.7 million. To ease its already enormous debt to the federal government, the SRVWUA in 1937 created the Salt River Project Agricultural Improvement and Power District, with boundaries and interests practically identical to those of the Association. Under Arizona law, the District received the rights, privileges, exemptions, and immunities granted political subdivisions of the state. Most important, formation of the District made possible the refinancing of outstanding Association bonds at a lower rate because interest on bonds issued by public agencies is tax exempt. Under contract, all Association properties were transferred to the District, but the Association continued to operate all of the Salt River Project as agent of the District.[13]

At the same time, federal financial assistance allowed the city of Phoenix to develop its water system to accommodate increased demands. Funds from Washington were used to rebuild municipal pipelines, extend water services, and locate new water supply sources. By 1940, the Phoenix system each day could deliver enough water to serve one hundred thousand users.[14]

Phoenix leaders during the 1930s kept promoting the city as a winter tourist attraction and health mecca, and thousands of people responded. Barry Goldwater and other boosters encouraged this means of bringing new revenue into Phoenix and the valley. In 1940 Goldwater declared, "The natural thing to which to turn was the capitalization of our climate, our natural beauties, and the romance of our desert." These "natural resources were subjected to a national advertising program," and the "benefits from it can never be fully estimated." It "is safe to say that Phoenix would not be in the prominent position which she now occupies, near the top of the per capita spending column of the nation, if it were not for the thousands of winter visitors and tourists who call Phoenix their home during a few months of the year." According to Goldwater, "The stimulus from the injection of these tourist dollars into the veins of our economic being have been felt by every person doing business in this area. The farmer has sold more produce. The hotels have filled more rooms. The merchants have sold more goods. It is easy to see, therefore, why businessmen are so unanimously enthusiastic about the continuance and enlargement of a proper advertising program."[15]

In 1934 a local advertising agency, looking for a more appealing name for the Salt River Valley, came up with "The Valley of the Sun"; its use became popular as the impact of amenities on the economy of Phoenix grew stronger and publicity techniques improved. During the last half of the decade, the Phoenix Chamber of Commerce, the Phoenix-Arizona Club, and other booster organizations used the term in many of their national advertising campaigns, and by 1940 it was well established. The city also financed Valley of the Sun ads in leading newspapers and magazines across

Arizona Biltmore, c. 1930. Arizona State Library and Archives, Phoenix.

the country. Potential visitors were promised "paradise on earth." As one ad proclaimed: "A person coming to the Valley of the Sun is fascinated by the thousands of acres of green and gold citrus groves; marvels at the date gardens with their graceful, swaying palms, and the soft, grey-green olive trees." It was asserted that visitors would "find an urge to claim for their own the wide-sweeping cactus-dotted deserts and towering craggy mountains— for these are the much-talked-of 'great open spaces' where there is room enough to breathe, to laugh, to exercise, to relax, to 'sun gaze' the days through and 'star-gaze' the nights away."[16]

During the winter season of 1939–40 it was estimated that 35,000 visitors came to the Phoenix area, and without exception the hotels, resorts, and guest ranches reported gains in the number of guests. The exclusive Camelback Inn announced that business in December 1939 represented an increase of 68 percent over December 1938 and a rise of 107 percent over December 1937. The war in Europe encouraged the influx to Phoenix, for tourists, now prohibited from going abroad, often chose to visit Arizona, and

those who did so in 1940 spent about $30 million in and around
"The City of Palms."

The Phoenix area not only offered the best in luxury accommodations, but it also claimed to be "the motor court and motel
capital of the world." Visitors of all income levels found their way
to the place where "summer comes to winter." Four major federal
highway routes entered the Phoenix oasis, and as New Deal road
improvements were made during the decade, more tourist accommodations and service facilities appeared, especially along Van
Buren Street and Grand Avenue. Because of the range and number of its facilities, the Valley of the Sun increased its appeal as
a convention center, attracting groups from all over the state and
beyond to attend thirty-four gatherings in 1938 and fifty in 1939.[17]

During the Great Depression, Phoenix promoters continued to
recognize the importance of cultural and social amenities. More
churches and schools, for example, came into being. The number
of churches increased considerably during the decade, providing
spiritual aid to their members and also serving as social rallying points during trying times. They conducted charitable as well
as religious activities. Protestant, Catholic, and Jewish benevolent associations were closely connected with the congregations.
In attempting to care for their own, these organizations provided
a valuable service.[18]

More educational facilities opened during the decade. Phoenix
Union High School, with eleven buildings and over five thousand
students in 1937, remained the principal secondary institution.
In 1938 construction on North Phoenix High School started with
the help of federal funds on a thirty-acre site at Twelfth Street
and Thomas Road and was completed a year later. Designed to
accommodate two thousand students, the eight-building school
was equipped with a fifteen-hundred-seat auditorium and a three-
thousand-seat stadium. It helped relieve overcrowding at Phoenix
Union, in 1937 one of the largest high schools west of the Mississippi River, and quickly became another object of local pride.
Federal funds also made possible the completion in 1939 of a new
thirty-acre Phoenix Junior College campus facing Encanto Park
on Thomas Road. Larger and more appealing in its new setting,
the school attracted more than eight hundred students in 1940;
Phoenix Technical School, a vocational training institution, occupied the old Phoenix Junior College buildings at Seventh Street
and Fillmore.[19]

Both North Phoenix High School and Phoenix Junior College were WPA projects. The WPA also supported the development of the Pueblo Grande Museum and the Federal Art Center in Phoenix. The former, along with the Heard Museum, allowed Phoenicians to continue to preserve important links with the past, while the latter, opened in July 1937, provided relief for local artists and afforded the public "opportunities to participate in the experience of art." The program of the Federal Art Center proved to be one of the most patronized in the United States, and it helped lay the groundwork for the future Phoenix Art Museum. Additional cultural offerings were the plays performed by the Phoenix Little Theatre and the concerts sponsored by the Phoenix Symphony Association.[20]

For those who preferred to socialize in Phoenix parks, the New Deal provided expanded facilities. In 1930 the federal government abolished the Papago-Sahuaro National Monument east of the city and designated part of the land for public recreational use. Under the New Deal, Phoenix received three Civilian Conservation Corps camps, one located in Papago Park and two in South Mountain Park. During the decade, CCC members worked hard to improve both facilities, making them into major local attractions by 1940. In that year, at Papago Park, visitors were especially pleased with the new Desert Botanical Garden. Late in the decade, federal funds also inspired the development of Phoenix Municipal Stadium and Encanto Park, as well as improvements to Eastlake Park, Grant Park, and other neighborhood recreational areas. As a Phoenix observer declared in 1940, "Without the 'Depression' the park system would still be only a dream."[21]

Some events, such as the annual Arizona State Fair, were canceled during the Great Depression years, but others, such as the annual Masque of the Yellow Moon pageant, continued to attract Phoenix residents and visitors. Sports events also remained popular, with the annual Fiesta del Sol Football Classic and Phoenix Open Golf Tournament drawing large crowds. In 1938 the Phoenix Chamber of Commerce established the Royal Order of Thunderbirds, a special group of promoters patterned after the Tournament of Roses Association of Pasadena, California. Consisting of forty select members, the Thunderbirds, who pledged themselves "to work for the glorious future of Phoenix," took charge of promoting key events every year to "mark the official beginning of the winter season in the Valley of the Sun."[22]

As in the past, Phoenicians enjoyed a variety of social activities, not all of them constructive. Sometimes a social situation ended in tragedy. For example, early in the decade Phoenix received more publicity than it wanted when Winnie Ruth Judd, a local secretary known as the "Trunk Murderess," went on trial. Judd, a very attractive young woman, was accused of killing two female friends while in a jealous rage allegedly brought on by problems in her love life, sawing them into pieces, and sending the pieces to Los Angeles in two trunks. Leaking blood upon their arrival in the California city, the trunks were opened and their contents discovered. Judd was arrested in Los Angeles, returned to the Arizona capital, and put on trial for murder in October 1931.

The case attracted national attention; for example, a *Chicago Tribune* reporter filed the following lead paragraph from Phoenix: "From Hollywood, San Bernardino, and San Diego, and from Omaha, Denver, and Salt Lake, from Chicago and even from New York the sort of people that have the time, the money, and peculiar taste for the sensationally gruesome are alighting from every train." He called the trial "the biggest thing that has happened in Phoenix since it emerged from the sage brush two generations ago." Some local promoters, of course, felt it would help the tourist business, but most deplored the negative publicity. Judd was eventually convicted and sent to the Arizona State Prison at Florence; later she was transferred to the Arizona State Hospital for the Insane in Phoenix.

Sensational murder trials were rare in Phoenix, but destructive social behavior retained a place in community life. The end of prohibition in 1933 may have made law enforcement easier, but the Great Depression created new problems. Phoenix never hired enough police officers or built enough jails or detention centers to handle the great influx of transients. Drug trafficking also increased in the city during the 1930s. In 1935, according to W. D. Chesterfield, a private investigator hired by Mayor Joseph S. Jenckes, Phoenix served as "one of the main distribution centers of narcotics in Arizona." He called the problem "quite flagrant, very extensive, and too large for the city to handle." He urged federal authorities to get more involved.

In addition to drugs, prostitution and gambling persisted in Phoenix. In 1934, a new police chief pledged to end all "dilly dallying with vice in forms of prostitution and gambling, which

have been much of the time, open and notorious." Despite periodic attempts to purify the urban center, the "business of sin"
prevailed. Brothels concentrated on Jefferson, Madison, and Jackson between Central and Fourth Street. Gambling places could be
found throughout the city. Brothels and gambling places closed
and reopened, and closed and reopened. "The way the situation is
being handled is just to let prostitution and gambling run" and
"every once in a while to bring the participants in and fine them,"
complained one critic.

Private investigator Chesterfield reported in 1935 that nothing
would change until the police department was reorganized and
"purged of some of the crooks." He claimed he knew of "men within
the police department who are in direct collusion with malefactors
of the community and the underworld and are double-crossing the
chief." Similar accusations were made throughout the decade, but
public apathy reigned and few constructive changes occurred. In
1940, the fines levied on prostitutes and gamblers continued to
provide an important source of revenue for the city treasury. In
April 1940, for example, the *Arizona Republic* reported that the
Phoenix "red light" district contributed a "steady income to the
city hall":

> The operators used to pay a flat $50, but lately the "fines" have
> been changed to a basis of $25 for each "resident" of their hotels,
> making some of the levies $150 per month. A city that a year
> ago said it would not tolerate prostitution collected in excess of
> $9,000 in "fines" from these women in the last six months.

A week prior to the *Republic* article, eighteen new cases of syphilis and eleven of gonorrhea in Phoenix were reported to state
health authorities, but city health reports failed to mention them.
This failure to report venereal disease happened time and again.
Despite such problems, few called for the complete eradication of
the "red light" district. Most residents who cared to venture an
opinion felt it was "a necessary evil, which should be regulated,
localized and kept under police supervision." "It is impossible to
cleanse the city of it entirely," asserted a Phoenix resident, "and
by driving it out of the business district, it infests the residential
section and becomes more of a moral hazard. Perhaps the only
satisfactory, practical solution is to allow it to operate under control."[23]

The integration of society occurred as much in the irregular economy as it did anywhere else in Phoenix. People of different classes and races often mingled openly in the establishments where gambling, prostitution, and drug use prevailed. At the same time, of the total population few members of racial minority groups or white groups were involved in such activities. However, second-class citizenship reflected the economic and social lot of minority group members more than of Anglos. In 1940, Mexicans remained the largest minority group in Phoenix with a population of 9,750, up from 7,293 in 1930. Mexicans continued to make up about 15 percent of the total population and blacks continued to make up about 5 percent. In 1940 blacks numbered 4,263, up from 2,366 in 1930. The 1940 census also revealed a Native American population of 250, a Chinese population of 430, and a Japanese population of 50, with each group representing less than 1 percent of the total.[24]

When the Great Depression arrived in the Arizona capital, minority group members often suffered the most; by October 1933, 59 percent of the Mexican population, 51 percent of the blacks, and 11 percent of the Anglos in Phoenix were on relief. Life proved especially difficult in the poorer neighborhoods of south Phoenix. In 1940 most of the city's two largest minority groups, the Mexicans and the blacks, still lived in that section of the city. Over the years, a sense of ethnic identity and cultural awareness, along with patterns of discrimination and segregation, had encouraged minority enclaves. Cheap housing and the availability of employment also drew Mexicans and blacks to these areas. Low-income jobs, including farm work, could be acquired. Buses often carried neighborhood residents to the fields to work. In the 1930s, adverse economic conditions had brought even more difficult times.

During that decade, the Mexican population concentrated in two areas. The poorest barrios were located between Sixteenth and Twenty-fourth streets from Washington south to the Salt River. The area contained blocks of shacks in the vicinity of the railroad tracks where many destitute Mexicans lived. A second area housing mostly Mexicans was south of Washington between Second and Fourth avenues. Blacks also concentrated in two south Phoenix neighborhoods. Most of them resided in low-cost housing located south of Washington and north of Buckeye Road from Central Avenue to Sixteenth Street. Other blacks lived in a poorer neighborhood, located between Seventh and Seventeenth avenues, from Madison Street to the south side of Buckeye Road.[25]

A heritage of poverty and a language problem, along with a lack of education and ambition, according to Anglo observers, allowed Mexicans little upward mobility. Take away the language barrier, and the blacks occupied a similar position, along with a history of racial segregation and discrimination. Segregated housing for blacks was strongly supported in Phoenix by white institutions. Banks and other lending agencies refused to give mortgages to blacks on homes in white areas, and the building and real estate industries would not sell homes in white neighborhoods to blacks. Firms vied with each other in offering property with the most rigid race restrictions.

Combined with legal segregation in the schools and discriminatory practices in hotels, restaurants, theaters, swimming pools, and other public places, the blacks' situation epitomized the second-class citizenship afforded racial minorities in Phoenix and the Valley of the Sun. Denied adequate educational and job opportunities, they were forced by their economic and social position to endure a lower standard of living than most whites. Black men, employed mostly as unskilled service workers downtown, or as common laborers or farm help, and black women, usually employed as domestic workers, faced rising unemployment in the 1930s. By 1940, it was estimated that "the average black family in Phoenix was living under crowded conditions in a poorly furnished home." In that year, federal census workers canvassed the neighborhoods in which blacks lived and found "only a few modern homes, and many wood shacks, trailers, tents, sheds, and abandoned stores." They reported "most homes are one to four room structures without benefit of running water or sewage."[26]

Ignored by the Anglo relief agencies in Phoenix early in the decade, blacks formed their own organizations to combat the situation. In 1931, the Phoenix Protective League, headed by Sidney Scott, H. D. Simpson, James L. Davis, and other black leaders, collected and distributed food and clothing to unemployed blacks; it also tried to find jobs for them. The Phoenix branch of the National Urban League and the local chapter of the National Association for the Advancement of Colored People also provided relief to the "colored needy." The black Masons, the black Elks, and numerous other black fraternal lodges made an effort to take care of their own jobless members and their families. All of these organizations demanded and succeeded in getting an "all Negro Division" of the Phoenix Community Chest during the 1930s. They also welcomed the arrival of federal funds and programs designed to help all Phoenicians in need of aid. Black voters, like the majority of white voters, were grateful, and throughout the decade they supported Franklin D. Roosevelt and his New Deal.[27]

Father Emmett McLoughlin, a Catholic priest who arrived in the city from California in 1934, was shocked by life in the poorer neighborhoods of south Phoenix, but he viewed them as "an opportunity and a challenge." With funds he acquired from "dinners, bazaars, barbecues, gambling, panhandling, and begging," he bought an abandoned grocery store located at Seventh Avenue and Sherman Street, in the center of one of the poorer black neighborhoods, and remodeled it into a church and social hall called St. Monica's Community Center. White Catholics in Phoenix contributed well, he noted, but he felt many of them only "wished a separate Negro church lest they might have to worship together before a common altar." He recalled the opposition from priests, nuns, and laity when he had "tried to gain acceptance of Negroes in the Knights of Columbus, parish societies, the parochial school (where only a token few were taken), and the Catholic school of nursing."

The social hall fared better than the church, especially after Father McLoughlin installed a jukebox. It "packed the social hall more effectively than the Pied Piper of Hamlin. Many youngsters played and danced till they were too tired to fight or steal or molest. Juvenile delinquency dropped." Health problems especially interested the priest, and when the owner of an adjoining barbershop donated his property, McLoughlin remodeled it into a maternity clinic, the first in Arizona. Free care was administered by volunteer doctors and nurses, many of them from St. Joseph's Hospital. Other free clinics followed, including a venereal disease clinic, another first for Arizona. It became necessary because "too many babies had ophthalmia neonatorum, gonorrhea of the eyes, or congenital deformity due to syphilis."

St. Monica's Community Center, also known as Father Emmett's Mission, became an institution in south Phoenix. Despite his critics, including some black religious leaders who felt he was competing with them, the white priest continued to pursue his goals: "I had to humiliate myself, to beg, to accept insults, to wait in offices, to explain the needs of the poor, to be brushed off like an unwanted salesman and to persist for the sake of my people till I was tossed the crumbs that would send me on my way." In the process, he expanded his operation in many directions, from playgrounds to housing projects. By the end of the decade, Father Emmett was receiving the support of the United States Public Health Service, the Surplus Commodity Corporation, the Farm Security Administration, the Works Progress Administration, the National Youth Administration, the Arizona Department of Health, the Maricopa County Health Department, the City of Phoenix, St. Joseph's Hospital, and the Phoenix Community Chest.

Federal funds and programs played a crucial role in the improvement of housing conditions in south Phoenix. In 1938, Father McLoughlin began emphasizing in public the large number of substandard dwellings in the area. Time and again he called for New Deal programs to change the situation. With the aid of *Gazette* reporter Bob Macon, who ran headline stories with photographs, the priest further documented his case by taking motion pictures of "the leaning shacks, 'one-holers,' and congested fire-traps. One of them was actually a horse stable on a fifty-foot lot, which had been converted into one-room shelters housing twenty families— of people, not horses—at $20 per month per family." The priest "showed the pictures to and pleaded with Catholics, Baptists, Methodists, Presbyterians, Orthodox and unorthodox Jews, Kiwanians, Rotarians, Lions, the PTA, the YMCA, the YWCA, and the man on the street."

When state legislators met in Phoenix in January 1939, Father McLoughlin and his supporters lobbied hard to convince them to approve public housing under the United States Housing Act of 1937. The priest had managed to be appointed a chaplain at the session, and he quickly violated the nonpolitical nature of his appointment by arguing public housing with representatives from every part of the state. He even threatened to "forget to bless the members" if they refused to approve the necessary legislation. At the end of the session, the legislators finally passed the enabling law that allowed federal funds for the eradication of slums in Arizona.

The Phoenix City Commission soon appointed a housing authority and named Father McLoughlin as chairman. As chairman of the Phoenix Housing Authority, he realized that "the fight had just started." Three sites, all located in slum areas, were chosen for housing projects; but, according to Father Emmett, "The cries that rose to the city commission would have led bystanders to believe that we were about to tear down the country club." The property owners led the protest.

The dogs that barked showed who had been hit. Several were Roman Catholics. Some were also Irish. They had complained for years of the grinding, exploiting tactics of the British. Now they were caught owning properties in slum areas, covered with shacks, from which they extracted rents that returned their investment within a year. No money was needed for maintenance. A single outside toilet would suffice. Because it rarely rained, roof repair was unnecessary. And none of the shacks was ever painted.

The golden goose was about to be slaughtered. And if it were, the clergy was told, what would happen to their church collections? I presided at a meeting in the city hall after the police had taken a shotgun from one irate citizen. I heard myself denounced as a disgrace to the clergy and as a renegade Irishman who had out-Cromwelled Cromwell.[28]

Dangerous times for Father Emmett, but other members of the Phoenix Housing Authority backed him and the sites were approved. Condemnation of the properties followed and the odious shacks were demolished. After receiving a grant of $1.9 million from the federal government, Phoenix officials ordered the construction of three housing tracts, and homes for six hundred low-income families were completed in 1941. Since they were built without graft, construction costs turned out to be the lowest in the nation; rents were as low as ten dollars per month. The developments were the Marcos de Niza Project for Mexicans and the Matthew Henson Project for blacks, both located in south Phoenix, and the Frank Luke, Jr., Project for Anglos, located in east Phoenix. These projects proved popular and quickly filled with residents. Thus some progress was made on the housing front largely as a result of New Deal programs and the persistent leadership of "the people's padre," Father Emmett McLoughlin, also known in the local minority group press as the "Guardian of the Southside of Phoenix."[29]

Other institutions and leaders emerged in south Phoenix in the 1930s to combat problems intensified by the Great Depression. Hispanic voluntary associations, including Protestant churches and fraternal lodges, became more numerous. The Catholic Church remained a force, but small Protestant congregations made up of Baptists, Methodists, Presbyterians, Episcopalians, Seventh-Day Adventists, and others were evident. Joining the Alianza Hispano Americana and the Liga Protectora Latina as popular organizations for Mexicans was the Latin American Club, created by Luis Cordova in 1932. Friendly House also remained a center of Hispanic community life in the 1930s. Like St. Monica's Community Center, it provided south Phoenix residents with a number of valuable services. Poor whites and blacks arrived in the city during the decade to compete with Mexicans for menial jobs. As unemployment rates soared, relief agencies strained to meet the demand for aid. Friendly House not only continued its "Americanization" programs but also became the chief relief agency "for all Spanish-speaking residents."[30]

In 1931 Mrs. Placida Garcia Smith replaced Carrie Green as director of Friendly House. A native of Colorado and a college graduate, she had done volunteer work at Friendly House since her arrival in Phoenix. A dedicated teacher, she was determined to carry on the "Americanization" programs associated with Friendly House, but the unemployed were desperate for relief in the form of food, clothing, and jobs. When not assisting in the repatriation of Mexicans to their native land, Garcia Smith and her staff provided food and clothing to the Hispanic needy. Friendly House also provided the Anglo community with trained Mexican domestic workers; by the end of the decade it had achieved a reputation for providing efficient and reliable help. For the Mexican workers, who were mostly female, this exposure to "American" culture in the homes of north Phoenix Anglo families was seen as a positive experience.

By 1933, federal funds and programs became available, and Friendly House increased its services. Since the government required citizenship for individuals to be eligible for relief programs, more English and other "Americanization" courses were offered. Day care nurseries for Mexican children and projects for Mexican "musicians and actors" were started. Garcia Smith's aggressive promotional work made Friendly House a widely admired community asset during the Great Depression. In September 1935, the *Republic* described it as "an institution devoted to the economic and social welfare of Spanish-American citizens of Phoenix." In the late 1930s, Garcia Smith became a supporter of Father Emmett McLoughlin in the drive for public housing projects in south Phoenix. Noting the deplorable conditions in the poorer neighborhoods, she declared in 1938, "The greatest thing we could do to relieve the situation would be to inaugurate a slum clearance program. By providing clean homes for underprivileged families, we can give them a foundation on which they can raise themselves and their children to a better standard of living."[31]

The few Indians in Phoenix also experienced difficult times during the 1930s. They continued to congregate at the railroad depot and other public places in the city to sell their wares to tourists and residents. Theaters maintained separate seating areas for Indians, and they were denied the right to vote or to marry whites. The Phoenix Indian School remained a source of cheap labor for Phoenix employers. Female students took courses in cooking, sewing, housekeeping, and child care, while males took subjects such as agriculture, carpentry, plumbing, masonry, and printing.

The school utilized New Deal funds for physical development. By the end of the decade, the campus covered 187 acres and its buildings included office structures and dormitories, classrooms and shops, a hospital and a gymnasium; five hundred students from throughout the state and beyond were in residence. In 1940, when it opened for its forty-ninth year, the Phoenix Indian School remained one of the leading Indian institutions of learning in the nation and a local landmark of considerable interest.[32]

In the early 1930s, the small Chinese population continued to concentrate in Chinatown. Organizations ranging from the Chinese Chamber of Commerce to the Chinese Salvation Society did what they could to alleviate hard times during the Great Depression. Opium smoking and gambling posed persistent problems for local and federal authorities, although many local Anglos participated. The Chinese lottery especially appealed to a broad spectrum of the Phoenix population; W. D. Chesterfield reported in 1935 that "hundreds of local citizens are gambling at Chinese lottery."

Chinatown, a fixture in Phoenix since the nineteenth century, began to break up late in the 1930s. Successful Chinese business and professional leaders led the way in leaving the area, located mainly on Madison Street between First and Second streets. They felt the area encompassing Chinatown would inevitably deteriorate, and rather than become part of a "skid row" in downtown Phoenix, they began moving and scattering to various outer city neighborhoods. Gambling and drug trafficking had given Chinatown a bad image, and upwardly mobile Chinese wanted to avoid being part of that image. Chinese business interests also realized that "Phoenix would grow and that commercial enterprises would have a better chance of success if they were in areas of expansion." D. H. Toy, for example, moved his restaurant and food service business from Chinatown to Sixteenth Street and Camelback Road.[33]

The Japanese made up the smallest minority group in Phoenix; only about fifty of them resided within the city limits in 1940. Several hundred lived outside the city in the valley, and most of them engaged in agricultural work. Confronted with incidents of discrimination and segregation, and possessing a sense of ethnic identity and cultural awareness, the Japanese in the Salt River Valley created their own communal structure. Beginning in the 1920s, the Japanese Association of Arizona, organized to protect the general interests of members, maintained an office on South Third Street in Phoenix. The Japanese Community Hall and the Japanese Language School building opened in 1928, and in 1932 the Arizona Buddhist Temple was formed in the Glendale home of Hiboshi Yamamoto. It listed more than one hundred members from Phoenix, Mesa, Tempe, Glendale, and Tolleson. Affiliate organizations were the Buddhist Women's Association and the Young Buddhist Association. Like other groups making up the demographic mosaic, Japanese secular and spiritual organizations and institutions helped alleviate problems that members faced individually and collectively during the Great Depression. The construction of a building to house the Arizona Buddhist Temple was completed in May 1935, near the corner of Indian School Road and Forty-third Avenue. Through the last half of the decade, it served as a center of life in the Japanese community.

The Japanese proved particularly successful as lettuce and cantaloupe growers, but competition with white farmers in the 1930s caused conflict. In the past, the Japanese in Phoenix had been subject to segregation in public places, such as theaters and swimming pools, and state law prohibited them from marrying whites. Restrictive laws in the early 1920s limited the entry of Japanese immigrants into the United States, and state legislation such as the Arizona Alien Land Law of 1921 denied Japanese aliens, who by law were ineligible for citizenship, the right to "acquire, possess, enjoy, transmit, and inherit real property or interest therein." Although the law was designed to prohibit Japanese aliens from living on or owning land in Arizona, some Japanese gained access to agricultural lands through lease contracts with accommodating whites or through their American-born children.

White farmers in Arizona did not test the land law until the Great Depression. In August 1934, frustrated at the continued success of the Japanese vegetable and fruit farmers in the Salt River Valley, several militant white farmers organized the Anti-Alien Association and began calling for the strict enforcement of the law. Japanese farms were damaged and destroyed, and Japanese farmers were harassed and attacked. The Anti-Alien Association, which soon had hundreds of members, organized "anti-Jap" motorcades to drive throughout the valley to protest the "Yellow Peril" and to demand the removal of "the Japs" from Arizona. As acts of violence escalated, the Japanese community complained and representatives of Japan and the United States, reflecting on the "bombings, shootings, floodings, and burnings," asked Arizona Governor B. B. Moeur to settle the dispute. As Tomokazu Hori, Japan's consul general in Los Angeles, put it to Moeur:

> Such wanton and barbaric assaults upon the law-abiding Japanese are damaging to the name of your state as well as to the friendship between the United States and Japan. Both for the sake of your state and American-Japanese friendship, I beg you to redouble your efforts in suppressing the agitators and vandals, and thus safeguarding the lives and properties of the Japanese.

Only after United States Department of Justice agents arrived did the violence stop. Especially effective was the warning issued by New Deal authorities in Washington that if the situation did not change, there might be a problem in granting Arizona federal funds and projects. With millions of dollars needed for relief and recovery, Arizona officials received the message and ultimately proved reluctant to commit the state to any policy strenuously disapproved by the federal government. By March 1935, the crisis was over. The Arizona Supreme Court ruled against the Alien Land Law of 1921, and the Arizona State Legislature, under a great amount of international, national, and local pressure, failed to pass similar measures. The crisis, however, established the Phoenix area as a focal point of racial prejudice and discrimination against the Japanese, a circumstance that contributed to the breakdown of Japanese-American relations that led eventually to World War II. During that war, members of the Japanese population in Phoenix

Table 3. Phoenix and Neighboring Communities, 1880–1940

City	1880	1890	1900	1910	1920	1930	1940
Phoenix	1,708	3,152	5,544	11,134	29,053	48,118	65,414
Tempe	300	500	900	1,154	1,963	2,495	2,906
Mesa	100	400	700	1,700	3,036	3,711	7,224
Glendale	—	—	300	1,000	2,737	3,665	4,855
Scottsdale	—	—	100	300	500	700	1,000
Chandler	—	—	—	—	400	1,378	1,239

SOURCE: U.S. Census of Population, 1880–1940.

and the Valley of the Sun would be subject to relocation to concentration camps constructed in remote areas of the Arizona desert.[34]

A number of small agricultural centers surrounding Phoenix, including Tempe, Mesa, Glendale, Scottsdale, and Chandler, had emerged by 1940. They all lagged far behind the capital city in population, however, and none of them ever threatened its prominence. Phoenix remained the hub of central Arizona life, and the adjacent farm towns looked to it for a wide range of goods, services, and amenities. At the same time, they contributed a great deal to the desert center, and in some instances they achieved a particular identity that added valuable new attractions for local boosters to promote.

Tempe, founded in 1871, and Mesa, founded in 1878, continued to dominate life in the eastern part of the Salt River Valley. Charles Trumbull Hayden led the way in Tempe. A prominent merchant and mill owner, he urged fellow Arizonans to recognize the importance of educational institutions to the growth of the territory. An ardent booster, in 1885 he helped influence the legislature to select Tempe as the site for the new Arizona Territorial Normal School, now Arizona State University. Hayden and other supporters purchased five acres of Tempe land and donated the site for the institution, which in 1886 opened its one classroom to thirty-one students.

In 1887, the Maricopa and Phoenix Railroad, connected to the Southern Pacific transcontinental line to the south, arrived in Tempe and crossed the Salt River into Phoenix. That same year, outside investors organized the Tempe Land and Improvement Company, purchased 705 acres of property from Hayden and other settlers, and began to promote a townsite. Lots were sold, and new homes and businesses appeared. The Normal School building, as well as the new homes and businesses, were constructed of fired

red brick and sawed lumber; adobe was abandoned for a more "American" look. In December 1888, the local newspaper declared, "Tempe's building boom is still on the rampage." Tempe was incorporated as a town in 1894, and its promoters looked forward to more progress.[35]

Tempe was a small but growing farm and college town by 1900. As the irrigated acreage around the town increased, so did the population and the volume of business. Tempe's location on the railroad made it the shipping point for the east side of the valley. Because of the college, local promoters also began calling Tempe the "Athens of Arizona" despite sarcastic remarks made by critics in Tucson, home of the Territorial University of Arizona, who claimed the same title for their urban center.[36]

While banks and hotels, churches and schools, new railroads to Mesa and new bridges to Phoenix came into being, Tempe residents lived with the uncertainty of the Salt River, experiencing floods and droughts. Roosevelt Dam and its extensive support system brought relief, and Tempe enjoyed the benefits of the "cotton boom" until hit by the "cotton bust" in the early 1920s. During the economic depression, hard times enveloped many residents, especially those who lived in "Mexican Town." Since the beginning, the Mexican population of Tempe had been increasingly excluded from Anglo-dominated society; in 1915, for example, residents officially endorsed the segregation of Tempe schools. When hard times returned in the 1930s, the Mexicans suffered the most among the various groups in Tempe.[37]

In 1931 contractors completed the new Tempe bridge. It assured a dependable Salt River crossing that strengthened the link between Phoenix and Tempe and other east valley towns. The project provided jobs for many unemployed workers, whose presence reflected the hard times that affected Tempe and the Normal School. Enjoying progress and prosperity in the 1920s, the institution provided Tempe with prestige as well as a steady source of economic betterment. In 1925, the Normal School was renamed Tempe State Teachers College. Four years later it became Arizona State Teachers College.

With the advent of the New Deal the college president, Dr. Grady Gammage, supported by Arizona Governor and Tempe physician B. B. Moeur and Arizona Senator Carl T. Hayden, son of Tempe pioneer Charles Trumbull Hayden, began successfully applying for federal grants and projects. From 1934 to 1940, Washing-

Tempe Railroad Bridge washed out by flood, 1905. The Herb and Dorothy McLaughlin Photographic Collection.

ton officials approved several million dollars' worth of PWA, WPA, NYA, and other government agency improvements, including the construction of at least a dozen college buildings and the complete landscaping of the campus. By 1940, Arizona State Teachers College at Tempe, with an enrollment of 1,300 students, was a leader in the educational system of the valley and the state.[38]

Incorporated in 1883, the town of Mesa, located eight miles east of Tempe, served as another commercial link for area agricultural interests. The Mormon farmers who predominated turned to Mesa to serve their economic and social needs. Francis M. Pomeroy, George W. Sirrine, Charles J. Robson, and other townsite promoters, influenced by the plan of Salt Lake City, allowed for generous lots, broad streets, public squares, groves, and gardens. The town grew slowly as freighters and merchants catered to the nearby mining towns of Globe and Superior as well as to local farmers. In 1895, the Maricopa, Phoenix and Salt River Valley Railroad was completed to Mesa from Tempe, tying the Mormon town into regional and national railroad networks. The construction of Roosevelt Dam provided another boost to the local economy during the years 1903 to 1911. Mesa was the gateway to that immense project, and merchants, freighters, and others involved benefited directly and indirectly. Improvements in the water supply system, including more canals, opened more land to irrigation and the volume of crop production increased.

With the arrival of the railroad, architectural changes occurred in Mesa. Brick and wood replaced adobe in the construction of buildings, and new homes and businesses were "modest imitations of popular Eastern styles." Local residents moved quickly to construct brick Queen Anne and other Victorian-style dwellings. By 1910 Mesa was a bustling "American" community with 1,700 residents. It contained stores and banks, hotels and restaurants. By that year, church services were being held by Baptists and Methodists as well as Mormons, although the latter remained in the majority. Voluntary associations such as the Masons and the Odd Fellows tried to meet the needs of population elements.

"Mesa is in the midst of a wide area of productive farming land," noted an account in 1914. It added, "In addition to vast fields of alfalfa, cantaloupes and brown sugar beets do well, the seedless grape is cultivated, and oranges." Citrus became increasingly popular and profitable, and, like much of the rest of the Salt River Valley, the Mesa area experienced the cotton boom and bust during World War I and the postwar years. The local economy recovered slowly in the early 1920s, and leaders welcomed the arrival of the Southern Pacific main line to Mesa in 1925. An industrial district began to develop in the vicinity of the new Southern Pacific Railroad depot, located along Broadway.

Mesa's population reached 3,711 in 1930. Blacks and Mexicans lived in separate neighborhoods, and Anglos dominated life in the town. Among the Anglos, the Mormons remained the most numerous. In the rest of the valley prejudice against them continued to be evident, but in Mesa they were in charge. The "Mormon Capital of Arizona," Mesa in 1928 celebrated the completion of the Mormon Temple, the most impressive structure in the town, which served as the center of Mormon activity in the state.

The early 1930s proved to be difficult years for Mesa, but the New Deal provided substantial relief. Federal help allowed city officials to erect a new post office, build more schools, pave and curb Mesa's streets, and finance other desirable projects. Project jobs offered hope to the unemployed, and many of the projects, once

Mesa in the 1930s. Arizona Historical Foundation, Hayden Library, Arizona State University.

Mormon Temple in Mesa, c. 1930. The Herb and Dorothy McLaughlin Photographic Collection.

completed, improved the physical appearance of Mesa. During the decade, the little city doubled its population to 7,224 and secured its position as the second largest community in the Salt River Valley.[39]

Glendale, another principal town of the Salt River Valley, was founded in 1892 and incorporated in 1910. Located along Grand Avenue nine miles northwest of Phoenix, the community at first contained Dunkard farmers from the East. William J. Murphy, developer of the Arizona Canal, promoted the settlement of Glendale. A temperance advocate, he urged Chicago resident and Church of the Brethren colonizer Burgess A. Hadsell to recruit Dunkards as settlers. Religious, sober, industrious people, they irrigated their farms with water from the Arizona Canal and shipped their crops via the Santa Fe, Prescott and Phoenix Railroad. In the 1890s Murphy had negotiated with the railroad, giving it property along Grand Avenue in exchange for assurance the line would run through Glendale, and most likely make it a significant shipping center. Murphy also boosted the construction of the Glendale Sugar Beet Factory in 1906; though sugar beets proved too difficult to grow and harvest in the area, and the factory closed in 1912, it remains a local landmark.

Glendale experienced steady growth, and observers noted that it erected "schoolhouses and churches but no saloons or gambling houses." Following the completion of Roosevelt Dam, it prospered and plummeted while it participated in the cotton boom and bust. Of German, Polish, and Russian stock, Glendale farmers succeeded despite setbacks, and in time their community became known as "the Vegetable Capital of the Southwest." Along with progress came problems, especially during the Great Depression. Glendale farmers experienced economic hardship in the early 1930s, and many of them joined in the anti-Japanese crusade during those years. Better times arrived later in the decade, and Glendale evolved into the leading town in the west valley, recording a population of 4,885 in 1940, up from 3,665 in 1930.[40]

In February 1888 Winfield Scott, a well-known promoter of immigration, received an invitation to visit the Phoenix area and observe its potential. After taking a tour of the valley and talking to residents, he purchased 640 acres of land that in time became the center of Scottsdale. Watered by the Arizona Canal, it proved to be productive property. The New York-raised Scott, a Civil War veteran and a military chaplain, traveled throughout the country

Farm equipment store in Glendale, c. 1925. The Herb and Dorothy McLaughlin Photographic Collection.

boosting his new home. He called it a better place to grow fruit than California, and he urged farmers seeking a future to move to the Salt River Valley. While Scott served in the United States Army, preached at revival meetings, and promoted his new home, his land was turned into a prosperous fruit ranch by his brother George. The Scotts, determined to make the area "the orange capital of the West," soon ranked among the leaders of commercial citrus production in the valley.

In 1893 Scott retired from the army and began devoting full time to fruit ranching and Baptist preaching. The following year he supervised the subdivision of land located just south of his ranch into a townsite called Orangedale. Scott did a fine job, and in that same year, in recognition of his role in the founding of the town, its name was changed to Scottsdale. Settlers, including health seekers, soon began arriving and slowly a town emerged. A school opened in 1896, and a post office in 1897. In the latter year, the population reflected the influence of Scott when it formed the first Anti-Saloon League in Arizona Territory. Scott preached temperance, a Phoenix reporter observed, and "It is the determination of the first settler of Scottsdale never to let alcohol get a foothold in this part of the valley." By 1900 the town contained about one hundred residents, and they no longer had to travel to Tempe or Phoenix for essentials. Winter visitors also increased in number, and they were welcome as long as they were sober.

With the completion of Roosevelt Dam, land sales accelerated in the Scottsdale area, and the town attracted more residents and businesses. Promoters advertised the community as "an earthly paradise where every project pleases," and in October 1913 the *Gazette* called it "a lovely oasis where olives and fruit vie with cotton and alfalfa in paying tribute to soil of great richness." The cotton boom helped boost Scottsdale's population to five hundred in 1920, but the cotton bust took its toll.

The Great Depression also retarded the development of Scottsdale, the number of residents increasing to only about one thousand by 1940. By that year, however, several hotels, including the Jokake Inn and the Camelback Inn, had opened in the vicinity, making it a center of luxury resort living in the Valley of the Sun. Moreover, artists of the caliber of Philip Curtis and Lon Megargee began arriving in the 1930s, and in 1937 Frank Lloyd Wright began constructing the architectural school that became Taliesin West. All three helped to establish Scottsdale's early reputation as a receptive place for those interested in the fine arts.[41]

Dr. Alexander John Chandler, a veterinarian from Detroit, visited the Salt River Valley in 1887. Backed by eastern capitalists, he purchased land south of Mesa and began irrigating and cultivating crops. Chandler incorporated the Consolidated Canal Company, which allowed him to divert more water to his land. By 1900, the forty-one-mile Consolidated Canal dominated water distribution south of the Salt River, and Chandler had developed several thousand acres. In that year, he led the way in providing hydroelectric power to pump groundwater to supplement river irrigation. The Chandler Ranch soon served as another model agricultural project in the area.

Along with William J. Murphy, Dwight B. Heard, and other Salt River Valley speculators, Chandler and his backers acquired thousands of acres that offered potential for huge profits from land sales. The land increased in value in 1909, when the federal government purchased the existing canal systems in the valley, including the Consolidated, as part of the Roosevelt Dam project. The assurance of an adequate water supply to irrigate the land was essential to the success of Chandler and other speculators.

Land could be sold for prices much higher than the original purchase price. After Roosevelt Dam was dedicated in 1911, Chandler began subdividing his 18,000-acre ranch, and in 1912 he founded the town of Chandler to serve those who bought and settled his land. According to promotional campaigns, the builders of Chandler did not expect it to compete with Phoenix as an urban center; they wanted it to be "the Pasadena of Arizona," a well-planned example of the "City Beautiful" movement popular throughout the nation at that time.

Chandler's organization conducted a national promotional and sales campaign, and the public responded. Chandler, it was declared, offered a better future than California. Special excursion trains transported hundreds of prospective investors to the townsite and its surrounding acres. The most popular locations proved to be the more expensive lots adjacent to the proposed San Marcos Hotel, destined to become one of the nation's leading winter resorts. Designed by Arthur Burnett Benton of Los Angeles, the San Marcos Hotel opened in November 1913, and soon wealthy and prominent people from throughout the country were seen at the luxurious winter resort, many of them becoming annual visitors.

San Marcos Hotel in Chandler, c. 1915. The Herb and Dorothy McLaughlin Photographic Collection.

Peoria ranch house, c. 1890s. The Herb and Dorothy McLaughlin Photographic Collection.

The cotton boom brought population growth to Chandler, which incorporated in 1920. The cotton bust hurt, but the influence of Dr. Chandler and the Chandler Improvement Company remained strong, and local officials in the late 1920s continued to try to foster a spirit of planned development. In 1926, for example, they adopted a zoning ordinance "with a view to conserving the value of buildings and encouraging the most appropriate use of land throughout the town of Chandler." The Great Depression, however, brought economic problems to the striving town, and hard times undercut enthusiasm for plans of any kind. Chandler was the only major town in the Salt River Valley to lose population during the decade, dropping from 1,378 in 1930 to 1,239 in 1940. Severe conditions existed in Chandler in the early 1930s, but soon New Deal programs involving the CCC, PWA, CWA, WPA, NRA, and other federal agencies inspired an upward trend that continued, with occasional recessions, into World War II.[42]

Several other small agricultural communities existed in the Phoenix metropolitan area by 1940. Northwest of Glendale on Grand Avenue, the settlement of Peoria, founded in 1888 by Illinois friends of William J. Murphy, served as another shipping point along the Santa Fe, Prescott and Phoenix Railroad. At the west

Table 4. Metropolitan Southwest, 1880–1940

County	1880	1890	1900	1910	1920	1930	1940
Maricopa County (Phoenix)	5,689	10,986	20,457	34,488	89,576	150,970	186,193
Pima County (Tucson)	17,006	12,673	14,684	22,818	34,680	55,676	72,830
El Paso County (El Paso)	3,845	15,678	24,886	52,599	101,877	131,597	131,067
Bernalillo County (Albuquerque)	17,225	20,913	28,630	23,606	29,855	45,430	69,391

SOURCE: U.S. Census of Population, 1880–1940.

end of the Salt River Valley, migrants from Ohio settled Buckeye in the late 1880s, and after the turn of the century Tolleson (1910) in the west valley and Gilbert (1912) in the east valley appeared. Smaller hamlets also emerged, and by 1940 Maricopa County contained a population of 186,193, compared with 72,830 in Pima County, home of Tucson. In 1940, Phoenix retained its ranking as the second largest city in the Southwest and the center of the largest metropolitan area in the region.

By 1940, the urban framework of the Valley of the Sun was well established. The agricultural capital of the Southwest and the home of the capital of Arizona, the area functioned as an economic, political, and social focal point in the region. A national tourist attraction, it was linked to the rest of the country by road, rail, and air transportation networks. During the 1930s, a strong relationship evolved between the federal government and the desert urban center, and New Deal programs helped especially to alleviate problems that surfaced. The Great Depression retarded progress, but in the future that relationship between Washington and the Phoenix area would grow stronger and the metropolitan complex would eventually develop to proportions undreamed of in the past, with the city of Phoenix continuing as its vital hub and dominant force. An economic boom and a population explosion during and after World War II would quickly push Phoenix toward metropolis status.[43]

6 THE BOOM YEARS, 1941-1960

During the next twenty years, Phoenix emerged as the leading city in the Southwest. Surpassing El Paso in the 1950s, the Arizona capital was well established at the top of the regional urban hierarchy by 1960. The optimistic attitude of promoters during the period and the atmosphere it encouraged helped the Phoenix Standard Metropolitan Statistical Area (Maricopa County) to more than triple its population between 1940 and 1960, and it easily extended its lead over rival areas. Despite problems of growth, shared by other vital urban centers in the nation, Phoenix expanded in scope and prominence as economic and population trends favored it.

The coming of World War II triggered an economic boom and population explosion in Phoenix. To begin with, the war years saw the activation of several military installations in the area, followed by the establishment of defense industries. As early as 1939, Phoenix aviator Carl (Pappy) Knier initiated the Civilian Pilot Training Program at Sky Harbor Airport. With the conflict in Europe emerging, the federal government contracted with fliers throughout the country to conduct such "war preparedness" programs. California investors bought out Knier in October 1940 and expanded the Sky Harbor operation under the name of Southwest Airways. Six months later, the new company opened Thunderbird

Field, north of Glendale, and signed a contract with the Army Air Corps to provide primary training to cadets. Soon another contract was signed with England's Royal Air Force to train its cadets, and a new base northeast of Mesa, called Falcon Field, was opened in September 1941. The success of both operations indicated the importance of being prepared for an air war in the near future.

The success of the training schools caused Phoenix promoters to become increasingly air-minded. With federal funds the city improved Sky Harbor, and it encouraged Southwest Airways' expansion. A municipal aviation commission, along with the Chamber of Commerce, represented by its national defense and aviation committees, worked to create "a huge air program in the sun." The area offered air bases fine flying weather and "the availability of a vast uninhabited territory, near at hand, for gunnery range purposes." Level surfaces, little rainfall, and the "rarity of high winds" also helped make it appealing. Local representatives in Washington, particularly Senators Ernest W. McFarland, Jr., and Carl T. Hayden, did their best to attract attention to potential Phoenix military installation sites.

In January 1941, the *Republic* announced the government's plan to establish "a big advanced aviation training field in the Valley." Military inspectors chose a site two miles north of Litchfield Park and eight miles west of Glendale. Phoenix officials quickly purchased the 1,440-acre location for $40,000 and leased it to the War Department for a dollar a year. Local boosters celebrated for good reason; one of them noted, "Base development will bring to the Valley an estimated income of $3,500,000 per year, in addition to the $1,500,000 initial cost of establishing the field. This seems good business in anybody's language." The Phoenix Military Airport, constructed by local contractor Del Webb, opened ahead of schedule in June 1941. The complex, which included 126 buildings, was capable of accommodating 2,500 men. Senator Hayden sent a telegram to the *Republic* announcing that the new facility would be named Luke Field, after Frank Luke, Jr., the Phoenix flying ace of World War I fame. On August 15, forty-three members of the first graduating class received their wings.

At about the same time, the *Republic* received a telegram from Senator McFarland announcing that the Army Air Corps had selected a site south of Mesa and east of Chandler for a basic or intermediate flying school. The Phoenix area thus could provide "all facilities necessary for developing in progressive stages fledg-

Luke Field, 1942. Luke Air Force Base History Office.

ling fliers into full-fledged Army pilots." Mesa Military Airport, a reporter observed, "will add to the thousands of men already stationed in the Phoenix vicinity some 3,000 officers, cadets and enlisted men. The field itself will be nearly as large as the Litchfield Park post." Senator McFarland estimated the cost of the 160-building base to be $4.7 million. Changes in plan brought expansion before it was completed, and Del Webb employed 2,500 men on the project. Mesa Military Airport, also called Higley Field, opened in September 1941. Renamed Williams Field after a former Army Air Corps pilot in January 1942, the base helped make the Phoenix area one of the nation's outstanding army air centers.

Following Pearl Harbor, other fields came into being: Thunderbird II, a primary training school opened north of Scottsdale in June 1942, and Litchfield Naval Air Facility, a testing station, opened in Litchfield Park in October 1943. Thousands of American and foreign cadets trained at Valley of the Sun installations. By the end of the war, for example, Luke was the world's largest advanced flying training school; by August 1945 more than 13,500 pilots had received their wings at the post.[1]

The Arizona desert attracted army camps as well as air bases. West of Phoenix several desert warfare training installations emerged in 1943 and 1944, notably Camp Horn and Camp Hyder. At one point in 1943, Camp Hyder contained over thirty thousand troops. As many as fifteen military trains serving the posts passed through Phoenix every day; on one occasion twenty-five railroad cars carried nearly two thousand soldiers. At Union Station, volunteers kept busy serving complimentary coffee and doughnuts to traveling soldiers around the clock; one afternoon five volunteers served 6,900 soldiers.

For those troops given time off from duty at the camps, Phoenix became "the desert's greatest oasis." They filled every available facility, including temporary quarters erected at the Arizona State Fair Grounds. An observer of the 77th Infantry Division, training at Camp Hyder, noted, "Best of all were the visits to Phoenix. This city, one hundred miles to the east, was a recreation spot for the dehydrated soldiers, and its hospitality was appreciated." In its "modern hotels and homes they scrubbed off desert dust and drank cool liquids." Its "parks contained green grass and trees."

Trains, buses, trucks, and other vehicles helped transport as many as ten thousand soldiers to Phoenix. Former Mayor Newell Stewart later recalled, "They'd just walk through town and buy everything there was—meat and cigarettes and liquor." At the camps, "they had about eight men in a tent. One man from the tent might come to town and buy for eight people." George Luhrs, a local hotel owner, recalled, "At night the sidewalks on Washington Street on both sides of the street, on Central Avenue, you would have thought you were in New York City. The traffic of pedestrians was from buildings to the curb." Local women working for the Red Cross canteen at Union Station, the USO, and in two servicemen's clubs, one for whites and one for blacks, served countless men in uniform. Red Cross volunteers also operated a canteen at Sky Harbor. Elizabeth Nehf, a participant, later recalled, "Planes arrived from the Pacific carrying the very sick, maimed and blind soldiers to hospitals in the East. We served hot soup along with any other food we could get."[2]

Thousands of defense workers arrived in Phoenix during the war, seeking employment in the new plants. The area offered defense plants an inland geographical position protected from possible air attacks, an important consideration in light of the federal government's dispersal policy. Phoenix organizations such as the Chamber of Commerce worked closely with Arizona's representatives in Washington to secure these valuable assets. Induce-

ments were offered and every form of cooperation was pledged, for
Phoenix promoters realized that defense plants as well as military
bases meant millions of dollars to the local economy.

In July 1941, city officials announced that Goodyear Aircraft
Corporation planned to open a plant west of Phoenix at Litchfield Park: "The project brings Arizona its first large defense industry and is expected to herald many other major industries
for the Phoenix area." Paul W. Litchfield, head of the Goodyear
Tire and Rubber Company of Akron, Ohio, knew the Valley of
the Sun, and had recommended its potential to Washington influentials. At Litchfield Park, a town he had helped develop and
where he often stayed at the luxurious Wigwam, the Defense Plant
Corporation, a federal government agency, built a $500,000 air-
plane parts plant on leased land south of an eighteen-thousand-
acre cotton ranch owned by Southwest Cotton Company, another
Goodyear subsidiary. The government-owned, Goodyear Aircraft
Corporation-operated plant opened in November 1941. As the *Republic* put it, "We owe a debt of gratitude to Paul Litchfield for his
unbending faith in the present and future of this area." The new
facility, Litchfield pointed out, "is another step toward decentralization of America's program for the production of vital defense
materials. It is well inland and thus protected from any possible
air attacks."

In the next few years, the plant expanded to twice its original
size and at its wartime peak employed 7,500 workers. They came
from the Phoenix area and throughout the country. A Goodyear
executive recalled, "We had recruiters in all areas of the country looking for labor to staff this plant or the plant at Akron. . . .
We trained cotton pickers galore out of Tennessee, Mississippi,
Arkansas, Kentucky. . . . We had a lot of women that were well
worth their salt in the plant. I was amazed at some of the younger
women whose husbands were overseas. They were very adaptable.
They were really sincere." In October 1943, Litchfield Naval Air
Facility was established to accept modified planes from Goodyear,
test-fly them, and deliver them where they were needed. As more
civilian and military personnel arrived, new communities such as
Goodyear appeared. Emergency housing was financed by the federal government, but it never succeeded in meeting the demand;
many workers came from Phoenix and other towns by car or bus.

Transportation proved to be a problem. Car pooling allevi-
ated gas rationing, but a bus shortage caused difficulties. Mayor

Stewart later recalled that Phoenix furnished transportation to the defense plants and military installations. "We had an awful time getting buses. You just couldn't buy buses and automobiles, so we had men going all over the country finding secondhand buses, any condition as long as they ran. We'd drive them back here and fix them up." The plants never closed, and roads deteriorated from constant use. J. W. Robison worked for the Goodyear Aircraft Corporation during the war, and he later noted that Phoenix buses usually managed to "get all our people out in the morning for the day shift, bring the second crew out and take the first shift back, and so on. We had a street full of buses down in front of the Goodyear plant."

Local promoters celebrated the arrival of Goodyear Aircraft Corporation. "It seems that the ice has been broken," exclaimed Sylvan C. Canz, president of the Chamber of Commerce, in July 1941, "and that from now on Phoenix will become increasingly important, and properly so, as an industrial center. . . . This is exactly the type of enterprise for which the Phoenix Chamber of Commerce has been striving and for which it will continue to strive." In the next few years several defense plants located in the area, notably Alcoa and AiResearch. In March 1942, the Defense Plant Corporation joined with the Aluminum Corporation of America to build a plant on a three-hundred-acre site located at 35th Avenue and Van Buren Street. Employment at the facility soon reached 3,500, and workers were complaining about the housing shortage in the area.

Despite housing shortages and other obstacles, business concerns faced with emergency production expansion and military requests for dispersal during the war continued to locate in the Valley of the Sun. In November 1942 AiResearch, an airplane parts plant, took possession of a Defense Plant Corporation manufacturing facility south of Sky Harbor Airport. The government-owned plant reached a wartime peak of 2,700 employees. To help ease the housing shortage, federal government agencies built public housing projects for the defense workers: Alzona Park across from Alcoa and Duppa Villa in east Phoenix, not far from AiResearch.

In November 1942 the Phoenix War Housing Committee appealed to "all patriotic citizens of the community who have a spare bedroom to make it available to those working for victory on the war production lines here." The committee, headquartered downtown, registered all available units, and members hoped to secure

"Share Your Home" program was successful during World War II in Phoenix. The Herb and Dorothy McLaughlin Photographic Collection.

enough of them "so that war workers will not have to live in the streets and parks." Committee chairman Cavett Robert reminded residents that "Phoenix invited war plants here at a time when accommodations were available. Now that war plants are going into heavier production we must meet the housing needs of their workers." Mayor Stewart supported the plea, noting, "War plants in this area already have lost hundreds of prospective employees because of a lack of quarters." Valley residents responded positively to the "share-your-home" program; moreover, the committee aided the federal government in the conversion of large buildings in the area into apartments for war workers, but the end result of these and other measures fell short.

As at Goodyear Aircraft, women as well as men worked for Alcoa and AiResearch. "I was Rosie the Riveter," Oleta Schlichting, an employee of AiResearch later recalled. At AiResearch her husband, Robert, supervised thirty women who assembled intercoolers for B-17 and B-29 bombers. He noted that the city tried to provide for the female and male shift workers:

We were working all three shifts, twenty-seven hundred people at the peak. Movies like the Fox and the Orpheum stayed open all night for swing shift people. We used to go out on moonlight horseback rides at Weldon Stables. The swimming pool at Fortieth Street and Thomas, Nelson's Beach, used to stay open for us.[3]

World War II brought problems as well as opportunities to Phoenix. The inconveniences and shortages that existed elsewhere in the nation were intensified in the Arizona capital by the presence of thousands of military personnel and defense workers. Insufficient housing, inadequate transportation facilities, and underdeveloped social services tended to cause occasional conflict in the community. Explosive situations could lead to violence. For example, off-duty black soldiers from the 364th Infantry Regiment stationed at Papago Park frequented the Phoenix "colored neighborhood." On the night of November 26, 1942, in a cafe at Thirteenth Street and Washington, one of them struck a black female over the head with a bottle. A black military policeman tried to arrest the soldier, but he resisted with a knife. When the military policeman shot and wounded the soldier, black servicemen protested.

Many of them had been drinking, and they were difficult to control. Military policemen soon assembled about 150 of the soldiers at Seventeenth Street and Washington in order to return them to Papago Park. Buses were brought in, but before the soldiers could be transported back to camp, they became excited and broke ranks when a jeep full of armed blacks appeared. A "lone shot from somewhere" was fired, according to accounts, and it ignited a riot. "This does it," an observer declared, "now all hell will pop." Soldiers scattered widely while pistols, rifles, machine guns suddenly "snapped and barked." There began a "hunt for all who might be involved."

All available law enforcement officers joined the military police, and twenty-eight blocks were cordoned off and searched. A number of hunted soldiers hid in the homes of friends in the area. To flush them out, the military police utilized armored personnel carriers. Another observer later recalled, "They'd roll up in front of these homes and with the loudspeaker they had on these vehicles, they'd call on him to surrender. If he didn't come out, they'd start potting the house with these fifty-caliber machine guns that just made a hole you could stick your fist through." Before the episode ended, three men died and eleven were wounded. Most of the 180 men arrested and jailed were soon released, but some of those who bore arms during the conflict were later court-martialed and sent to military prisons.[4]

Violent occasions did little to improve community-military relations in Phoenix, but more damaging was the steady rise in venereal disease cases among servicemen. Phoenix officials had been repeatedly warned by military authorities to do something about "vice conditions in the city and the extremely high venereal disease rate." As in the past, local officials ordered periodic raids on houses of prostitution, but the problem remained. Early in 1942 the houses of "Red Light Row" in the southeastern part of downtown Phoenix were closed, but they soon reopened, minus their "glaring neon signs." Many politicians and their followers continued to tolerate contained prostitution, noting that if it were outlawed, it would scatter through the city. Others disagreed and called for its abolition. Finally, on November 30, 1942, a few days after the riot, Colonel Ross G. Hoyt, commander of Luke Field, declared Phoenix out of bounds to post personnel; other post commanders followed Hoyt's lead. Hoyt and his colleagues made it clear, however, that the order had "no connection with the Thanksgiving night riot." Hoyt emphasized that "the order is concerned solely with the venereal disease situation."

The *Republic* sympathized with the military and accused the city of "failing to enforce its own laws and of making no sincere effort to eliminate what has been called everything from 'a disgraceful situation' to much worse." It quoted a federal government investigator, Edwin Cooley, who had announced, "In the three weeks prior to Phoenix being declared out of bounds, and these facts have been carefully checked, there were nine houses of prostitution running, containing fifty inmates, two disorderly bars or joints which were headquarters for prostitutes, and one disorderly 'massage parlor.'" The action of the military, the *Republic* lamented, "is a distinct blot on Phoenix, the ill effects of which will last a long time. . . . The question is, are the people going to remain passive as they have in the past, or are they going to demand that something drastic be done to remedy the situation?" Moreover, the military's new policy affected not only the city's moral image but also the economy; as one merchant pointed out, "The army's payrolls constitute one of the community's largest sources of revenue."

Again city officials promised to clean up Phoenix. Proposing "direct action of a more stringent nature," they deplored the laxity of the past and assured Hoyt and his colleagues that they planned to "control the incidence of venereal disease in the community." Local authorities would enforce the laws and they would organize "an immediate drive on all loose women, have them examined for venereal disease and if they are diseased place them in the new city venereal disease clinic for treatment 'no matter who it hurts.'" Colonel Hoyt reminded them, "The city will stay out-of-bounds until it has become untenable for prostitutes." He also stressed that the "military authorities had no wish to be belligerent, that it took the out-of-bounds action reluctantly," but "it was mandatory as long as the venereal disease rate among the military personnel steadily was rising." He asserted that the number of venereal disease cases at Luke Field alone had tripled in the past four months, and something had to be done. Above all, he wanted results.

When few results materialized, concerned Phoenix citizens called for the appointment of new, responsible, nonpolitical city administrators, particularly in law enforcement. Led by the board of directors of the Phoenix Chamber of Commerce, a group of citizens joined with elected officials on December 17 in an emergency evening meeting in the card room of the Hotel Adams. Claiming to speak for the community, board members demanded that the city "restore confidence" in the administration of law enforcement in Phoenix by replacing the current city manager, chief of police, city clerk, and city magistrate. The meeting lasted until early morning and, feeling the pressure, most members of the City Commission agreed that new administrators were needed. They were duly drafted. Charles A. Carson, one of the Chamber of Commerce directors, declared that the changes did not involve charges. The "question that the board considers essential to the welfare of the community is that the confidence in the enforcement agency be immediately restored in order that the army's out-of-bounds order may be raised." It is "imperative for the restoration of the good name of the city of Phoenix."

Bad for business and bad for the city's image, the out-of-bounds order had to be revoked. The "lack of confidence in government" complaint was heard time and again, and it reflected a vigorous awakening on the part of the business community regarding the future of the city. At the Hotel Adams card room meeting, another Chamber of Commerce director, prominent local lawyer

Frank Snell, pleaded with the politicians. "We're asking you," he told Mayor Newell Stewart and the commissioners, "to restore unquestioned confidence of the community in its government." The city manager, police chief, city clerk, and city magistrate should be discharged because "we don't have confidence in them and we don't believe the community has confidence in them." He also noted, "We don't know that they're bad or inefficient or that there's anything else wrong with them, but we just don't have confidence in them."

The changes at city hall pleased military leaders, and they looked forward to more results. The *Republic* also looked forward to a new era. "By their action," the paper reported, "the chamber directors have made it the solemn duty of all citizens and taxpayers to take a greater interest in and a more definite position with respect to the government of the community than has been the case heretofore." The importance of the issue could not be overestimated:

> There is more involved in having a clean city than merely the removal of the out of bounds order. There is a moral question involved that affects the citizens more than it does the military personnel of the fields which is more or less transient. The future of the city also must be considered. The progress and growth of Phoenix depends entirely upon the type of city it is. As a wide open town, naturally there would be an increase in population but not the kind that makes substantial communities. The type of people that would be brought to the city under such conditions would not make Phoenix the kind of community in which home-loving, law-abiding folk would desire to live.[5]

On December 21, three days after the shake-up at city hall, Colonel Hoyt revoked the order placing Phoenix out of bounds for military personnel. The lifting of the ban, Hoyt added, would be in effect "only as long as venereal diseases among men stationed at the airfields show a decrease." Arrests and convictions increased under the new administrators, who pursued a policy of "strict repression" against those involved in professional prostitution. Critics, however, noted that "all organized houses here are closed, but the bars, hotels, and auto courts are not being checked closely enough." Also, a problem with "amateurs" persisted. As one report asserted, it is very difficult to establish adequate controls over women who have "serviced the military personnel as a patriotic duty." The "failure to proceed against parents and establishments which wittingly or unwittingly are, in effect, contributing to the delinquency of minors, many of whom have been guilty of illicit relations" presented a problem. To parents of girls of "the impressionable age," Mayor Stewart issued an appeal: "Guard them zealously and supervise their activities—particularly after sunset." He promised rigorous enforcement of the recently enacted curfew laws.

Mayors, commissioners, and administrators changed during the war years, but no final solution to the venereal disease dilemma ever emerged. Moreover, houses of prostitution and gambling establishments continued to exist, despite periodic shutdowns. Vice and corruption persisted, as did patronage and favoritism. Despite objections, cronyism prevailed, and inefficient, inadequate government continued to operate. No more out-of-bounds orders were issued by the military, but the realization that Phoenix suffered economically and socially from a tarnished image encouraged local reformers to hope for better days ahead.[6]

Following the war, it became evident to Phoenix promoters that if the city were to grow and prosper, it needed to replace the small-time politics of city hall with modern, progressive structural and social reform. For years, Phoenix, under an inefficient, inadequate commission-manager system, had been governed in an undistinguished manner. Frequent change and chronic instability, rather than modern, progressive administration marked Phoenix government in the years following 1914; mediocre leadership, petty factionalism, and "politics as usual" continued to reign, to the detriment of the city. As one observer later put it, "Phoenix had a crummy reputation around the country."[7]

Ray Busey, a local businessman, successfully ran for mayor in November 1946, promising to work for charter reform. In October 1947 he appointed a Charter Revision Committee composed of forty prominent citizens to look into structural change. Chaired by lawyer Charles E. Bernstein and made up of business and professional leaders, the committee met on a regular basis from January to August 1948, to discuss specifics. Members studied material on local government obtained from the National Municipal League, and that organization's Model City Charter exerted a strong influence on the committee's final recommendations.

Most important, the committee called for the amended charter to exempt the city manager from the local resident requirement; no longer would the office of city manager be the choicest plum of all. A trained professional manager from outside was to be appointed for an indefinite period on the basis of his qualifications as an administrator. In a further effort to eliminate politics from city hall, the amendment forbade elected officials to meddle with the appointive and removal powers of the manager. Reformers wanted to prevent city council members from manipulating the city manager and controlling various municipal departments, which had been a major problem in the past.

Along with a strong manager, the committee recommended changing the name of the city's governing body from commission to council and enlarging its membership from five to seven, including the mayor. The mayor and incumbent councilmen were to appoint the two additional members, and all were to serve until the next election. Rather than overlap, terms of office were to run concurrently, with biennial rather than annual elections; the committee deemed it especially important that the mayor and council members all be elected at the same time. Moreover, the council could dismiss the city manager only by a four-to-three vote for cause or a five-to-two vote without cause. The reformers hoped that by strengthening the city manager's position and by removing politics from city hiring and firing, Phoenix could make progress in the elimination of vice and corruption.[8]

At a special election in November 1948, voters approved the committee's suggested revisions by a three-to-one margin. The committee conducted an intensive campaign throughout the city, enlisting the support of many service clubs, church groups, and political organizations. The city's leading newspapers, along with several influential boosters of the Phoenix Chamber of Commerce, actively supported the charter amendment. The press hammered home the need to "take politics out of city hall," and the Chamber called it time to change "our horse and buggy charter." Among those opposed were a number of city employees, including City Manager James T. Deppe, and City Commissioners H. W. Blaine, Ray D. Stone, and W. F. Tate. Other interested citizens, including paint store operator and reputed "invisible boss" Ward H. "Doc" Scheumack, a supporter and beneficiary of the traditional system, also did their best to defeat the charter revision movement.

With the successful adoption of the charter amendment, Phoenix reformers looked forward to living in a city equipped to seek progress and to remedy problems. Unfortunately, the three commissioners who had opposed the structural changes still controlled

Phoenix in 1949. The Herb and Dorothy McLaughlin Photographic Collection.

the City Commission. Following the adoption of the charter amendment, they remained a majority bloc and appointed Thomas J. Amler and Wallace W. Caywood, both of whom shared their views, as the two additional councilmen. The new City Council reappointed James T. Deppe as city manager, so few significant changes occurred in city government. The same type of individuals who ran city hall before the charter amendment continued in power and, to the dismay of reformers, good government did not result.

When it became apparent that neither the City Council nor the city manager had any intention of effecting improvements, reformers were disappointed and angry. Unless the City Council supported charter changes, they were worthless. One observer remarked in April 1949: "There are many persons in Phoenix who believe that, with an eye to the municipal elections next November, it would be prudent to form a citizens' organization as a safeguard against possible neglect by the council and manager to take advantage of the opportunity for better government offered by the charter amendment." Such an organization could "spearhead the drive for development of more effective municipal government." In July, a number of concerned citizens' groups met, under the direction of businessman and promoter Alfred Knight, in the boardroom of the Phoenix Title and Trust Company and organized the bipartisan Charter Government Committee (CGC). Formed for the purpose of offering a slate of candidates committed to the implementation of the revised charter, the CGC became the force that truly changed the direction of Phoenix city government. Made up largely of businessmen and professionals, the CGC eventually grew to more than a hundred members.[9]

The CGC recruited candidates, raised campaign funds, and directed the campaign of its slate in the November 1949 election. In that election, and in every election during the next decade, the committee enjoyed total success in getting its selections for mayor and council elected. In 1949, the Civic Achievement Group, representing the old order, assailed the CGC, but Phoenix voters were determined to go for reform. They turned out in record numbers and gave the CGC slate a clean sweep. CGC candidates, promising to implement charter revisions, appoint a professional city manager, and install efficient and economical government in Phoenix, gained an easy victory. Casting twice as many votes in 1949 as in 1947, citizens of the growing urban center voiced their approval of change by giving a majority vote in each section of the city to the CGC ticket, with the north side voting strongest in its favor. Soon after taking office in January 1950, the new council dismissed City Manager Deppe on charges of administrative incompetence, and replaced him with Ray W. Wilson, a trained professional who since 1940 had worked under L. P. Cookingham, highly regarded city manager of Kansas City, Missouri. Wilson would remain city manager of Phoenix for the next eleven years.[10]

In 1949 CGC candidates supported nonpartisan, at-large elections, the council-manager plan, and "a businesslike approach to government," and they were enormously successful. As Michael Konig and others have noted, they brought a positive image to city government; the old image of the past promoted by mediocre leadership, petty factionalism, and "politics as usual" quickly faded into obscurity. Credit for this transformation belongs to numerous organizations and individuals, including Eugene Pulliam, since 1946 the owner of the city's two major newspapers, the *Arizona Republic* and the *Phoenix Gazette*. A newspaper publisher from Indianapolis and a frequent winter visitor to Phoenix, Pulliam soon turned the *Republic* and the *Gazette* into powerful organs for political conservatism and business growth in a city "ripe for a civic and economic boom." He agreed with Alfred Knight, Walter Bimson, Frank Snell, Sherman Hazeltine, and other local leaders that political change was necessary in Phoenix, and his newspapers played a crucial role in the success of the charter reform movement.

Pulliam helped select Barry Goldwater and other victorious members of the 1949 CGC slate that swept into office; "he was the one who talked me into it," Goldwater later recalled. The *Republic* and *Gazette* engaged in an aggressive editorial campaign denouncing vice and corruption, favoritism and inefficiency. "It couldn't have worked without Gene Pulliam," remarked Dick Smith, a member of the original CGC. And in future elections, declared his biographer, "the committee always cleared the slate with Pulliam before announcing it." A very influential figure in Phoenix—too influential, according to his critics.[11]

Barry Goldwater also was encouraged to run for City Council in 1949 by his good friend Harry Rosenzweig, jewelry store owner and member of an old and respected Phoenix family. Himself a candidate, Rosenzweig helped convince department store executive Goldwater that he could make a contribution. Goldwater served one term on the City Council. In 1952 he successfully ran for the U.S. Senate, and in 1964 he unsuccessfully ran for President; although he lost badly, both Phoenix and Arizona became known as "Goldwater Country." While Goldwater was attaining a national reputation and spending most of his time in Washington, his good friend and adviser Harry Rosenzweig, and Harry's brother Newton, remained in Phoenix, where they vigorously promoted the growth of the city and the valley. Active in Republican Party affairs, Harry became one of the most powerful and influential men in Arizona. His brother and partner in business, Newton, another strong supporter of Charter Government, also contributed much to Phoenix life, especially as a leader of community organizations.

In the 1950s, with supporters like Pulliam and candidates like Goldwater, the CGC was the dominant political force behind Phoenix city government. Businesslike, honest, growth-oriented, flexible, and pragmatic enough to meet any serious opposition, the organization succeeded during the decade because it reflected the ideals of most Phoenicians. The CGC welcomed the first All America City Award Phoenix won in 1950, for it contributed to the desired image of the Arizona capital as a city with "a good,

Two aspects of Barry Goldwater. Barry Goldwater Collection, Arizona Historical Foundation, Hayden Library, Arizona State University.

clean, competent government," run by the "right people." One observer noted that the "leadership of the CGC . . . reads like a list of the social and economic elite of the city." Another declared, "An overwhelming majority of the Committee members are white, business-oriented, highly educated, and generally could be placed in middle or upper-middle classes." Critics complained that the CGC-endorsed City Council was "unrepresentative and stacked in favor of upper economic and social classes," but opponents had little influence. Nearly all of the CGC candidates in the 1950s were businesslike individuals who lived in the affluent north side areas of the city. Reflecting a philosophy akin to Republican conservatism, they easily won at-large, nonpartisan elections time and again. This trend, evident in cities throughout emergent Sunbelt America during this period, seemed natural in the rapidly growing and developing Southwest urban center.[12]

During the 1950s city services in Phoenix tried to keep up with population gains and physical expansion. City utilities, including police and fire protection, were upgraded, and new streets, sewers, parks, and public buildings appeared. Sky Harbor Airport, purchased by the city in 1935 and developed into a jet-age facility over the years, became one of the busiest airports in the nation. Local leaders initiated a freeway system and a water development program, and citizens displayed their faith in CGC-oriented Phoenix government by voting millions of dollars in bonds for necessary improvements.[13]

During the 1950s the population increased a remarkable 311 percent, the highest rate of growth among the nation's fifty largest cities during the decade. By 1960 Phoenix was the largest city in the Southwest, with a population of 439,170, up from 106,818 in 1950 and from 65,414 in 1940. While the CGC encouraged changes in the political structure and the national image of Phoenix, the Chamber of Commerce and other booster organizations kept trying to attract more business and industry to the area.

During the Cold War military installations such as Luke and Williams Air Force bases continued to serve as part of the national defense effort, and former war plants looked not only to the military but to civilian markets as well. A multiplier effect took hold, and as more manufacturers moved to the area, they attracted others. Predominant were light and clean industries, especially electronics firms that flourished in the low-humidity climate so necessary to their success. Electronics plants used little water,

*Motorola plant in the 1950s. The Herb and Dorothy McLaughlin
Photographic Collection.*

and they produced high-value, low-weight goods that could easily
be shipped anywhere. Phoenix's relatively isolated location was
no problem in electronics production because, as one observer declared, "a truckload is worth a million dollars."[14]

It was important to tourist businesses in the "clean city" of
Phoenix that pollution-free industries settle in the area. City developers encouraged smokeless plants in order to preserve "the
sunshine and pure atmosphere" of the oasis. In the Arizona capital, the sun shone 85 percent of the time, a statistic that pleased
manufacturers. Business could meet production schedules without
being interrupted by adverse weather; absenteeism fell; and outdoor testing of particular products, such as weapon systems, went
undisturbed by "nature's battle plan." Executives and workers appreciated the nearby mountains, the man-made lakes, and the
active but casual year-round lifestyle that emphasized informal
outdoor leisure living.[15]

The Motorola experience is representative of the sort of success
story that would be repeated over and over in Phoenix, and it aptly
illustrates the attractions the city held for corporations. Early in

1948 officials of the company, a leading independent concern in the rapidly growing electronics industry, decided to establish a new research and development center devoted exclusively to military electronics in Phoenix. The Cold War and national defense considerations encouraged Motorola to locate in a primary dispersal area in line with the federal government's decentralization program.

Phoenix drew attention because of its favorable business climate and its excellent location midway between the national-defense-oriented industrial supply houses of Albuquerque and southern California; moreover, nonstop six-hour air service was available between the desert city and Chicago, Motorola's main base, and nearby Arizona State College at Tempe offered the potential for the development of quality engineering programs. The most important factor, however, was the city's "outstanding climate and its nation-wide reputation as a resort and health center." It was felt that the climate and health factors would be "potent aid in attracting the desired personnel."

The Motorola operation in Phoenix proved to be a success, and expansion followed. Only one drawback was voiced: the intense heat of midsummer. Yet, as Daniel E. Noble, a leading executive, wrote in June 1954:

> The agreement is quite general among the Motorola families that they will take the four months of summer weather in preference to the winters in the north and the east. . . . They point out that a hundred-mile drive north from Phoenix will take them into the cool, wooded mountain areas of pine trees and streams. Where, they ask, in the north or in the east, can they drive out of the snow and ice and the cold in a hundred miles? And then there are the coolers. . . .
>
> Experience with evaporative coolers showed that they worked very well the greater part of the time, but that refrigeration in the laboratories insures perpetually satisfactory working conditions for the staff during the summer months. . . . Staff members are installing refrigeration units in their homes to provide an equally satisfactory control of temperatures for the family. . . . Motorola management feels that refrigeration cooling is the complete solution to the Phoenix summer heat problem. Refrigeration cooling has transformed Phoenix into a year-round city of delightful living.[16]

By 1960 Motorola operated three electronics plants in Phoenix, and the company payroll of five thousand employees was the largest in the city. With Motorola setting the pace, manufacturing had become the city's number one source of income by 1955, with farming and tourism in second and third places. Between 1948 and 1960 nearly three hundred manufacturing enterprises opened their doors and manufacturing employment in the metropolitan area tripled. The annual income from manufacturing rose from under $5 million in 1940 to over $435 million in 1963. As a result, in this important sector urban rivals in the Southwest such as El Paso, Tucson, and Albuquerque were left far behind.[17]

In the postwar years, Phoenix achieved economic diversification and the Valley of the Sun emerged as the metropolitan center of commerce and industry in the Southwest. Major firms in the Phoenix area in the 1950s included Motorola, General Electric, Kaiser Aircraft and Electronics, Goodyear Aircraft, AiResearch, and Sperry Rand. They represented the type of industry local promoters wanted to attract: clean and employing thousands of trained workers.

Suitable conditions for both work and play seemed to meet in the city, and its opportunities and amenities drew people to it like a magnet. "The principal reason we're here," Robert W. Barton, a Motorola manager, declared in 1957, "is the serious shortage of engineers. We can run an ad in the trade magazines mentioning three places to work—Phoenix, Chicago and Riverside, in California. We'll draw 25-to-1 replies for Phoenix compared with the other cities.... We don't have to pay a premium to get engineers and other skilled employees to live here, either. The premium is free—sunshine."[18]

Phoenix booster organizations worked hard to attract and serve industry. The Phoenix Chamber of Commerce, under the leadership of Lew Haas and Floyd A. Rains, conducted extensive national advertising campaigns in the postwar years. Especially through its monthly publication, *Phoenix Action*, the chamber sought to make Phoenix one of the most publicized cities in America. Related groups actively pursued special projects. For example, in September 1955 the Municipal Industrial Development Corporation, a group of determined business leaders, played a key role in bringing Sperry Rand to the Valley of the Sun by raising $650,000 in seventy-two hours. The organization bought the company a fac-

Sperry Rand Phoenix plant, 1959. The Herb and Dorothy McLaughlin Photographic Collection.

tory site, paid for improvements to a nearby airport, and arranged other inducements.

Influential Phoenicians helped to get changes in state tax laws that made the business climate of the Phoenix area even more attractive. Most important was the repeal in December 1955 of a state sales tax on products manufactured for sale to the federal government. The day after the legislature acted, Sperry Rand headquarters in New York announced that it would definitely locate its aviation electronics division plant and research center in Phoenix. The change also encouraged a number of other companies to move and inspired the expansion of several local electronics and aerospace firms that did business with the federal government.[19]

In the postwar years, the CGC and its candidates agreed with prominent booster organizations that tax reform to benefit business was necessary if the city hoped to achieve progress and prosperity. In November 1949, when the first CGC ticket was elected, voters approved ordinances that eliminated or lightened many of the tax burdens of business. A few critics complained that the new approach cost Phoenix tax revenue, but Walter Bimson, Barry Goldwater, Eugene Pulliam, and other promoters predicted that

the city would more than make up for the loss by increasing industrial production and employment. Their prediction proved correct
at the state and local levels in the following decade, with Sperry
Rand only one example of what was accomplished. In Phoenix a
close relationship persisted between the business community and
local government; often one represented the other. The Pulliam
press and the majority of the citizens approved of this united approach. The ongoing cooperation of Phoenix business and political
leaders assured the development of an environment attractive to
industry, and hundreds of establishments, large and small, appeared.[20]

Phoenix boosters in the postwar years were aware that an
area having little organized labor often appealed to industry, and
they successfully backed right-to-work legislation. Always weak
in Phoenix, labor unions proved ineffective in the prewar years;
most of the work was open shop. During the war, organized labor
made some gains in Phoenix, and following the conflict it asserted
itself in defense of the closed shop. The Phoenix Chamber of Commerce and other influential business groups encouraged industrial
growth, but discouraged union activity and worked against the
closed shop. In March 1946 Herbert M. Williams, a veteran of
the war and a local contractor, lost a bid on a construction job
because his workers were nonunion. The outraged Williams soon
formed the Veterans' Right-to-Work Committee, an organization
that quickly gained wide support. It filed an initiative petition
to put a state constitutional amendment on the November 1946
ballot. The amendment guaranteed that in Arizona an individual
would not have to join a union in order to hold a job.

Most citizens supported the amendment, including many unemployed veterans shut out of closed shops in Phoenix because
of their nonunion status. An aggressive, pro-initiative, anti-union
campaign spearheaded by the Pulliam press brought results, especially after several strikes occurred in the Valley of the Sun prior
to the voting; the initiative was approved by a substantial majority. Overreacting to the initiative, "labor's stand approached
paranoia." An editorial in the *Arizona Labor Journal*, published
in Phoenix, spoke of "The Right to Starve" law. The law banned
the closed shop in Arizona, retarded the organization of labor in
Phoenix, and helped to attract industry to the area. Attempts by
labor to reverse the decision during the period failed.[21]

In the 1950s urban leaders in the Southwest wanted their cities to develop economically, but some worked harder than others to realize that goal. Phoenix promoters often led the way; the Thunderbirds, an arm of the Chamber of Commerce, proved to be especially adept at recruiting firms to relocate. Small as well as large industries were attracted to the Arizona capital, resulting in such impressive statistics as a 1,500 percent increase in the value of manufacturing in the city during the period. Businessmen in other cities noted the aggressive tactics employed by Phoenix leaders. In Phoenix, an El Paso businessman observed, "industrial scouts are met at the plane, entertained, offered free land, tax deals, and an electorate willing to approve millions in business-backed bond issues." By comparison, he lamented, "El Paso does nothing." As a result El Paso lost its spot as the number-one city in the region. The businessman declared, "Unless we start hustling after new industry, we're going to wind up in serious trouble."[22]

Agriculture, despite urban encroachment, continued to be important to the area, with hundreds of thousands of acres of cotton, grain, vegetables, citrus, and other crops being cultivated each year. By 1955 it had fallen behind manufacturing as a source of income in Phoenix, but Maricopa County still retained a high ranking in the country in the value of agricultural products. And it showed; having seen cultivated areas from an airplane, an observer declared, "The burgeoning green of the irrigated Valley overlays the desert as if painted there with shining lacquer."[23]

At the same time, the tourist business in the Arizona center remained vital, and income from it rose considerably as facilities and services multiplied to meet the rush. Tourism continued as the Phoenix area's third biggest source of revenue, behind manufacturing and agriculture, and accommodations ranged from luxurious hotels to modest motels. Traditionally most tourists came to seek relief from harsh northern winters, but thanks to air conditioning some visitors came in the summer.

The mass production of air conditioners in the 1950s and the consequent age of refrigeration not only attracted manufacturers and brought an extended tourist season to Phoenix, it also made the city more comfortable for those permanent residents unable to leave for the coast or the mountains during the hot summer months. In addition, many of the military veterans who had served in the area, and many of the steadily increasing number of winter visitors, wanted to come back to live permanently in the air-conditioned oasis. "Even cars have air coolers," declared an observer. By the end of the decade a national magazine called Phoenix "the most thoroughly air-conditioned town on earth."[24]

During the 1950s signs of growth appeared everywhere in the capital city. The value of construction in the area, for example, jumped from $22 million in 1955 to $94 million in 1960. New city, county, state, and federal buildings reflected increased government activity at all levels, and the number of new private-sector structures was equally impressive. Del Webb, David Murdoch, John F. Long, and other big project builders led the way. "All of Central Avenue," noted a reporter, "is becoming a great commercial artery." Central Avenue "skyscrapers"—notably the twenty-story Guaranty Bank, the tallest building in the state—and sprawling subdivisions appeared during the decade. Developers created bedroom suburbs such as Maryvale and Arcadia; retirement communities, notably Youngtown and Sun City; and such large shopping centers as Uptown Plaza and Park Central. When Uptown Plaza opened at the corner of Central Avenue and Camelback Road in north Phoenix in August 1955, it was billed as "the largest single shopping center between Dallas and Los Angeles" and "dramatic evidence of the importance of suburban shopping centers in modern living . . . a symptom, and a healthy one, of a great demand for goods that will grow as metropolitan Phoenix grows."

There was more construction in Phoenix in 1959 than in all the years from 1914 to 1946 combined. In that year a total of 5,060 dwellings, mostly single-family residences, were constructed, along with 429 swimming pools, 115 office buildings, 94 stores, 167 industrial buildings, and 15 educational facilities. Each year records were broken in practically every category, as the city experienced phenomenal growth. *Time, Newsweek, U.S. News & World Report*, and other national publications contained glowing stories of the economic and demographic explosion in 1950s Phoenix. In 1960, a Phoenix observer noted: "The mood is here; the word is out; this is the place. The city is going somewhere, and it is attracting more than an average share of people who want to go somewhere with it."

Explosive new growth and development prompted an exhibit of the exploitative but traditional philosophy of progress. Like the upstart western cities of nineteenth-century America, Phoenix and other boom towns of the Southwest in the mid-twentieth century attracted men of enterprise, new pioneers willing to promote their cities for their own kind, with all, in their view, to share in the benefits. Reflecting on the frontier spirit that pervaded the area in the 1950s, a new Phoenix millionaire asserted: "This country pumps new life and energy and thinking into a man! Back East, there's nothing left to make the blood circulate; hell, it's all been done before your time by your grandfather. For the big and small alike, out West there is release from the staid, old ordinary ways of life and thinking. The same thing is true today in Phoenix as in the Gold Rush, except in a more civilized way." The lure of Phoenix included the chance to "make it big," declared a reporter; in the growing desert center "new millionaires breed like forced hothouse flowers," and "behind them are more candidates on the heels of the initial successes."[25]

Annexation of land was vital to Phoenix's population growth. In 1940 the city had a population of 65,414 in an area of 9.6 square miles; the totals by the end of 1955 were 156,000 population and 29 square miles. At that time the City Council, in its *75th Anniversary Report*, announced: "The rapid growth of Phoenix and its surrounding area has brought your city to a crossroads in its development." Phoenix, the report declared, "faces the choice of being a large city capable of planning for sound growth throughout the area and providing the type of services and facilities a large city requires or of being a relatively small city surrounded by a number of satellite 'bedroom' towns benefiting from a number of city facilities and services but making no financial contributions toward their costs." In May 1956 the city charted its course by approving a basic plan for the growth of a greater Phoenix. The plan consisted of a "stepped up year-round program of annexation" and the "development of a long-range capital improvement program to take care of present and future needs of the growing city."

Although some outlying towns, notably Scottsdale and Tempe, resented this type of urban imperialism, the annexation program moved ahead. The *Republic* asserted, "Phoenix faces a problem common to all growing metropolitan areas. It must keep pushing its limits out into the county as new housing and industrial developments are built up. Otherwise, the new areas will become incorporated and Phoenix will find itself hemmed in by a group of independent satellites." Efforts to throttle the growth of the city failed, for most people in the unincorporated areas wanted to live in Phoenix, especially since the success of the CGC-backed city government. Considered a model of civic virtue that mirrored the new image of Phoenix, it received enormous support from the population and the press. City officials, working closely with the Phoenix Chamber of Commerce, had gained the allegiance of industrial elements who were interested in maintaining a desirable business climate, including such inducements as "reasonable" tax rates and building codes.

So extensive was the annexation program that by 1960 approximately 75 percent of the people living in the city were residents of areas that had been annexed during the previous decade. In one operation in 1959, the city more than doubled in area and added over one hundred thousand people to its population; by December 1960 Phoenix contained 187.4 square miles and a population of 439,170. Pulliam, Bimson, and other boosters believed annexation to be a key to urban development; as Pulliam put it, they were determined to keep Phoenix "from being a one-horse town."

An aggressive annexation policy during the 1950s helped Phoenix to increase its population fourfold and enabled the city to increase its physical size elevenfold. In the process it kept money in the city, greatly broadened the tax base, and made it unnecessary to raise the property tax during the decade. In this manner Phoenix expanded and retained its influence in the metropolitan area; its suburbs were never able to overwhelm it. As a local official later put it, "We wanted to avoid the St. Louis model, where suburbs strangle the city. . . . We didn't want white flight, or brain drain, or whatever you call it, so we annexed."[26]

While the Phoenix suburbs developed rapidly during the 1950s, the city's central business district (CBD) went into a decline from which it never recovered. As residential dispersal progressed, business decentralization, especially of retail outlets, increased. During World War II, retail business in downtown Phoenix recorded spectacular growth, but following the war the increasing population began to spread out. Streetcars stopped operating in 1948, and automobile drivers increasingly declined to deal with the severe lack of downtown parking. As the *Gazette* put it at the time, "The price paid for allowing inadequacy of parking in a commercial area is loss of trade to an outlying section where parking is available. That trend has already begun in Phoenix." During the 1950s shopping centers outside of downtown appeared to serve affluent, automobile-oriented suburban customers. Goldwaters, for example, relocated in 1957 from downtown to Park Central, a major new shopping center north of the CBD at Central and Osborn Road.[27]

As downtown Phoenix declined and the outlying suburban areas expanded, the city's transportation system proved to be less than adequate. Phoenix had increased its physical size in square miles from 17.1 to 187.4 during the 1950s, and by 1960 the city limits reached Sixty-seventh Avenue on the west, Cactus Road on the north, Papago Park on the east, and South Mountain Park on the south. A transportation system to serve such a vast area was considered by some observers a high priority, but it never materialized.

Buses took the place of streetcars, but they proved unpopular. Most Phoenicians preferred to ride in cars and trucks. The physical dimensions of the city encouraged an automobile culture. A drive-in society featuring residential suburbs and shopping centers increasingly became part of the good life offered in the Valley of the Sun. The "car city" concept produced problems as well as progress, however. Congested streets and garish commercial strips often made driving an undesirable chore. Drive through the streets of Phoenix, a critic noted, and view

> . . . the surrounding turbulent sea of ugliness. Become engulfed in the towering billboards, the animated signs, these evidences of our willful and unrestrained hucksterism which blot out the natural beauty of the landscape; be shocked by the blinking, blinding neon signs; be appalled by the flimsy shacks with the whimsical phony fronts designed to sell hot dogs, pizza pies and hoola hoops. Be disgusted by the disorderly array of industrial buildings, the junk yards, the "tortilla flats," the shanty towns of our civilization.

There were calls for better city planning. Because of growth and its problems, air pollution increased in the 1950s. Weatherman Louis R. Jurwitz declared, "The normal result of living is to pollute the air . . . there's a heap of living going on here now." Much of the "smust" was caused by the smoke and dust of a city on the move: burning dumps, unpaved streets, construction sites. Automobile exhausts also proved guilty; according to one observer, "Ride on a main thoroughfare some morning and notice the blue haze lying over the street." Desert temperature inversion contributed greatly to the problem, especially during the winter months. There were days when you could not see the mountains. Concerned citizens formed a committee, but little was done. Even promoters ignored the pollution; in the words of one, "A lot of this is just the price we're paying for growth, and much of it will take care of itself."

In 1960, the *Wall Street Journal* called Phoenix the city with the dirtiest air in the nation.[28]

Rapid growth made it difficult to keep up with the need for new roads and highways. Following World War II, federal funds became available for freeways. Cities throughout the nation benefited, but Phoenix political and business leaders hesitated before taking advantage of federal aid. Local interests also argued over freeway plans; each route seemed to threaten the business interests of particular groups. Old streets were repaired and new streets laid out in Phoenix, but slowly, and freeways remained elusive until passage of the 1956 Interstate Highway Act.

Taking advantage of that act, city officials finally cooperated with state and federal representatives, and received sufficient funding to institute a freeway system in the city. It was a beginning, but by 1960 Phoenix remained far behind other cities in its freeway facilities; indeed, in that year the first freeway in the city opened. In May 1960, Wilber Smith and Associates of San Francisco presented an ambitious plan calling for the improvement of existing streets and the construction of 140 miles of freeway by 1980. Local officials and business leaders considered the estimated cost of $532 million prohibitive, and they failed to promote implementation of the plan. The lack of an adequate freeway system would continue to plague metropolitan Phoenix.[29]

Water from underground sources and reclamation projects remained essential to area growth. In 1952, the Salt River Project (SRP) made a deal with Phoenix to provide it with more water for the city's rising population. Under the 1952 Domestic Water Contract between Phoenix and the SRP, the city became the first in the valley to use the utility's water as a domestic supply. The agreement served as a model for other cities within the Project's boundaries, and most of them signed similar contracts. As Phoenix expanded during the decade, it developed its own supply and delivery system more fully: for example, with revenues raised by bond issues it purchased many private water companies and incorporated them into its own sprawling network.

Since urbanization and manufacturing used less water than agriculture, Phoenix area developers did not worry about that precious commodity being lost when irrigated lands were transformed into housing and business sites. Prior to 1948, only 22,000 acres of irrigated land had been lost to subdivisions, but in the decade following 1948 another 32,000 acres of irrigated land were taken

Salt River Project and central Arizona, c. 1950. Salt River Project.

out of agricultural production and converted to residential or commercial use. Forecasters predicted more record-breaking statistics in the future.

As in the case of transportation, city officials never implemented comprehensive water plans for the future; rather, they tended to respond to less expensive emergency situations. After all, declared one water expert, in the past it had always rained. But support was forthcoming for the Central Arizona Project (CAP). Believing that economic and demographic pressures would continue to put a strain on surface and subsurface sources of water, influential Phoenix promoters supported the 1947 plan to transport Colorado River water to central Arizona. However, this plan to alleviate potential water problems in the area did not receive final authorization from Washington until 1968. California objected strongly to Arizona's goal, but during the struggle Senators Hayden and Goldwater proved instrumental in securing eventual acceptance of the federally funded project; moreover, by 1968 CAP promoters had become more vocal regarding the need for future sources of more water, especially for nonagricultural use.

As the urbanization of the desert continued, SRP built numerous generating stations and became increasingly involved in supplying electricity. Following World War II, Arizona Public Service (APS) joined with SRP to lead the way in providing energy for the boom. Since 1886, under a variety of names, APS had sold gas and electricity to Phoenicians while it erected power plants throughout the area. It became known as the Central Arizona Light and Power Company (Calapco) in 1920, and four years later it became part of the American Power and Light system. Expansion followed to meet the demands of its growing service area.

During this period, a movement evolved to return Calapco to local ownership. Led by Frank Snell and Walter Bimson, a group of prominent Phoenix promoters bought a controlling interest in the company in 1945; in turn, a majority of them became directors of the company. In the postwar years, Calapco expanded its operations throughout Phoenix and Arizona to meet unprecedented demands for utility service. It merged with Arizona Edison, a large Tucson-based power company, in 1951, and out of this union Arizona Public Service Company was born. Henry Sargent, president of Calapco, became president of the new company, and former board members of both organizations served on the board of APS. APS and SRP entered into territorial agreements, thus eliminating costly competition.[30]

During the decade many elementary schools, as well as West, Camelback, South Mountain, Central, and Carl Hayden High Schools, opened. Higher education also underwent change. Phoenix College experienced unprecedented growth, and in 1958 Arizona State College became Arizona State University. The enrollment at Arizona State College at Tempe rose rapidly following World War II, increasing from 553 in 1945 to 9,708 in 1958. University of Arizona interests opposed university status for ASC, but Phoenix-area promoters worked hard to gain recognition for their school. They supported academic and athletic programs, and they pressured the state legislature. The University of Arizona, however, continued to be a powerful force in that body, so Arizona State boosters organized an initiative petition drive to put the issue to Arizona voters.

The Pulliam press strongly backed the drive, and by July 1958 nearly 65,000 signatures, more than double the amount needed, had been collected. A vigorous campaign in greater Phoenix and the rest of Arizona on behalf of the name change preceded the November election. Supporters noted that metropolitan Phoenix was the only urban center of its size in the nation that lacked a university, and organizations such as Citizens for Arizona State University labored tirelessly in Maricopa County and elsewhere to rectify the situation. "See that Arizona State becomes a university in name as well as in fact," the *Republic* declared to voters, and they responded by voting two-to-one in favor of the name change. Pima County, home of Tucson and the University of Arizona, voted against the change, but its opposition proved to be a lost cause.

The Phoenix Chamber of Commerce and other booster organizations made up of leading business and civic leaders appreciated the name change. No longer, observers noted, should "Greater Phoenix be educationally retarded." The change enhanced the business and engineering programs so valuable to Valley of the Sun economic interests; to secure companies of the caliber of Motorola and General Electric, it was necessary to upgrade the status of the institution. ASU also served as a cultural and intellectual focal point in metropolitan Phoenix and the state of Arizona, each year improving the quality of its general programs and cultural offerings. In addition, the school improved its image as a sports power; the Sun Angels and other booster organizations predicted that Sun Devil teams would soon attain national rankings in intercollegiate athletics. A record-breaking 11,128 students enrolled at ASU in 1960, and the rapid growth of the institution reflected the magnitude of the boom occurring in metropolitan Phoenix.[31]

Phoenix business and civic leaders supported a variety of cultural offerings during the period. Although an occasional critic would describe Phoenix as "a cultural void," by 1960 the city contained a number of new institutions, including a modern library, a little theater, an art museum, and a symphony orchestra; the library, theater, and museum were located in the new Phoenix Civic Center complex at Central Avenue and McDowell Road, on land donated by the Heard family. Promoters viewed these cultural attractions as enticements to draw desirable people and businesses to Phoenix. The proper combination of amenities and opportunities was needed for the desert center to continue to grow and develop. The image of the new Phoenix demanded a civilized atmosphere, and boosters tried to provide it during the postwar years. CGC-backed city officials, anxious to increase the economic and demographic growth of Phoenix, offered support.[32]

Collectively and individually, there were people in Phoenix who sought to improve the cultural condition of the city. Outstanding in this respect was Mrs. Archer E. Linde, who worked tirelessly to bring culture to the Arizona capital. Archer and Jessie Linde had arrived from Chicago in 1920. A health seeker with a musical background, Mrs. Linde served as the major impresario in town for the next forty years. According to one observer, "There were times when Mrs. Linde simply couldn't stuff culture down Phoenix throats. But she tried." The Phoenix Union High School auditorium proved inadequate at times, so she promoted a new auditorium, but it was not built until after her death. In the 1950s Phoenix audiences preferred Liberace to Horowitz, but she loved them both; indeed, she presented to Phoenicians a wide variety of offerings. As one grateful supporter put it:

> We got Horowitz and Heifetz and Victor Borge and Pavlova and Van Cliburn and Rubinstein and Duke Ellington. We had the Philadelphia Orchestra and the Israel Philharmonic. Lauritz Melchior and Marion Anderson sang for you. Tyrone Power, Agnes Moorhead and John Gielgud acted for us. H. G. Wells lectured and the Ballet Russe danced. And there were more— in all some 700 concerts, recitals, plays, etc., over that 40-year span.[33]

When not enjoying local parks and playgrounds, backyard barbecues and swimming pools, and nearby lakes and mountains, many Phoenix residents played golf and tennis or attended the annual Rodeo of Rodeos or watched major league baseball teams in spring training, or ate dinner at the Green Gables Restaurant or spent an evening at the Sombrero Playhouse, often called "the desert outpost of Broadway." The casual, leisure-oriented lifestyle appealed to many newcomers. In 1957, a former New York City executive explained:

> I used to commute from Oyster Bay on Long Island to Wall Street everyday—an hour and a half each way. Now I live on the desert just beyond town, and it takes me only 20 minutes to get to work. I can go home at lunchtime and take a dip in my pool. After work or on weekends, I play tennis and golf. Sometimes I go prospecting for uranium in the Superstition Mountains with an Indian friend of mine. I just enjoy life about 10 times as much.[34]

Not everybody enjoyed the good life in Phoenix. Minority groups, for example, continued to grow in size in the 1940s and the 1950s but most of them faced difficulties. The number of Native Americans in Phoenix increased rapidly, although their share of the total population remained less than 1 percent. The 1960 census listed

Phoenix subdivision in the 1950s. Note the cooling units on each house. The Herb and Dorothy McLaughlin Photographic Collection.

3,538 Indians, up from 325 in 1940. Encouraged by the relocation programs promoted by the federal government to move from reservations to urban centers, they sought a future in the cities of Arizona, especially Phoenix. Most of them remained poor and lived in the deteriorating downtown neighborhoods, including the Deuce. Others lived near the Phoenix Indian School, the Phoenix Indian Hospital, and other federal institutions located on Indian School Road. These places offered employment as well as services, such as educational opportunities and health care, to urban Indians.

While Indians working for the federal government made economic gains, others occupied the bottom ranks. Alcohol abuse and other stability problems continued to contribute to high unemployment rates. Although federal policy encouraged the movement of reservation Indians to the city, it failed to provide enough help to urban Indians; reservation residents received the bulk of government aid. Also, federal institutions such as the Phoenix Indian Hospital often proved reluctant to serve poor urban Native Americans. A variety of private organizations, ranging from the Phoenix Indian Center to the Central Presbyterian Indian Church, tried to help urban Indians overcome their problems, but inadequate funds always limited their success. Tourists, of course, continued to be attracted to Native Americans selling their wares on the busiest streets of downtown Phoenix.[35]

The Chinese population in Phoenix increased from 431 in 1940 to 1,113 in 1960, but their percentage of the total population actually decreased. During the period the Chinese population decentralized and Chinatown disintegrated. Located throughout the community, the Chinese worked diligently to achieve economic status; a number of them graduated from college and entered the professional ranks. Voluntary associations continued to play a vital role in the success of the Chinese; for example, the large Ong, Yee, and Wong Family Associations raised permanent funds to subsidize new family enterprises. These and other organizations also served social and cultural purposes; the First Chinese Baptist Church, formed in 1957 with eighty members, was particularly active.[36]

The scattered Japanese population in the Valley of the Sun met hard times during World War II. Following the attack on Pearl Harbor in December 1941, persons of Japanese ancestry in California, Arizona, and several other western states were placed under restrictions and eventually removed from "prohibited zones" near "vital war industries and military establishments." In May 1942, hundreds of Phoenix-area Japanese were relocated to distant detention camps in the Arizona desert, where they suffered deprivation and dishonor. Located at Sacaton on the Gila River Indian Reservation and Poston on the Colorado River Indian Reservation, the two camps housed 31,000 Japanese from California and Arizona. The internment policy not only seemed necessary as a defense measure, it also pleased perennial "Jap haters" and economic competitors of the Japanese. The Arizona Farm Bureau Federation praised the government's action in furthering "the safety of the United States." The attitude of many valley residents was summed up by a leading local grower when he declared: "We don't want them."

Not all valley Japanese were evacuated to the relocation camps during the war. Those not living in "prohibited zones" were allowed to pursue their farming and other endeavors. Limited to "free zones," they could not enter parts of Phoenix and other prohibited areas. Upon their release from the camps, those Japanese not entering the military service returned to their former homes in California and Arizona. Those who had engaged in farming in the free zones during the war helped many of the returning Japanese resume their places in the community. Along with farming, including flower growing, gardening became a popular occupation. An active social and cultural life also developed; for example, after the war the Arizona Buddhist Temple reopened and flourished throughout the period.[37]

Phoenix Hispanics served in the armed forces during the war; they also worked in defense plants and at military bases. Following the conflict, the G.I. Bill offered Hispanic veterans new educational opportunities. At the same time, most Hispanics in Phoenix continued to labor in the bottom ranks of the work force. Their representation in the skilled trades was minimal, and they made up less than 1 percent of the area's professionals. Upward mobility remained low, leaving many poor Mexicans and Mexican-Americans with no choice but to live in the substandard housing offered in the barrios or the city's segregated projects. In general, the housing conditions of the residentially segregated Mexican-Americans were deplorable.

Hispanic students in the barrios of south Phoenix continued to attend "racially isolated" schools. Their residential neighborhoods reflected their low economic status. Inadequate schooling, housing, and employment opportunities made life difficult. During the period imported farm workers from Mexico, along with advances in mechanization in agriculture, weakened the economic position of local workers, and the number of Hispanics on the welfare rolls rose. Hispanic leaders in Phoenix called for an end to the importation of braceros from Mexico, but the practice continued. As many as five thousand Mexican nationals worked valley fields each year. Manuel Pena, Jr., speaking for Phoenix Mexicans, declared, "As long as we have the imported worker, the local worker will never get a decent living wage." Anglo farmers preferred imported labor, for it was cheaper and easier to control.

Among the Hispanics, Pena noted, "a fortunate few have succeeded." With a population of 61,460, 14 percent of the total in 1960, Hispanics remained the largest and fastest-growing minority group in Phoenix. Up from 16,000 in 1940, the Hispanic population needed all the help it could muster. In the barrios of south Phoenix, however, little was done; as Phoenix philanthropist Robert B.

Choate, Jr., put it, "Social welfare in that part of town, from any possible direction, is insufficient for the demand." His organization, Careers for Youth, was especially concerned with the problem of improving the effectiveness of education in poor south side neighborhoods.

A variety of voluntary associations served the community by trying to improve employment, housing, and educational opportunities. The Greater Phoenix Council for Civic Unity and the Phoenix All-American Council for Equality opposed discriminatory practices in areas of public accommodation. Organizations such as the League of United Latin American Citizens and the Committee for Americanism and Inter-American Solidarity worked on behalf of the Hispanic community in general, and local institutions such as the East Madison Settlement House and the Southside Benefit Club brought a range of social services to the barrios.

The most important center of activity in the Hispanic community remained Friendly House. Supported by the Phoenix Community Council and other financial sources, Friendly House retained its Americanization program and expanded its educational and charitable work. The beloved director of Friendly House, Placida Garcia Smith, served as the Mexican community's representative on important civic committees. At Friendly House, she was ably assisted by Adam Diaz, who served as president of the private agency during the postwar years. A firm believer in education as the answer to Hispanic problems, Diaz proved to be a great fund raiser. He was the first Mexican-American to be elected to the Phoenix City Council, having been selected as a CGC candidate in 1952.

In 1956, with United Way as its biggest financial contributor, Friendly House increased its offerings. Citizenship and English classes, along with domestic training and employment programs, multiplied. Of utmost importance, Friendly House served as a meeting place for Hispanic groups and as an informal community center where Hispanic problems could be discussed and resolutions considered. The gracious and talented Mrs. Smith led Friendly House in fulfilling its motto of "Helping People Help Themselves." An advocate of the belief that education provides the key to progress, she was widely acclaimed for her leadership qualities. "Friendly House has given innumerable services to the community and especially to *la colonia Mexicana*," observed an admirer in 1961. "Mrs. Placida Smith has been at the lead of this great work which has been conducted with intelligence and, above all, with a great deal of heart."[38]

Father Emmett McLoughlin, deeply involved with the development of housing projects for those in need, also became a driving force behind the construction of St. Monica's Hospital, the first hospital to serve south Phoenix. In the early 1940s, the influx of military personnel and defense workers strained health care facilities in the valley, and the poor minorities often were the last to receive medical treatment. At the same time Father Emmett was contemplating a hospital for the south side, military authorities were complaining of the high rate of venereal disease among post personnel. Air field commanders blamed "the promiscuous women of Phoenix" for the outbreak of syphilis among the flyers, while angry Phoenix officials claimed that the "lecherous" flyers and soldiers stationed in the area were "contaminating the purity of Phoenix womanhood."

Father McLoughlin discussed the matter with the commander of Luke Field, who recommended that the federal government, under the Lanham Act, approve and fund a new hospital "on condition that the proposed bed capacity be doubled and that half the beds be reserved for the treatment of the female syphilitics of Phoenix." The priest quickly agreed, and in August 1942 President Roosevelt approved the hospital and the financial appropriation needed for its construction. Fund-raising events and personal donations allowed Father McLoughlin to purchase a hospital site in a slum area one mile south of the railroad tracks at Seventh Avenue and Buckeye Road, but the material demands of World War II delayed the completion of the project.

Senators Hayden and McFarland exerted pressure in Washington, and it helped. Finally, in February 1944, the 230-bed nonsectarian St. Monica's Hospital opened. The first integrated hospital in Phoenix, it soon introduced the first interracial nurses' training program west of the Mississippi River. The neighborhoods of that section benefited greatly as St. Monica's, a haven for all races, evolved into Phoenix Memorial Hospital by 1951. During the following decade its reputation as "the hospital with a heart" increased.[39]

Jim Crowism, however, flourished in Phoenix. Theaters, restaurants, hotels, and other places of public accommodation segregated blacks from other patrons, but it was official only in the public schools. Black elementary schools and a black high school continued to exist by law in the city. In 1942 Phoenix Union Colored High School was renamed George Washington Carver High School. W. A. Robinson, who became principal of the high school in 1945, found conditions appalling. Twenty years after it opened, he declared, the school still had "no library, no music equipment, no modern home economics, no shop equipment, no art equipment. ... The only athletic equipment in the school consisted of some worn-out parts of football and basketball uniforms marked with names of other schools in the system." Under Robinson's leadership, in the next several years the school made remarkable strides. Improvements in facilities and faculty brought the institution, according to Robinson, "up somewhere near the legal requirement that a segregated Negro high school be as good as the segregated white schools," but problems remained. The 450-student school also proved costly to operate.

For several years a growing protest had been developing in Arizona against school segregation. The Arizona Council for Civic Unity and other state organizations effectively lobbied the legislature in 1951 and secured a law giving local school boards the option of voluntary desegregation. School districts in Phoenix remained subdivisions of state government and independent legal entities; thus their funding and policymaking procedures were not dependent upon city hall, and they refused to abolish segregation. Liberal lawyers William P. Mahoney, Jr., and Herb Finn, both white, and H. B. Daniels, a black, filed suit in 1952 on behalf of three black children seeking admission to Phoenix Union High School, naming its governing school board members as defendants.

Basing their arguments on recent California cases, which held that the segregation of pupils for ethnic reasons at the discretion of school boards was an unconstitutional delegation of legislative power, the lawyers won. They succeeded by getting declared unconstitutional a law they had urged the legislature to pass. After hearing the case, Superior Court Judge Frederic C. Struckmeyer, Jr., ruled in 1953 that such segregation laws were invalid. "A half century of intolerance is enough," he declared. Phoenix Union High School District board members voted to abide by the court ruling.

Daniels and Finn also filed suit in 1953 against Wilson Elementary School District in Phoenix, and Judge Charles E. Bernstein ruled that segregation in elementary schools was unconstitutional. Wilson School board members also accepted the court's ruling. The Phoenix decisions were rendered before the United States

Supreme Court delivered its famous ruling regarding the desegregation of America's schools in the *Brown* v. *Board of Education
of Topeka* case in 1954. In that case, the Arizona experience was
taken into consideration.

The costly George Washington Carver High School soon closed
its doors, and its students were instructed to attend high schools
in their residential zones: Phoenix Union and South Mountain.
Phoenix elementary school districts also failed to achieve racial
integration by requiring all students, regardless of race, to attend
schools in their respective neighborhoods. Because of economic
and residential patterns in Phoenix, minority students usually
ended up in minority neighborhood schools. As it worked out, the
plan placed many Mexican-American children in the former black
schools and many black children in some of the former Mexican
schools. Only a few blacks lived in the zones of white schools.
There existed in Phoenix, W. A. Robinson lamented, "a sort of
belief that desegregation can be carried out successfully without
greatly disturbing the former pattern of school attendance and
teacher employment." At the same time, he noted, the situation
was superior to "the former pattern of complete segregation in the
schools."

De facto segregation continued to plague blacks in the 1950s,
and education, housing, and employment continued to pose problems. In 1960, the black population reached 20,919, up from 4,263
in 1940. The percentage of blacks in Phoenix actually decreased
from 6.5 to 4.8 percent of the total population in twenty years.
According to the local chapter of the Urban League, at least 95
percent of blacks still resided south of Van Buren in the worst
housing areas in the city. As a report of the Urban League put it,
"Of the 21,000 Negros in Phoenix 19,000 live in 9 of the city's 92
census tracts, with 7 of these south of the Southern Pacific Railroad tracks. Three of these seven tracts contain roughly one-half
of the city's Negro population." North Phoenix remained a white
preserve during the decade, offering its inhabitants the best educational facilities and the best housing developments.[40]

The failure of city influentials to recognize and do something
about conditions in parts of south Phoenix led outsiders to point
to pockets of poverty in that section of the city that "could match
misery for misery and squalor for squalor" with any city in America. CGC-inspired administration of city affairs won plaudits from
the majority of Phoenix residents, especially those residing on the

north side, but a small minority of critics pointed out that not everybody was suitably represented. When you look at Phoenix, one observer noted, you see that "the only areas being developed are ones where councilmen are interested. Look south of the tracks. Nothing's being done there." The people there "are not represented on the council."[41]

While progress in minority relations lagged behind, greater Phoenix developed as one of the fastest growing urban areas in the nation. Newcomers and residents alike generally displayed an optimistic attitude, and the atmosphere it encouraged helped the Phoenix Standard Metropolitan Area (Maricopa County) to more than triple its population between 1940 and 1960, and to extend its lead as the major metropolitan center in the region. During this period the booming oasis had exerted a dominant influence on the civilization of Arizona and the Southwest. It represented the essential point around which the state and the region developed; and in the years ahead, despite continuing problems of growth shared by other vital urban hubs in the nation, Phoenix would expand in size and prominence as economic and population trends persisted in favoring it. As a capital of the emerging Sunbelt and a prime example of the new urban America, Phoenix moved rapidly ahead during the next two decades.

7 SUNBELT CENTER, 1960-1980

During the next twenty years Phoenix emerged as a major Sunbelt center. In December 1960, business and civic leaders from the regional metropolitan centers held a conference in Phoenix to discuss the progress of their respective communities in the "Southwest Sun Country." They had good reason to celebrate, for during the preceding decade the cities of the area had become magnetic growth centers in the burgeoning Sunbelt, a new American region that lay south of the thirty-seventh parallel and extended across the country from North Carolina to southern California. Since World War II, the ongoing decline of the old Snowbelt urban centers in the Northeast and Midwest had caused a shift in economic and demographic power toward the rising urban centers of the Sunbelt in the South, Southwest, and southern California. As the decade of the 1960s opened, observers of Phoenix were predicting even more explosive growth for the desert cities of the Southwest Sunbelt.[1]

The Charter Government Committee-endorsed mayors and city councilmen remained popular in Phoenix during the early 1960s, despite attacks from the far right and the liberal left. Moreover, as the decade progressed, they turned increasingly to the federal government for aid in solving the problems of Phoenix. For example, Mayor Milton Graham, elected in 1963, became aware of national opinion linking high crime rates to racial discrimination and minority poverty. He accepted War on Poverty funds to alleviate that affliction in Phoenix, and he responded to racial tension and violence in a responsible manner.

When members of the local chapter of the Congress of Racial Equality (CORE) engaged in a protest demonstration in 1964 to draw attention to the plight of residents in south Phoenix minority neighborhoods, Graham created an advisory council later called Leadership and Education for the Advancement of Phoenix (LEAP). It soon became the clearinghouse for federal programs designed to better conditions in the city's pockets of poverty.

Persistent racial tension led to racial disturbances. In 1967 rioting in Phoenix resulted in two hundred arrests, but it also led to more requests for federal aid to support more education, employment, and housing programs. Much of the federal aid, however, went to fighting crime. "City Council members are concerned by the ever increasing crime rate in Phoenix and understandably so," the *Gazette* declared in November 1968. "They have poured extra millions of dollars into the Police Department budget and have authorized the hiring of new police officers," the paper stated, "yet none of the moves have brought the hoped-for result—lowering of the crime rate."

Mayor Graham, who had been easily reelected as a CGC candidate for an unprecedented third term in 1967, on a platform emphasizing the crime issue, and the CGC-backed City Council welcomed new federal funds to improve law enforcement. Residents usually against the use of federal funds to support social programs generally approved their use to strengthen police agencies; even the Pulliam press was less strident in its opposition. Selective acceptance of federal funds helped make it possible to improve law enforcement and to slight or ignore anti-poverty programs; it allowed Charter Government to establish philosophical priorities, maintain a low tax rate, and stay within state budget limits on city expenditures. During the decade, it became increasingly difficult for Phoenix to reject opportunities offered by the money pipeline connecting the federal government and the nation's cities. More and more Mayor Graham and other Phoenix officials tried to provide necessary services to their constituents by seeking selective federal aid even while they denounced Washington's increasing involvement in the city's affairs.

When Graham decided to run for a fourth term in 1969, the CGC and the Pulliam press refused to support him. In turn, Graham spoke out against Charter Government and the Phoenix newspapers, and formed his own slate, the Citizens' Ticket. The CGC, deploring Graham's attempt to win a fourth term, chose business and civic leader John Driggs to head its slate. Mayor since 1963, Graham had accumulated enemies who supported Driggs and other CGC candidates, and they won handily. Charter Government, however, lost one battle; Ed Korrick of the Citizens' Ticket won a seat on the City Council. It proved to be a significant victory, for Korrick's success represented the first city election loss experienced by the CGC in its twenty-year history. Driggs, a savings and loan company executive, received ample financing from his backers and unlimited campaign coverage from the Pulliam press. Indeed, when asked by a reporter what factors he attributed to his defeat, Graham replied, "$120,000 and the newspapers. I think that's probably it."[2]

Mayor Driggs spent more time pursuing federal money than any of his predecessors. Increasingly he lobbied Washington to secure funds not only for law enforcement but also for social programs conducted by LEAP and other agencies. While other cities raised taxes, Phoenix progressively relied on federal funds to service its growing population. Even the Pulliam press, aware of the fiscal crisis facing many major urban centers, relaxed its opposition. Strongly supported by the CGC and reelected along with a CGC-endorsed City Council in 1971, Mayor Driggs, a friend and supporter of Richard Nixon, proved especially adept at securing Phoenix's share of the federal funds made available by the president's revenue-sharing program.

Under the State and Local Assistance Act of 1972 and the Housing and Community Development Act of 1974, Phoenix received millions of dollars in federal aid. Much of it was automatic; and later Driggs, who actively supported the legislation, noted that it opened up "this whole new concept of the block grant— the no-strings-attached aid, or return of the federal income tax to the state and local governments for their discretionary use." As Phoenix accepted more federal aid in the 1970s, critics increasingly worried about an overreliance on federal aid, but their concern had little impact on the new money pipeline to Washington. The funds served the population in many ways, from police recruitment to poverty programs; they even enabled the city to drop its unpopular liquor tax.[3]

Despite Phoenix's phenomenal growth, there was never enough money to run it adequately. Property and sales taxes, along with other local sources of revenue, were minimal; thus federal aid helped. Services always seemed to lag behind the population explosion, so complaints multiplied. In 1973, CGC candidate for mayor Timothy A. Barrow emerged victorious, but Gary Peter Klahr, an outspoken critic of Charter Government who ran as an independent, won a seat on the City Council; CGC candidates retained the other seats, but three of them were seriously challenged in the election. The influence of the CGC was waning, political analysts declared, and they predicted more defeats for that body in 1975. Many observers, however, remained reluctant to forecast the end of CGC influence; after all, they said, through the 1973 elections the CGC elected eighty-nine out of the ninety-one candidates it nominated for office. Yet two defeats in recent years encouraged opponents; they believed that after twenty-five years Charter Government was finally vulnerable. Rumors of dissension within the organization's ranks spread, and talk of significant changes in the concept of Charter Government could be heard.[4]

The end came in late 1975, when the mayor's office and four out of six City Council seats fell to non-CGC candidates. Mayor Barrow, for personal reasons, chose not to run again. Margaret T. Hance, a travel and tourist television show producer and CGC-endorsed City Council member, failed to receive that organization's nomination for mayor, so she ran as an independent and won. Hance and Lyman Davidson, a businessman and the CGC's candidate for mayor, both agreed that crime remained the big issue. Davidson listed public safety as the first priority of the Charter slate, and Hance agreed that better law enforcement was an urgent need. The image of Phoenix as the most crime-ridden city in the United States continued to irk the press and the public. Regarding crime and other city matters, Hance and Davidson both represented the CGC philosophy. The CGC simply preferred Davidson as a candidate, so Hance, the daughter of a local banker and the widow of the vice-president of one of Arizona's largest insurance companies, chose to run as an independent, but she retained the conservative philosophy of that organization. The Pulliam press recognized the similarity in outlook of the candidates when it urged citizens "to vote for either Davidson or Hance in order to guarantee strong leadership in what will be a very important period for Phoenix."

Opponents dwelt on the elitist and undemocratic nature of the CGC. They noted the voter apathy it inspired, with only 14 percent of the vote turning out in 1973. They also labeled it out-of-date, and called for a change to meet the many needs of the growing, sprawling metropolis. Citizens for an Independent Council formed a slate, and three of its candidates—Joy Carter, Rosendo Gutierrez, and Calvin Goode, a black—emerged victorious, along with Ken O'Dell, another independent, and Hance. Two CGC candidates, Amy Worthen and William Donahue, managed to win City Council seats, but the organization no longer controlled Phoenix government.[5]

In the 1977 election, the CGC failed to field a slate for the first time in nearly thirty years; an era had passed. The organization supported several candidates, including Mayor Hance, but few of them wanted to represent Charter Government directly. Like Hance, a number of them shared the basic CGC philosophy, but they did not consider its support essential. As candidates, they preferred to be as independent as possible; being tied to Charter Government could be detrimental. Summing up the changing times on the eve of the 1977 election, the *Gazette* stated:

> For more than a quarter of a century the CGC (Charter Government Committee) has been the conscience of good government in Phoenix. Its success in electing non-career politicians to municipal posts has been near perfect. Not a single Charter councilman has ever been tainted by scandal. . . . But Charter has fallen on hard times because it hasn't kept up with the times. Charter leaders are aging, at a time when Phoenix boasts one of the nation's youngest median ages. . . . Charter's noble principle of slating candidates who represent virtue and civic achievement seems esoteric at a time when more down-to-earth problems trouble big city residents.

Persistent urban problems, including crime, dominated campaign rhetoric, and Hance won reelection. She had said crime was her first priority, especially after *Republic* investigative reporter Don Bolles was murdered in June 1976, and she was proud of the fact that during her first term the percentage of major crimes had dropped. Keeping taxes low also remained a top priority; in 1977, the property tax was based on $1.89 per $100 assessed valuation. In order to maintain low property taxes, sales taxes and utility rates had risen. Like her predecessors, Mayor Hance often criti-

Margaret Hance, Mayor of Phoenix, 1976–1983. Photograph by Gittings. City of Phoenix Public Information Office.

cized urban America's reliance on federal funds, but she worked diligently to get Phoenix's share, for the city needed it to adequately service its exploding population. And she succeeded; the amount of federal aid to Phoenix rose from $14 million in 1972 to $89 million in 1978, an increase of 534 percent.

Accepting federal aid was considered better than raising taxes or reducing services. Also, most Phoenix officials, while calling

themselves fiscal conservatives, had a "take what you can" attitude, feeling that the New Federalism entitled their city to a fair
share of tax sharing. As Senator Goldwater put it on national television in June 1979, "The most vociferous citizens of the cities of
my state against high taxes and federal control are also the most
vociferous citizens calling for federal aid to cities."

The Pulliam press and the public criticized the federal role in
local affairs, but they, too, were concerned about Phoenix's image.
In this view, there were priorities; social welfare programs, for
example, were seen as less essential than police services. The
"relatively low tax assessment when combined with skillful use
of federal funds," observers noted, "permitted Phoenix to have the
best of both worlds: low taxes and essential services." This combination appealed to satisfied Phoenix boosters and businesses who
"escaped the increased tax burdens of large urban areas, while still
allowing them to receive the benefit of an impressive police force
and other adequate selected services, such as fire protection."

Mayor Hance's comments on the "evils of federal aid," along with
her success in securing money from Washington for essential services in Phoenix, helped her win a third term in November 1979;
no serious candidate opposed her. City Council incumbents also
experienced no difficulty in getting reelected, making for a dull
election, according to reporters. The popularity of the candidates,
along with voter apathy, received the blame. Hance not only appealed to most of the voters, she brought national attention to the
city when Phoenix became the largest city in the country to have
a woman mayor. Feminists in search of a heroine, however, faced
disappointment. According to observers, "She got there without
help from the local women's political caucus, she took no stand on
the Equal Rights Amendment, she happily admits using her sex to
its greatest advantage, and she has charmed her city with a vein
of wit that Steinem et al. might like to see strip-mined."

The Hance years would prove to be transitional. With the defeat of the CGC in 1975, the Phoenix power structure began to
change. Walter Bimson, Frank Snell, Eugene Pulliam, and other
established leaders had either retired or died. No longer could one
group of influentials dominate and determine the city's future. A
few months before the 1975 election, Eugene Pulliam died. In one
of his last exertions of power, he helped organize the Phoenix 40,
a group of business and professional leaders concerned about the
city's image as a crime center. Most of them were younger than

Eugene C. Pulliam, Phoenix newspaper publisher. Phoenix Newspapers, Inc.

Pulliam, and he urged them to get more involved in community problems. Critics scorned the organization as a "white-collared executive group of crime-stoppers" whose members were similar in many ways to the CGC; membership in the all-male, all-white group, for example, was by invitation only. The Phoenix 40 may have been appropriate in the 1950s, declared critics, but Phoenix in the 1970s was growing and changing, and it no longer accepted without question the good intentions of self-appointed elite groups.

The CGC never recovered from the 1975 election, but critics, including minority leaders, continued to maintain that a larger City Council and a district system of elections were needed to meet the varied problems of the increasing population. They complained about a lack of services in some city areas, and a lack of neighborhood concern on the part of City Council members elected at large. They kept asking for structural change in the political system. Mayor Hance and her supporters, many of them former CGC stalwarts, disagreed with the critics. The latter became more vocal and more organized, however, and they emerged victorious in the early 1980s.

In the meantime, city officials and workers grappled with the problems of phenomenal growth, trying to provide basic services such as police and fire protection, and street, sewer, and sanitation expansion, along with more recent programs encouraged by state and federal government assistance. Phoenix did not have primary responsibility for some of the more costly functions provided by city governments elsewhere, such as welfare, public health, and public education; the state of Arizona, Maricopa County, and independent school boards took care of those important issues.[6]

While the political climate underwent change, the economy continued to boom. Despite occasional setbacks, Phoenix experienced rapid economic development during the twenty years after 1960, easily exceeding national rates of growth during that period. Overall, its diversified economy expanded and remained strong. Opportunities and amenities continued to increase in the desert center while cities elsewhere became increasingly less inviting. Having moved to the top of the urban hierarchy of the Southwest in the 1950s, Phoenix remained there during the following two decades, with manufacturing holding its lead as the most dynamic growth sector. The growth-oriented CGC and the Phoenix Chamber of Commerce, among other booster groups, continued to cooperate in providing the best business climate possible for industry.

By the end of 1977, the Arizona capital had 74.5 percent of the total manufacturing employment in the state, and the annual income from manufacturing in the Phoenix area had increased to $2.5 billion. Electronics and aerospace plants dominated the industrial landscape in the Valley of the Sun, and in 1980 the area was competitive with leading high-tech centers across the country.

General Electric plant in 1965. Note encroachment of industry and housing on agriculture. The Herb and Dorothy McLaughlin Photographic Collection.

Motorola continued to set the pace, and by 1980, with eighteen thousand employees, was still the largest corporation in the area. AiResearch, General Electric, Goodyear Aerospace, and Sperry Rand, along with newcomers Digital, Litton, ITT, General Semiconductors, Honeywell, Intel, and GTE, also were important electronics firms.[7]

AiResearch, an established company, employed six thousand workers. Small new arrivals like GTE also had an impact on the economy that pleased local promoters. While GTE contemplated joining the high-technology companies along the Black Canyon Freeway in northwest Phoenix in 1977, Phoenix Chamber of Commerce head George Reeve told the Downtown Kiwanis Club that he figured $66 million worth of business could be generated by GTE's estimated 350-person payroll of between $12 and $15 million annually. GTE employees, he declared, would spend $30 million on new housing, which meant 210 construction jobs worth $3.7

million, plus another 438 jobs worth an additional $4.5 million for allied industries. "That's just the tip of the iceberg," he continued. "Builders, for example, will spend $5.4 million for lumber and building materials and the new homeowners will spend an average of $3750 apiece on furnishings. In terms of taxes, homeowners will pay $4.5 million in property taxes, and pay property insurance premiums of $52,000 during the first year. The city of Phoenix will receive $19,000 in city sales tax; the state $79,000 in transaction privilege taxes. In addition, GTE itself will generate tax revenues for city, county, state and federal taxing entities."[8]

Business promotion was a priority in Phoenix. As a bank president in El Paso put it at the time, "I hate to express it publicly, but it's true our leadership has been sort of mediocre. We didn't have the influx of well-educated people in the industrial and commercial world. Phoenix did." Another El Paso businessman remarked, "We haven't always done a selling job of what we've got. Phoenix has done a better job."

Not all of the new businesses emerging in Phoenix belonged to the world of high technology; many of them served other needs. Some of them made Phoenix their corporate headquarters, such as American Express, State Farm Insurance, and the Greyhound Corporation. "Chicago is a good business city," declared Greyhound Corporation head Gerald H. Trautman in 1971, "but Phoenix offers us a substantial reduction in expenses—wages, rentals, communications. The survey we had done about relocation concluded that Phoenix was best for us."

As more job opportunities opened up, people flocked to the city. Although salaries were often lower in the Arizona capital than in the bustling urban centers of the East and California, so was the cost of living. The California influx, or the "California slopover," as it was called by critics, was especially imposing. And why not leave, it was asked, considering the outrageous cost of housing and other essentials in the Golden State. In Phoenix, people usually received more for their money. Moreover, many observers considered the quality of life in Phoenix and Arizona superior to that in Los Angeles and California. "I talked recently to some friends in companies on the West Coast," a local electronics firm executive declared in October 1978, "and they are thoroughly disgusted with the high cost of land and housing and other problems of being there, such as smog, dense traffic and the fact that they have to live so far from work. They all said they would like to move to Arizona."[9]

Reasonable land and labor costs, along with an abundance of mortgage money, encouraged the construction industry to supply affordable housing for the hordes of newcomers. The growing savings and loan associations, led by First Federal Savings and Western Savings, along with the Valley National, Arizona, and First National banks, cooperated with home builders and buyers. In 1977, savings and loan figures soared to $3.2 billion, up from $2.8 billion in 1975. Phoenix remained the financial center for the state; banks headquartered in the city accounted for 65 percent of the total bank deposits in Arizona. State bank deposits totaled $6.7 billion in 1976; Phoenix accounted for $4.2 billion of that sum.[10]

Rapid urbanization continued to encroach on agricultural land, but agriculture, especially cotton production, remained a major factor in the economy. It progressively moved out of the urban area into the "wide open spaces." As the land became worth more than crops, many urban-area farmers sold their acreage to developers. In some instances, land worth $250 an acre in 1940 was selling for $25,000 an acre in 1980. According to spokesmen, the most persistent problem faced by metropolitan farmers was urban pressure. By 1977, ten thousand acres a year were being withdrawn from agricultural use. Yet Maricopa County, one of the top five agricultural counties in the nation in 1980, remained the agricultural capital of the Southwest.

Agriculture, however, was declining in importance. In 1980, agriculture was using 89 percent of the water consumed in Arizona, while the cities were using 7 percent and industry 4 percent. Experts were predicting that in the years ahead, more of the water supply would be diverted from agricultural to nonagricultural use.[11]

During the period 1960–80, in fact, tourism replaced agriculture as the Phoenix metropolitan area's second largest source of income. Many older establishments expanded and many new ones opened during the period, including places the caliber of La Posada and Mountain Shadows, and the Phoenix and Valley of the Sun Convention and Visitors' Bureau was kept busier than ever. National chains began buying famous local resorts; for example, in 1967 Jack Stewart sold the Camelback Inn to the Marriott Corporation. More high-rise hotels appeared; for example, the twenty-six-story Hyatt Regency opened downtown in 1976. By 1978, tourists were spending $1.6 billion a year in and around Phoenix.[12]

As in the past, many visitors to the air-conditioned Sunbelt center wanted to extend their visit or return to live there permanently. The amenities, as well as the expanding job market, kept drawing newcomers. "It's the lifestyle that's so attractive," remarked an observer from the East. Even more important than the sun culture, however, was the industrial expansion and economic growth. Job seekers escaping from difficult economic situations in the Snowbelt migrated in large numbers to the Phoenix metropolitan area. In 1980, in response to an informal survey conducted by the State Department of Economic Security, 29 percent of the Arizona job hunters said that the hope of employment was the primary reason they were moving to Arizona, compared with 22 percent who cited climate as the reason. Other reasons for their move were a change in lifestyle; friends or relatives lived there; and health. Encouraged by metropolitan Phoenix's comparatively low 5 percent average unemployment rate in 1980, the job seekers were optimistic about the chances of finding employment in the Phoenix area.

As the population rose, the metropolitan center not only continued to serve more tourists as well as its increasing resident population, it also remained the trading and distribution hub for a vast region of towns, farms, ranches, and mines in Arizona and the Southwest. Employment increases within the trade and services sectors accounted for a sizable percentage of the total increase in employment registered in the thirty years before 1980. The trade and services sectors provided the most jobs, and their importance as the dominant kind of employment in the local economy would be increasingly recognized in the future. The expansion of these traditional roles during the period under review may be seen in

Table 5. Metropolitan Phoenix Employment Trends, 1950–79

Employer	1950	1962	1970	1979
Manufacturing	8,800	38,700	70,900	105,500
Mining	200	300	300	200
Construction	6,700	15,500	21,300	54,100
Transportation and utilities	8,700	13,500	17,700	28,700
Wholesale and retail trade	21,300	51,600	81,000	156,000
Finance, insurance, and real estate	3,700	13,400	22,800	41,000
Services and misc.	11,500	32,200	55,000	121,900
Government	13,500	36,000	58,200	100,200

SOURCE: U.S. Department of Labor Statistics, 1950–79.

Table 5, which shows employment trends in metropolitan Phoenix.

Employment trends in the Phoenix area showed the persistent relationship of all levels of government activity to the economy. Substantial economic gains were due to the presence of Luke and Williams Air Force bases, and as a result of defense contracts negotiated with the federal government by local firms. As the capital of Arizona, Phoenix enjoyed the economic stimulus of state payrolls, and it continued to benefit as a county, state, and federal government service center. As Phoenix officials increasingly drew federal funds and programs to the city in the 1970s, the role of the federal government reached new dimensions in the Arizona capital. Present also was a growing institution of higher education that contributed much to the overall economic welfare of the Valley of the Sun. Arizona State University's enrollment increased to 39,431 in 1980, up from 11,198 in 1960, making it the largest university in the Southwest. As an intellectual center and an economic generator, its impact inspired local boosters to include it among the prime attractions in the metropolitan area; it served as an essential part

Del Webb's Sun City, 1970. The Herb and Dorothy McLaughlin Photographic Collection.

of their plans to keep the urban center at the forefront in the new world of high technology.[13]

The physical growth of the Arizona oasis in the years following 1960 was impressive. As time passed, the number of people and cars greatly increased, and a progressive conversion of land to residential and commercial use gave impetus to more urban sprawl. Developers were encouraged by the availability of large parcels of land. Supported by the federal government's housing policies (including loan guarantees) as well as the public's search for the good life, the developers transformed farmlands and desertscapes into new subdivisions featuring single-family homes and shopping centers.

Sprawling, low-density, auto-oriented suburban Phoenix proved inviting. A "growth is good" philosophy prevailed, a Boston reporter noted. "Nothing can keep out people who seek Phoenix's ultra-suburban, don't-tread-on-me, laid-back lifestyle." Not everyone admired it, but the majority accepted and appreciated it. "People who come to Phoenix don't want to move into an inner city," asserted another observer, "they've come to get away from that." Despite the costs in extended services, the "wide open spaces" seemed to offer an escape from the massive problems many newcomers had left behind in the older Snowbelt urban centers. Often a new housing development in the Phoenix area would be completely sold before there were any houses, streets, sewers, or utility lines on the land.

Rarely, in the 1950s and 1960s, did any of the cities of the Valley of the Sun adopt plans predicated on growth management. Local citizens who advocated stronger policies regulating urban area growth were ignored, and those who wanted the latest newcomers to be the "last settlers" were not taken seriously. Only in the 1970s, with the glaring appearance of energy and environmental problems, did controlled growth become a significant issue. By 1980 the "smaller is better" approach had not yet taken over, but steps to prevent the deterioration of the Phoenix metropolitan area were at least being discussed.

For example, city officials and civic leaders increasingly discussed the possibility of "infilling" lands leapfrogged by earlier development. "To the bird's eye," an observer declared in 1978, "the Phoenix area resembles an enormous patchwork quilt of developed and undeveloped property stretching almost from horizon to horizon." Expensive city streets and services expanded to meet

Eleventh and Northern avenues in 1950 (top) *and 1970* (bottom). *The Herb and Dorothy McLaughlin Photographic Collection.*

the needs of leapfrog development during the period, while empty spaces remained everywhere throughout the city. A reporter noted, "When a new development goes in, the land across the street increases in value. By skipping over that property and going out a little further the next developer can obtain land at a lower price. Once the leapfrogged parcel is bracketed by development, the value increases still more and often it stays empty, held by a speculator waiting for the right price." The city collected less revenue from undeveloped parcels than it did from developed properties already in the city service area.

In the late 1970s, Phoenix began considering a growth management program to encourage "infilling" the empty lands in the city. As late as 1980, 40 percent of the land within the city was vacant, and Mayor Hance emphasized, "Vacant properties within the city should be developed first, because the utilities, streets, fire stations, and parks are already in existence and can be used by additional thousands of people." Hoping to redirect some of the sprawling growth from the outlying areas, Hance and other city officials discussed offering incentives to developers to build on leapfrogged vacant land, but little was accomplished; indeed, the Phoenix growth pattern of leapfrog development continued into the next decade.

Since the success of Uptown Plaza and Park Central in the 1950s, shopping centers had multiplied in the Phoenix area, and they contributed considerably to the shift in retail trade from the downtown business district to the city's suburbs. By the late 1960s, all the leading department stores had abandoned downtown and moved to suburban sites. During the period Goldwater's, Diamond's, the Broadway, Sears, Montgomery Ward, and other department stores anchored Chris-Town, Thomas Mall, Camelview Plaza, Paradise Valley Mall, and other enclosed, air-conditioned shopping centers.

Huge regional shopping emporiums also helped to cause the shift as customers flocked to them; Metrocenter, described as one of the largest shopping centers in the world when it opened its doors in 1973, had parking spaces for 7,600 cars. The 312-acre mall, located in northwest Phoenix along the Black Canyon Freeway, was the first mall in the country to house five anchor department stores under one roof. It contained a host of specialty shops, restaurants, theaters, even a skating rink. Observers called Metrocenter

Metrocenter under construction, 1972. The Herb and Dorothy Mc-
Laughlin Photographic Collection.

a miniature city, and during the 1970s millions visited it; in 1979
alone, over fourteen million people entered the massive mall.[14]

As new subdivisions and shopping centers appeared, an aggressive annexation policy continued to allow Phoenix to increase its
physical and numerical size. Unlike so many central cities elsewhere in the nation, the desert hub was not hemmed in by incorporated suburban communities. In 1972, Phoenix ranked as the
third largest city in the nation in geographical area. A positive
attitude remained regarding annexation as an appropriate tool to
prevent overcrowding and other problems found in more compact
cities. Although expansion proved to be slower than in the previous period, Phoenix spread from 187.4 square miles in 1960 to a
sprawling 329.1 in 1980.

During the period, the rate of population growth in the Arizona
capital remained spectacularly high. Phoenix set the pace as the
fastest-growing urban center in that section of the Sunbelt; by
1980 it ranked as the ninth largest city in the nation, up from
twentieth in 1970.

Table 6. Urban Southwest, 1940–80

City	1940	1950	1960	1970	1980
Phoenix	65,414	106,818	439,170	584,303	789,704
El Paso	96,810	130,485	276,687	322,261	425,259
Tucson	35,752	45,954	212,892	262,933	330,537
Albuquerque	35,449	96,815	201,189	244,501	331,767

SOURCE: U.S. Census of Population, 1940–80.

Table 7. Population of Phoenix and Neighboring Communities, 1940–80

City	1940	1950	1960	1970	1980
Phoenix	65,414	106,818	439,170	584,303	789,704
Tempe	2,906	7,684	24,897	63,550	106,743
Mesa	7,224	16,670	33,772	63,049	152,453
Glendale	4,855	8,179	15,696	36,228	97,172
Scottsdale	1,000	2,032	10,026	67,823	88,412
Chandler	1,239	3,799	9,531	13,763	29,673

SOURCE: U.S. Census of Population, 1940–80.

In the 1950s and 1960s each of the satellite communities surrounding Phoenix retained an identity of its own. For example, Tempe was the location of Arizona State University; Mesa remained the "Mormon Capital of Arizona"; Glendale continued as a farming community; and Scottsdale billed itself as "The West's Most Western Town." The latter became famous as a winter resort for affluent winter visitors or "snowbirds." By the 1970s, however, it was becoming increasingly difficult for the towns to maintain their individual identities, for they were all undergoing population explosions and building booms. Each of them expanded into the surrounding desert, with more and more land used for the construction of housing tracts, shopping centers, industrial parks, and office buildings. As the urbanization of the suburban towns in the Phoenix area increased, each of them became more self-sufficient. The surrounding cities actually were growing at a much faster rate than Phoenix, and the capital city no longer demographically dominated the metropolitan area to the extent it once had.

As time passed, the metropolitan hubs of the Southwest, led by Phoenix, came to dominate the region more than ever. By 1980, for example, the Phoenix and Tucson metropolitan areas contained nearly 80 percent of Arizona's population, compared with about 70 percent in 1960; in 1980 the Phoenix metropolitan area alone contained more than 55 percent of the state's population. The central

Table 8. Metropolitan Southwest, 1940–80

City	1940	1950	1960	1970	1980
Maricopa County (Phoenix)	186,193	331,770	663,510	971,228	1,509,052
Pima County (Tucson)	72,838	141,216	265,660	351,667	531,443
El Paso County (El Paso)	131,067	194,968	314,070	359,291	479,899
Bernalillo County with parts of Sandoval County added in 1960, 1970, 1980 (Albuquerque)	69,391	145,673	276,400	333,266	454,499

SOURCE: U.S. Census of Population, 1940–80.

Arizona complex increased its numerical size more than sevenfold between 1940 and 1980, and in 1980 it was the fastest growing among the top thirty metropolitan areas in the nation. While the population of the city of Phoenix expanded by 1,107 percent between 1940 and 1980, the population of the Phoenix metropolitan area increased by 1,138 percent.[15]

While suburban development rapidly increased during the period, the downtown area continued to decline. In 1948, the Phoenix Central Business District (CBD) accounted for 35 percent of the total retail sales in Maricopa County. By 1963, this share had decreased to 7.7 percent. Retail sales downtown reached their peak in 1958, when the value totaled $133 million. Retail sales for the CBD totaled only $86 million in 1963, a 35 percent decrease from 1958; indeed, the 1963 figure represented $21 million less in sales than in 1948.

In 1963 Phoenix's 7.7 percent share of metropolitan sales compared with a national average of more than 13 percent and nearly 11 percent in the West. Even more striking was the fact that downtown Phoenix claimed 11 percent of the retail market within city limits in 1963, compared with an average of 23 percent for American cities in the population range of 400,000 to 750,000. And while downtown Phoenix sales rapidly declined in 1963, metropolitan Phoenix boasted record-breaking sales in that year: $1.1 billion, up 55 percent from 1958 and good enough in 1963 to rank third in the nation.[16]

In May 1966, *Republic* reporter Walter Meek called the center of Phoenix "a mercantile graveyard, and in many ways a slum." The figures, Meek noted, "indicate that since 1958 the central business district of Phoenix has suffered perhaps the worst decline in land use and commercial activity of any major American city." The effects in Phoenix "are worse because the loss has been more complete and because it happened in so short a time. . . . Other cities are answering their problems with corrective action, but Phoenix lies waiting, like an anesthetized patient, for the unknown surgeon to operate on its diseased heart." Meek and other observers agreed that the CBD could never again be the retail center of metropolitan Phoenix, but they felt it could be "the showplace of the Valley: a cultural, educational, and entertainment center by night and the business and professional hub by day. It could be a tourist mecca."[17]

In the 1960s, city officials realized something had to be done; for example, they talked a great deal about investing in an "auditorium-convention center complex, partly as a pump-primer for downtown redevelopment," but it remained a subject of discussion. Little income-producing activity replaced retailing in the CBD, for most of it occurred outside the downtown area, where the mushrooming growth was taking place. Attractive and convenient shopping centers, with their many amenities, drew hordes of customers who neglected, ignored, or forgot about the CBD.

The rise of the Phoenix Uptown Business District (UBD) in the 1960s also retarded CBD redevelopment. Between Osborn and Indian School on North Central a crop of high-rise buildings emerged early in the decade. David Murdock started the trend when he erected his twenty-story Guaranty Bank building in 1960, a landmark in the evolution of the Central Avenue corridor. One observer asserted, "The day they let Murdock build up there they began nailing the lid on the coffin of downtown Phoenix." Critics believed that the Phoenix Planning and Zoning Commission should have acted to prevent the construction of high-rise buildings on North Central, but as another observer put it, in those days the city's planning policy was "not to plan at all."

A few miles north of the CBD, the UBD attracted important segments of the business and financial sectors of the economy away from downtown. They occupied several high-rise office buildings constructed there, in part, because of lower land and tax costs uptown. Clustered in the UBD, the seventeen-story Del Webb building, the eighteen-story Financial Center, the twenty-six-story First Federal building, the twenty-three-story Del Webb Townehouse, and the twenty-story Rosenzweig tower impressed observers. Park Central Shopping Center also was located in the area. The new uptown emphasis, critics lamented, made downtown redevelopment "difficult if not impossible."

Phoenix in 1972 contained 5,189 of the valley's 8,545 retail stores, but only 201 of them were located in the CBD. In that year, downtown retail sales were only 2.9 percent of the city's $1.6 billion total. At the same time, however, downtown Phoenix continued to serve as the governmental, legal, and financial center of the metropolitan area. The construction of the Phoenix Municipal Building in 1963 and the Maricopa County Complex in 1965 signified the growing public presence; lawyers seemed to fill a number of core office buildings; and the erection of shiny new skyscrapers by the state's three largest banks, including the forty-story Valley National Bank Center, the tallest structure in the region, reflected downtown Phoenix's status as the banking hub of Arizona and the Southwest. The construction in 1972 of the Phoenix Civic Plaza, a new convention and cultural center downtown, prompted the appearance of two new hotels, the rebuilt Hotel Adams and the twenty-six-floor Hyatt Regency. In an effort to attract retail establishments and residential development downtown, city officials and civic leaders promoted the end of Phoenix's skid row, the Deuce.

Areas of the Deuce were razed to provide room for the Civic Plaza, a downtown complex extending from Monroe south to Washington between Second and Fifth streets. The Civic Plaza and Heritage Square, a cluster of historic buildings relocated to Sixth Street and Monroe, were planned to increase downtown's cultural offerings. Other attempts to clean up downtown included the development in 1974 of Patriots Square, a park that required the demolition of a whole city block of blight. By the late 1970s, a number of plans formulated by city officials and citizens' committees called for the erection of more high-rise office buildings downtown. They also recommended that government functions be confined to a mall running along Washington and Jefferson streets from the Civic Plaza on the east to the state capitol on the west. In 1980, the Central Phoenix Redevelopment Agency, charged with shepherding the plans to realization, noted the difficult task ahead but looked forward to more progress in the next decade. As one outspoken developer put it, "This is one of the most thriving cities in the country. But downtown is a mess. After 6 p.m., downtown Phoenix is a funeral home. We need to create an upper level environment, a street scene, a walking district with residential and retail development. We need a downtown with a pace, an excitement."[18]

The Central Business District (foreground) *with the Uptown Business District to the north, Phoenix, 1976. The Herb and Dorothy McLaughlin Photographic Collection.*

Phoenicians continued to be dependent on cars, which remained the primary mode of urban transportation. Few people used mass transit (meaning buses in Phoenix). The great majority preferred the privacy and mobility of the automobile, and low-density, horizontal expansion in the metropolitan area discouraged any official commitment to an adequate public transportation system. In 1970, for example, compared with 11,037 persons per square mile in San Francisco and 6,976 persons per square mile in Los Angeles, Phoenix had 3,103. As a result good roads, especially freeways, were considered by traffic engineers to be essential in the sprawling city. Not everyone in Phoenix agreed that freeways were necessary, however, nor did everyone in the city agree on where to put them. Their development proceeded slowly because of apathy and opposition. Environmental problems and funding problems also contributed to the delay in freeway construction in the traffic-congested city, where more than 95 percent of all personal travel was by automobile.

In 1980, there were thirty-two miles of freeway in Phoenix, up from seven in 1960, and most observers agreed that the situation was lamentable. In the 1960s, the scene was pathetic. As one observer declared in 1967, "In cities comparable to Phoenix in size, the freeways are carrying forty to forty-five percent of the traffic. That's better than five times the percentage of city traffic Phoenix freeways can carry." In that year it was pointed out that Phoenix had fallen behind cities of similar size in building freeways. Sacramento, with 300,000 people, had thirty-four miles of freeways built. San Diego, with 600,000, had seventy-four. Phoenix, with 500,000 people, had just twenty-two miles of freeways. At the same time, the area had experienced tremendous growth in numbers of people and cars. "There is no doubt that the long range solution is more freeways," asserted Phoenix traffic engineers.

Few gains were made during the 1960s, but in the early 1970s city officials and downtown promoters agreed that construction of the Papago Freeway "Inner Loop," that part of Interstate 10 designed to run through central Phoenix from the north-south Black Canyon Freeway on the west side to Twentieth Street (proposed north-south Squaw Peak Freeway) on the east side, was essential to the future progress of the downtown area. Charter Government and business leaders noted that state and federal funds could be utilized to help Phoenix catch up with the freeway programs of other urban centers. Study after study urged Phoenix to build freeways as fast as possible. Rapid population growth and "automania," along with low-density urban sprawl, called for more freeways. The city's traffic problems, it was said, would never be solved without an adequate freeway system.

Opposition to the proposed freeway system, particularly the Papago Freeway "Inner Loop," was led—surprisingly—by the Pulliam press. A staunch supporter of Charter Government and the business community on every other issue, Eugene Pulliam disliked freeways. And when the Citizens for Mass Transit Against Freeways, a small group of critics who opposed the establishment on this issue and warned of adverse effects of freeways on the city, including increased air pollution, protested to the federal government, the *Republic* and the *Gazette* supported them. Pulliam called the Los Angeles freeway system a mess, and he warned readers not to allow it to be repeated in Phoenix. He felt the Papago Freeway "Inner Loop" would divide the city and be an eyesore, since it would be elevated up to eight stories over the heart of Phoenix.

Determined to prevent the "Inner Loop" from being constructed, the powerful publisher launched what former *Republic* reporter Walter Meek later called "one of the dirtiest campaigns I had ever seen." Day after day, his newspapers were filled with blistering, one-sided, anti-freeway news stories and editorials. Derisive photographs and cartoons of freeway traffic and air pollution in Los Angeles and other urban centers also appeared, often on the front page. Pulliam's newspaper monopoly in Phoenix prevented pro-Papago Freeway voices from being heard; the *Republic* and the *Gazette* simply refused to give adequate news space to Pulliam's opponents, while they belted the public with their biased accounts. Pulliam, not about to change his views, left old friends and new opponents on this issue perplexed and bemused. Here he was allying himself with environmentalists and other "liberals." Some thought he was getting senile; others reflected that he was, above all, his own man.

Along with anti-freeway groups, the Pulliam papers kept demanding that citizens be allowed to decide for or against the freeway, and finally a nervous City Council reluctantly called for a vote. On May 8, 1973, the aggressive anti-freeway campaign of the Pulliam press and its allies paid off when the majority of the people voted against the Papago Freeway "Inner Loop." Pulliam had taken on practically everybody in the Phoenix power structure, and won; the influence of his newspapers on the Phoenix population was clear. His personal influence was compelling; as Frank Snell put it, "When he called you on the phone, you listened." Later observers would remark that the 1973 vote in Phoenix "set back transportation improvements more than a decade." It was a major defeat for the freeway forces, and public officials and business leaders blamed the Pulliam press. As James Walsh, a leader of the freeway opposition, put it regarding the vote: "There is no question that the newspapers almost single-handedly killed the freeway."

In May 1975 a new group called Unity (Use Now I-10 Effectively) took out initiative petitions to once again place the issue of the Papago Freeway "Inner Loop" on the ballot. The Pulliam press opposed its construction, but by this time the majority of voters were convinced that freeway development was badly needed in rapidly growing Phoenix, and on November 5, 1975, they voted in favor of it. The elevated part of the design that had proved so distasteful was eliminated.[19]

The lack of freeways proved frustrating to Phoenix officials, business leaders, and countless drivers. To others, the lack of public transit posed an additional transportation problem. As Phoenicians intensified their love affair with the automobile in the post-World War II years, they neglected the unpopular city bus system. The increasing physical size of sprawling Phoenix and the decline in bus passengers discouraged the City Council from supporting an unprofitable system. In 1959, the city sold its buses to a private line. In the 1960s, privately run lines in Phoenix also failed to make a profit. In 1971, feeling a sense of responsibility to Phoenix residents not involved in the auto culture, Phoenix once again acquired the bus system; at the time less than 1 percent of the population used buses. Private bus service no longer proved financially feasible, but the city had to provide bus service for the city's poor and others who relied upon it for transportation. The city subsidized the Phoenix Transportation Company to continue to operate the buses.

During the 1970s, federal grants for urban mass transit enabled Phoenix to expand and improve the bus system to meet increasing demands. By the end of the decade, the system operated two hundred buses, up from ninety utilized when Phoenix took it over in 1971. During this same time period, daily bus ridership in the city rose from an average of ten thousand to fifty thousand, but auto-crazy Phoenicians continued to reject the bus as an alternative mode of transportation. "Although our bus ridership is up enormously, the population is up, too," Mayor Hance declared in 1977, "so we're still serving only a half of one percent of the population." She noted, "There's a love affair with the automobile country-wide, but especially in a city that's so spread out as this one." Freeways, she added, reflecting the feeling of most Phoenix residents, were what was really needed.[20]

During the period, Sky Harbor International Airport was the one bright spot in the transportation facility picture. With ample funds from revenue bonds and the federal government, the facility remained one of the fastest growing in the nation. Since it was located only a few miles east of downtown, some wanted to move it to the suburbs, but in 1972 Phoenix aviation director William J. Ralston noted, "It's close to most of the people who use it. To put the same kind of property together, we'd have to go out twenty or twenty-five miles. We have a fifty million dollar investment here and we can get an awful lot of years of good use out of this facility."

Additional terminals and runways allowed the airport to keep pace with the jet age.

At the same time, airport expansion forced the destruction of adjacent neighborhoods and the relocation of their inhabitants, mostly members of minority groups. Done in the interest of "progress," the process contributed to strained relations between city officials and minority group leaders. Hispanic barrios and other affected neighborhoods were old but dear to many displaced residents. The experience proved to be highly emotional; and airport expansion, like earlier freeway displacement on the south side, reinforced a long-held feeling that the neglected and often ignored minority groups in Phoenix had enjoyed little success against the Anglo establishment.[21]

New water sources and water system facilities in the public and private sectors managed to keep up with the burgeoning population. Surface and subsurface water remained in sufficient quantity and quality to satisfy promoters. Experts declared that water shortages would not stem from the population influx, because more of the water supply could be diverted from agricultural to nonagricultural users.[22]

At the same time, pessimistic observers called for more restrictive water policies, and conservation became a planning priority on the state and municipal levels. In 1980 the Arizona Groundwater Management Act was passed to regulate the use of water by irrigators and to require better water management by the cities. Designed to force groundwater conservation in the metropolitan areas, it passed largely because of the pressure placed on Arizona by Secretary of the Interior Cecil Andrus. Without a strict groundwater code allowing for renewal and replenishment of depleted subsurface water, Washington would not allocate the funds necessary to complete the long-awaited Central Arizona Project, scheduled to bring water to the Phoenix area from the Colorado River in the 1980s. Supporters hoped the 1980 Arizona Groundwater Management Act would serve as a model for the region in the following decade.

City officials and concerned citizens encouraged voluntary water conservation programs in Phoenix. In the late 1970s they suggested that higher water-use rate structures and a public education program would cause a considerable reduction in water consumption. In addition, both the public and private sectors were urged to adopt a wide variety of waste prevention and water conservation measures. These included cutbacks in use, the utilization of water-saving devices, the use of waste water, the promotion of desert landscaping, and the improvement of irrigation methods. Making water conservation an acceptable way of life for many residents would pose a challenge in the 1980s.[23]

Phenomenal growth led to record-breaking numbers of new homes, churches, and schools. More than ever, promoters tried to offer cultural and social amenities as well as economic and employment opportunities. They encouraged the support of churches and schools, and increasingly they realized the need for a superior higher education system. During the 1960s and 1970s community colleges multiplied in the valley and Arizona State University experienced an enrollment explosion.

The university grew increasingly important. Its provision of advanced instruction in business and engineering to satisfy the demands of the new high-technology society it wished to represent attracted more firms to the valley. The institution offered to well-educated, highly trained staffs of the high-technology firms the Frank Lloyd Wright-designed Grady Gammage Memorial Auditorium (Gammage Center for the Performing Arts), one of the finest structures of its kind in the country. Dr. Gammage, president of Arizona State from 1933 to 1959, considered the new auditorium a dream realized. Before it opened in 1964, the valley had no quality performing arts center.[24]

Other efforts to upgrade cultural life in the area during the period followed, but they often fell short. Some progress was made, but it proved difficult to overcome the impression that Phoenix lacked culture. It may have been "culturally arid" to critics familiar with cultural life in New York, or Chicago, or San Francisco, but Phoenix was becoming a cultural center of the Southwest; it would, however, take time and experience.[25]

Theater performances, for example, improved in quantity but not substantially in quality. The Phoenix Little Theatre (PLT) underwent physical expansion and offered "what the public wants," but it rarely filled a cultural need, according to critics. Although the PLT persisted, it was said that the rivalry between it and professional groups retarded development. Economics played a role, but as critics declared in 1966, when the Arizona Repertory Theatre folded, the amateur PLT was largely responsible. It did not want to share its expanded facility, called the Phoenix Theatre

Center, with professional groups. Critics maintained that PLT members were "more interested in tea parties than good theatre" and that the PLT "would never have the courage or the resources to put on serious drama." Occasional imported theater remained the best Phoenix could offer; in 1980, an observer reported, "The Valley has not been able to mount its own professional theatre company. And attempts to move local community theatre to that status have not met with success on a level that would have given the project a fighting chance."[26]

The Phoenix Art Museum underwent expansion in 1965, and its holdings gained more attention during the period. Some critics wanted to see more western American art, but museum director Dr. F. M. Hinkhouse and other supporters insisted that "works of art springing from the inspiration of the American West" be "not simply western paintings and sculpture, but works of art that possess museum quality." Moreover, Hinkhouse noted, "This has to be a general museum due to the fact that we serve the largest land mass of any museum in America . . . so as a consequence we have become a general collection which will instruct the public and tell them about *all* aspects of Western and Far Eastern peoples, cultures and civilizations." Progress was slow, but in 1980 a Phoenix reporter covering the museum noticed "a rising quality of exhibitions in keeping with the increasingly large and cosmopolitan population here. You don't have to go out of town to see something first-class."[27]

The Phoenix Symphony Orchestra also made gains during the period. Encouraged by Lewis Ruskin, the orchestra's most influential patron, and other supporters, the orchestra in 1964 moved to Grady Gammage Memorial Auditorium at ASU, where it played for eight seasons before moving to the new Symphony Hall, part of the Civic Plaza complex in downtown Phoenix. The new concert hall, replete with crystal chandeliers, lush carpeting, mirrored walls, and a seating capacity of 2,575, added a touch of elegance to downtown redevelopment.[28]

As the population flowed into sprawling Phoenix, detached single-family homes remained the ideal; a Boston reporter suggested, "There's a land conscious mentality in Phoenix. People want their yards." The various housing forms helped to provide the good life to desert city dwellers, and the setting emphasized outdoor activity. Tennis courts and golf courses abounded. Countless houses were zoned for horse privileges. Phoenix became known

Residents enjoying "the good life" in Phoenix, 1965. The Herb and Dorothy McLaughlin Photographic Collection.

as the swimming pool capital of the world, and it boasted of more boats per capita than any place except Florida or California. Nearby lakes and mountains continued to draw Valley of the Sun residents of all ages. As local businessman Karl Eller put it in 1974, "I like the Phoenix way of life—the open air, open community type of living." A year later another business leader noted that his "employees work from seven till three and can be home in twenty minutes, swimming, playing tennis or golf, relaxing with their families."[29]

Phoenicians appreciated popular attractions and organized sports. Annual events such as the Phoenix Rodeo of Rodeos, the Phoenix Open Golf Tournament, and the Arizona State Fair attracted large numbers of patrons, and a number of athletic teams drew enthusiastic crowds. In 1968, thousands turned out to see the new Phoenix Suns of the National Basketball Association play in the 12,500-seat Arizona Veterans' Memorial Coliseum, constructed in 1965. The Coliseum hosted all kinds of big events, including annual performances by the Ice Follies and Ringling

Brothers Barnum and Bailey Circus. In the years ahead, the Suns represented big league sports in Phoenix, and there was talk of a National Football League team in the city's future. The ASU Sun Devils played to large crowds and gained a national reputation as a gridiron power. Also in the 1970s, the annual Fiesta Bowl football game became a major attraction.

It was, however, the Phoenix Suns who enabled local boosters to say, "Phoenix, a city with a future, has gone Big League." And the Coliseum helped make it possible to cultivate that attitude. As one booster declared after its first year of operation: "It opens a door to the best of the world's great productions in sports, entertainment and culture, an asset that helps industry attract to Phoenix Ph.D.-type engineers, scientists and executives of wealth. . . ." Another promoter called it "a great step in the maturing of the community."[30]

Parks and preserves served as recreational outlets for the growing population. In the 1960s the new Phoenix Zoo attracted the most attention, and in the 1970s local citizens joined in a move-

NBA's Phoenix Suns in action, 1970. The Herb and Dorothy McLaughlin Photographic Collection.

ment to preserve the Phoenix Mountains for future use. In the
early 1960s Dr. Robert E. Maytag, a wildlife conservationist and a
recent arrival in the Valley of the Sun, noted the need for a good
zoo in Phoenix. A founder of the Arizona Zoological Society and a
member of the wealthy Maytag (as in washers) family, he donated
half a million dollars of his own to the project and asked the people
of Arizona to raise the rest. The city of Phoenix supplied 120 acres
of Papago Park land for a dollar a year, and private contributions
ranged from school classroom collections of nickels and dimes to
$130,000 by the *Republic* and the *Gazette*. The Phoenix Zoo opened
in late 1962, and it proved immensely popular. It quickly expanded,
and in 1980 it recorded over 600,000 visitors, up from 400,000 in
1970. By 1980, it was the largest privately owned, nonprofit zoo
in the United States, and a generous public kept it competitive.[31]

Although the Phoenix parks system generally lagged behind
those of other cities of comparable size, some progress was made.
More neighborhood parks came into being, but Phoenicians especially supported the preservation of mountain land in the urban
area. In the 1960s, when builders began constructing more houses
on Camelback Mountain, the city stepped in and bought most of the
"hump" of Camelback above eighteen hundred feet. The development of the landmark mountain disturbed many, and a movement
to preserve such natural resources emerged. The protesters realized that the mountains in their midst gave their city an unusual
identity. Rather than see the mountains covered with houses and
other development, residents joined with ardent environmentalists and public officials in a movement to save the Phoenix Mountains.

Citizen committees met, and detailed studies appeared espous-
ing the cause. City officials placed moratoriums on building within
the proposed preserve, and in 1973 voters approved a $23.5 million
bond issue to finance the project. Mayor Driggs called the effort
"monumental." As he put it in 1974, "The saving of the Phoenix
Mountains is far and away the greatest accomplishment in my administration." Critics disagreed, asking, "What do we want to buy
a pile of rocks for?" Driggs's successors, especially Mayor Hance,
reaffirmed the city's commitment to make the Phoenix Mountains
"safe for tomorrow," and during the 1970s Phoenix bought more
mountain land with local and federal funds; by the end of the decade over $30 million had been expended.

Time and again developers challenged the Phoenix Mountain

Preserve, but the city continued to pursue its objective. By 1980, Phoenix owned almost 75 percent of the preserve land. In that year, observers asserted, "Had the city not undertaken the task of buying up the preserves, the mountains would now have houses all over them." Escalating land costs made acquisition difficult, but most advocates considered the effort to save the preserve for future generations an essential priority. As one of them stated in 1980:

> The natural beauty of our mountain horizon, our close-in mountain slopes and natural areas—this is the very substance of the natural environment that has been so instrumental in the population and economic growth of this region. The grand scale and rugged character of these mountains have set our lifestyle, broadened our perspective, given us space to breathe, and freshened our outlook. These mountains are the plus that still overweighs the growing minuses in our environmental account.[32]

A good many Phoenicians benefited from the soothing effect of the mountains. Caught up in the hectic pace of "making it" in the Valley of the Sun, they often suffered from physical and mental problems. As in the past, the urban frontier did not guarantee success; individuals experienced problems as well as progress. Alcohol and drug abuse, high divorce and suicide rates, and other social realities became major problems in the "new paradise." Moreover, air and water pollution increased during the period, and traffic deaths and the number of murders rose dramatically. There was a darker side to Phoenix life.[33]

Every conceivable kind of illegal activity seemed to flourish in the rapidly emerging metropolis, including white-collar and organized crime. Sharpers of all types, including con artists posing as legitimate business and professional people, abounded, fleecing countless victims in and out of the city and the state. The boom atmosphere in Phoenix and Arizona proved particularly conducive to land fraud. In the land of laissez-faire, few rules and regulations were imposed upon developers. Too many restrictions retarded progress and prosperity on the last frontier, it was said, and because of this wild West attitude, unscrupulous operators thrived.

For example, ex-Sing Sing inmate, master con man, and Arizona land fraud kingpin Ned Warren, Sr., practiced every deception in the book. The Phoenix-based Warren operated several firms in the 1960s and the 1970s, and he bilked thousands of investors

out of millions of dollars. He finally went to jail in 1977 for land
fraud, but not before he brought undesirable national exposure
to Phoenix and Arizona. Characters like Warren circulated easily
in boom town society. They contributed large amounts of money
to political parties, gave generous sums to cultural organizations,
and lived in expensive homes in elite neighborhoods. In Arizona,
"few people ask questions about strangers," noted an observer; and
another asserted, "There has been an atmosphere in the state for
some time that anything done by people wearing coats and ties
goes. Anything that purports to be business is not to be critically
examined."

An open, friendly atmosphere and ample western hospitality
made Phoenix another frontier of opportunity where men were
judged not by their past but by what they were up to in the present.
The newness of the city and the state made them attractive to
those in search of a future, and promoters used that appeal. As
Arizona Governor Bruce Babbitt put it:

> When I go out of state with business recruiters talking about the
> advantages of Arizona, I sell that as an advantage. I say, "Look,
> you want to crack the big time in Arizona? It's wide open." I say,
> "Look, you want to make your wife a society leader? Send one
> thousand dollars to your favorite charity and send her picture
> to the newspaper and she'll be a society leader. In New York
> you'd have to wait in line for five generations before they'd even
> acknowledge your presence. It just isn't true here." That's good
> in the sense of providing mobility, a sense of openness. If you've
> got a burning ambition to do something, there's absolutely no
> limits.

A democratic America was at work in Phoenix, and many honest and ambitious newcomers appreciated the welcome and the
opportunity; but as a result, Warren and other slick operators with
criminal intent penetrated the business and social life of the Valley
of the Sun. In many ways, much of the small-town-turned-boom-
town atmosphere that had prevailed in Phoenix since World War II
caused the local establishment to accept impressive newcomers
too quickly, and it suffered the consequences. One national television news commentator called Phoenix "the nation's biggest small
town." Despite the "big-city pretensions," Phoenix experienced the
problems of a twentieth-century West boom town, including the

influx of countless flim-flam artists who sought opportunity on the new urban frontier.

In this "live and let live" environment, Warren and others succeeded. According to Michael F. Wendland, "Warren himself seemed to epitomize much of what was wrong with Arizona. He had seen opportunity and seized it. No matter that he had broken the law. It was all some sort of marvelous game, a game without rules, to be won by the player with the most nerve." That "Warren felt no guilt and incredibly, was borne no animosity by his neighbors in Arizona," Wendland continued, "was evident by his plush Camelback Mountain home. Out front of his sprawling house, in bold, foot-high letters, the name 'N. J. Warren' was proudly posted next to his winding blacktop driveway. It was as if he was showing off the fruits of his criminality. And none of his neighbors seemed to mind." Phoenix, the reporter concluded, "was a world unto itself—a place where money was God and the hustler and con man were the priests."

Wendland and other reporters came to Phoenix in the fall of 1976 to look into the murder of *Republic* investigative reporter Don Bolles. Bolles had been compiling information on white-collar and organized crime in Phoenix and Arizona when he was killed by a bomb placed in his car. Three suspects were later convicted of the crime. When Bolles died, members of the national organization Investigative Reporters and Editors (IRE) descended on the Sunbelt center to uncover the circumstances surrounding his death. In the process, unwelcome national media attention suddenly focused on the Valley of the Sun. The *Republic* and the *Gazette* refused to publish the IRE's series of reports because, as they put it, the material lacked proof. "Above all, these newspapers strive always to be truthful and accurate," declared the *Republic*. A number of newspapers around the country also refused to publish the reports, calling them "insufficiently documented and inadequately supported."

Outraged critics voiced their disapproval and protested; even some of the *Republic* and the *Gazette* reporters objected, noting that the papers should have carried the series. Robert Greene, head of the IRE team, claimed that the papers' refusal to print the series "underlies what is terribly wrong in Phoenix and Arizona. People are not given a right to know what is going on." The *Republic* and the *Gazette* held out, and those who wanted to see the reports found them in the Tucson newspapers, other outside papers, and the *New Times*, a local weekly, or they heard selected portions of the reports read on radio and television.

The Bolles murder probe, and the exposure of land fraud king Ned Warren, convinced many observers that Phoenix's reputation as "the most crime-ridden city in the United States" was deserved, but they also led to reform measures in Phoenix and Arizona. By 1980, law enforcement agencies received more funding; a number of corrupt officials had been replaced; new anti-crime codes had come into being; and the court system was more effective and faster than it had been in responding to the problem. The Pulliam press, although it did not publish the IRE reports, continued in its own way to expose the crime problem. For example, the *Republic* published a special section entitled "CRIME!" in June 1978. It dealt with much the same material covered by the IRE reporters, but it failed to mention the names of prominent local individuals linked to the criminal element in the IRE series.[34]

As in the past, the 1980 population was largely Anglo. Blacks and Hispanics accounted for less than 20 percent of the total population in the Phoenix area. Hispanics continued to be the largest minority group in the desert center, with 14.3 percent of the total, while blacks constituted only 4.7 percent and Native Americans less than 1 percent. In Phoenix, problems for all persisted. At the same time, however, the civil rights movement brought educational and employment opportunities to many minority group members in the Arizona oasis; and, benefiting from new openings, they made significant gains in local economic and political circles. Yet critics continued to point out areas in which metropolitan Phoenix institutions could improve; for example, in the fall of 1981 only 4.2 percent (1,582) of the 38,075-member Arizona State University student body was listed as being Hispanic, while 2.2 percent (839) were black.[35]

Phoenix contained the largest black population in the Southwest, and while individuals from that minority group made meaningful advances in the twenty years after 1960, progress for blacks as a group proved to be slow. Problems such as high unemployment, poor housing, and lack of education plagued the black neighborhoods of Phoenix. In 1980, for example, in the two areas of Phoenix with the heaviest black concentration, 36 percent in one area and 26 percent in the other had less than a grade school education. In the summer of that year, following the black uprising in Miami, black leaders in the Arizona capital were asked if they felt the ingredients for a race riot were present in the city. In reply, spokesman Art Hamilton declared, "All the circumstances— the hopelessness, the helplessness—exist in Phoenix."

The long-standing problems of high unemployment, poor housing, and lack of education and attainment had been brought up in February 1962 at a U.S. Civil Rights Commission hearing in Phoenix. Black leaders representing the NAACP, Urban League, and other organizations noted that at that time black unemployment and underemployment in the private and public sectors far exceeded that of whites. In addition, both private and public housing units were occupied along racial lines in Phoenix, with over 90 percent of the black population residing south of Van Buren. Real estate interests continued to keep blacks from buying homes north of Van Buren. De facto school segregation still existed, and school districts north of Van Buren did not hire black teachers.[36]

As in other urban centers across the country, older black leaders in Phoenix had a difficult time becoming active in the civil rights movement in the early 1960s, but young blacks increasingly demonstrated in protest. Sit-ins and marches on city hall and the state capitol were utilized by blacks to make metropolitan Phoenix aware of their plight. The young protesters joined the Congress of Racial Equality (CORE) and other new groups, and they afforded new leadership to older groups such as the NAACP and the Urban League. Jim Williams, Austin Coleman, Clovis Campbell, Lincoln Ragsdale, the Rev. George B. Brooks, and others became spokesmen for blacks seeking civil rights. Sit-ins and marches helped secure a public accommodations ordinance from the city of Phoenix in July 1964, and a civil rights law from the state of Arizona in January 1965.[37]

Out of the Phoenix Human Rights Commission grew Operation LEAP (Leadership and Education for the Advancement of Phoenix), a public-private sector partnership agency established to combat poverty in the city. In January 1966, LEAP became a city department involved in federal War on Poverty programs, and some progress was made. A number of government-sponsored programs were offered, including new educational and employment opportunities. Mayor Graham and the City Council supported LEAP, and target neighborhood residents participated in its projects. Critics, however, remained dissatisfied; the situation had improved, but it needed more attention.[38]

Dissatisfaction centered on limited job training and the lack of minority hiring. There were complaints of the War on Poverty in Phoenix being "a day late and a dollar short." In May 1967, for example, a reporter declared that despite $15 million in new services, the "LEAP target area is more impoverished than in 1965." Despite all of LEAP's efforts, he continued, "people are still not working because they lack the ability to compete for work in the labor market." "The fact is that agency workers have been foundering in a sea of uncoordinated, limited programs that lead nowhere," noted another critic, and "all efforts have had a temporary Band Aid effect." A LEAP report in July 1967 noted only "52 job placements out of 250 contacts in Phoenix." At the same time, Arizona continued to pay its welfare recipients considerably less than the national average; indeed, wrote one observer, "For the poor Arizona is a tough state."

The 21.2-square-mile LEAP target area contained most of the blacks and many of the Hispanics in the city, and within its boundaries could be found some of the worst slums west of the Mississippi River. In July 1967 unemployment in the area was exceptionally high, and close to 30 percent of the residents lived on less than three thousand dollars a year. One observer asserted it "might be fairly termed a human disaster area in an affluent metropolis." It certainly pointed out that the boom in Phoenix benefited whites in the suburbs more than it did minority group members in core neighborhoods.

In similar neighborhoods around the country, blacks and other minority groups were rioting; and on July 25, 1967, Phoenix experienced a violent confrontation when firebombs were thrown and shots were fired at a police wagon on East Van Buren. Other disturbances occurred, and eventually a crowd of angry blacks gathered at the Sidney P. Osborn Project, a public housing facility located between Seventeenth and Eighteenth streets from Van Buren to Washington. Police sent to the scene were met with fierce hostility, but the rioting subsided. At a meeting at Eastlake Park the next day, Mayor Graham emphasized that he would not tolerate "stoning, gunfire and disorder in the streets." He also reiterated the city's intention to work toward racial justice. Young black leaders presented a list of grievances, noting especially the need for more job training and more jobs.

That evening rioting again erupted near the Osborn Project. Mayor Graham imposed a curfew and ordered police to enforce it. Arrests followed. About 280 people, including 38 juveniles, were taken into custody. A total of 376 Phoenix police officers were on duty at various times in the troubled area, their duties elsewhere in the city being taken over by 190 state highway patrolmen, 148 sheriff's deputies, and 64 Phoenix fire fighters. Isolated incidents continued to occur, but the curfew was lifted on July 30. On that date Mayor Graham, preferring to call the recent disorder a "serious civil disobedience" rather than a "riot," announced that Phoenix intended to provide more job training and jobs for minority groups. Also, to counter charges of police harassment in Phoenix, he promised a city effort to make community relations a vital function of the police force.

The city seemed intent on fulfilling its promises, but skeptics called for more police to enforce law and order. Blacks as well as whites opposed the violence. Many black parents objected to the riot, and they criticized the young participants. Moreover, declared one of them, "Eighty percent of all the kids who were making all the noise wouldn't take a job if you offered it to them—or if they did, they wouldn't work. They want to get paid, that's all." Others blamed the outburst on previous riots in Los Angeles, Detroit, and other urban centers; after seeing their vivid coverage on national television, Phoenix blacks, it was said, were merely conforming to the prevailing pattern.[39]

Problems remained in 1980, but progress was evident. National and local civil rights legislation, along with anti-poverty programs, helped make black organizations such as the NAACP and the Urban League influential forces in the community. In 1980, for example, the Phoenix Urban League, under the able direction of Junius A. Bowman, had a staff of over one hundred workers and operated programs that dealt extensively with job training, housing, education, health, and cultural enrichment. Administering a variety of projects from Head Start to Urban League Manor —a residence for the elderly and the handicapped—it proved to be one of the city's most respected professional social service agencies. It was especially adept at securing the support of white influentials and getting many large companies to establish affirmative action or fair employment offices. Individuals as well as organizations made progress in the private and the public sectors, especially the latter; for example, Doug Nelson advanced to assistant chief of the Phoenix Police Department, William Bell served as assistant city manager, and H. B. Daniels became the first black municipal judge in Phoenix's history.[40]

Neighborhood surveys and civil rights hearings described inadequate conditions in the Hispanic as well as the black community. Residentially isolated in the barrios of Phoenix, most Hispanics continued to experience low economic status. Inadequate housing, schooling, and employment opportunities made life difficult for them; for example, in some areas, education surveys indicated a lower level of attainment for Hispanics than for blacks. At the same time, as in the case of blacks, increasing numbers of Hispanic individuals made progress as more educational and employment opportunities opened up in the wake of the civil rights movement. Like blacks, Hispanics also made political gains. In the early 1970s Calvin Goode, a black, and Rosendo Gutierrez, a Hispanic, assumed influential roles on the Phoenix City Council while Art Hamilton, a black, and Alfredo Gutierrez (no relation to Rosendo), a Hispanic, were elected to the State Legislature. Many of the minority leaders were young, and they reflected the experiences of the civil rights movement.[41]

Alfredo Gutierrez, for example, was a student activist at Arizona State University in the late 1960s. He not only engaged in Chicano causes on campus, but he also helped form Chicano organizations in the Phoenix barrios to fight discrimination in the city. The new Chicano organizations attempted to go beyond the services provided by Friendly House; the new leaders and their organizations, notably Chicanos por la Causa (CPLC), represented a new determination and direction in improving conditions in the Hispanic community. In the fall of 1970, when conflict erupted at Phoenix Union High School (PUHS), for instance, CPLC organized a Hispanic boycott of the school until changes occurred. Gutierrez, Joe Eddie Lopez, Earl Wilcox, and other CPLC leaders and members of the Parent-Student Boycott Committee publicized the dissatisfaction of many Hispanics and made the public more aware of their plight. For a long time PUHS had needed programs more responsive to the needs of the minority group students who made up the majority of the school's enrollment, but few materialized. Calls for more minority teachers and counselors also went un-

heeded. Especially disturbing to minority parents was the incli-
nation of advisers to channel minority students "toward manual
rather than intellectual development, without consideration of the
fact that such a choice produces and perpetuates economic-racial
discrimination."

While the black and Chicano student population at PUHS rose
during the 1950s and 1960s, the physical facilities deteriorated
from age and neglect. White flight increased; from 1967 to 1970
alone, the number of Anglo students at the school declined from
35.1 to 19.3 percent. It had become a "minorities" school, but minorities had little voice in determining and conducting education
at the institution. Moreover, violence between blacks and Chicanos
played a large role in the day-to-day life of the school, with each
side blaming the other. Chicano parents and leaders from Chicano
organizations protested. Marches and demonstrations occurred,
and Chicano leaders demanded official action. Finally, on October
9, 1970, they called for a boycott of PUHS.

The participating leaders of CPLC and the Parent-Student Boycott Committee insisted that law and order on the campus was but
one of many grievances. The problem of student security was important, but they wanted the general quality of education at PUHS
to change so as to better reflect their aspirations for the Hispanic
community. In response to demands made by the leaders of the
Parent-Student Boycott Committee and CPLC, Valle del Sol Institute, Barrio Youth Project, and other Chicano organizations, school
officials promised to implement programs more responsive to the
educational needs of Chicano students. During the month-long
boycott, Barrio Youth Project operated classrooms for boycotting
students, and Valle del Sol Institute offered tutoring sessions during and after the boycott. During the 1970s these groups, along
with CPLC, joined Friendly House and other agencies in providing valuable educational, economic, and social services to Phoenix
Hispanics.[42]

The Alianza Hispano Americana and other older organizations
not attractive to younger Chicanos declined during the period,
while new and more timely groups such as CPLC gained ground.
In order to retain its importance, Friendly House adopted a more
aggressive approach in the 1960s and 1970s. In new quarters since
1961, it expanded its operations during the War on Poverty despite
objections from some Anglo board members. Mildred Brown, an
Anglo, took over as head of Friendly House in 1965, and under

her direction changes occurred; the Americanization programs remained most important, but more emphasis was given to welfare services. However, Friendly House's agenda failed to prevent young Chicano leaders from forming CPLC and other new Chicano-oriented organizations to represent the Phoenix Hispanic community.

Chicanos por la Causa, formed in 1969 to secure aid to confront the "oppressing problems threatening to overwhelm the Phoenix Chicano community," in the 1970s initiated many community service programs, including housing, counseling and rehabilitation, small business projects, job training centers, and neighborhood health clinics. By 1977 CPLC had an annual operating budget of $676,000; with heavy infusions of federal funds, it had grown to $6.3 million four years later. CPLC also served as a school of Hispanic leadership. Alfredo Gutierrez, Joe Eddie Lopez, and other Chicano activists, who founded CPLC to confront discrimination against the Hispanic community and improve barrio life in Phoenix, set the pace, while Ronnie Lopez (no relation to Joe Eddie), Tom Espinoza, and others later joined and contributed to the realization of many of the organization's goals. Espinoza, head of CPLC from 1974, proved to be especially effective in relating to and securing support from Anglo business and political leaders in and out of Phoenix.[43]

Despite gains made under the leadership of CPLC and other Chicano organizations, problems remained. By the end of the 1970s, south Phoenix residents still needed more of everything most north Phoenix residents already had or expected to have in the near future: more quality homes, more paved streets, more public parks, more health facilities, more libraries, more shopping centers, more police stations, more firehouses, and so on. Moreover, Phoenix Union High School and other educational institutions failed to do enough to spur confidence in their programs. Chicanos continued to head the dropout list, and the dropout rate contributed to high crime rates in Phoenix. In 1979 Reuben Ortega, a Phoenix police community relations officer and future police chief, declared, "More than half our crime problem is directly related to youth." In that year it was estimated that more than forty organized street gangs operated in Phoenix, many of them in Hispanic neighborhoods on the south and west sides.[44]

The Indian population in Phoenix increased from 3,538 in 1960 to 10,877 in 1980. Although they lived throughout the city, as did members of other minority groups, the Indian population in Phoenix continued to concentrate in a few neighborhoods; middle-class Indians, most of them employed by the federal government, lived near the Phoenix Indian School, the Phoenix Indian Medical Center, and the regional offices of the Bureau of Indian Affairs, all located uptown, while poorer Indians lived downtown in lower-income neighborhoods. For the latter, little schooling, menial employment, and inadequate housing made urban life difficult. In 1980, Indians in Phoenix had a 70 percent greater chance of being part of an impoverished household than did Hispanics, and a 20 percent greater chance than did blacks; at the same time, they suffered from extremely high alcohol abuse and suicide rates.

In the 1960s and 1970s, low-income Phoenix Indians gained some ground because of federal government social and economic programs administered by the Phoenix Indian Center and other organizations. Southwest Indian Development, Inc., formed in 1969, proved to be most effective during the 1970s. As in the case of CORE and CPLC for young blacks and Hispanics, SID served as a vehicle for Syd Beane, John Lewis, Gus Greymountain, and other Indian activists to press for more attention from the city. Phoenix was slow to respond, but it did create a special Indian advisory committee to keep city agencies such as LEAP informed of the needs of the Indian community. Cultural and social programs provided by institutions ranging from the Indian School to "Indian" churches to "Indian" bars helped to foster a sense of ethnic identity and awareness.[45]

In tandem with the economic boom and the population explosion in the Sunbelt center came the usual problems. Public services strained under the increasing numbers of residents and sometimes lagged in keeping pace with the city's extensive urbanization. To most people, however, the urban problems of Phoenix seemed relatively minor compared with those plaguing the older metropolitan centers elsewhere in the country. Many newcomers moving to the Valley of the Sun had left decaying, high-density, heavy-industry areas and, seeing what the Arizona capital offered, they heartily welcomed the change.

On the other hand, critics wondered if residents of the Phoenix oasis realized the difficulty of retaining the good life in the midst of rapid and uncontrolled growth that might damage or even destroy the very environment and existence they sought when moving to the city. Some critics, for example, were complaining about the "Los Angelization" of Phoenix and the "Californication" of Arizona. Indeed, in the 1980s, discussion would increasingly center on the achievement of a workable balance between continuing growth and the quality of life.

8 SOUTHWEST METROPOLIS: THE 1980S

The problems of growth continued to plague Phoenix, and Mayor Hance and the City Council remained committed to providing essential services. Social programs often suffered, while services such as police protection received more attention. "Despite efforts this year ... to reduce crime and respond to the juvenile issue," Mayor Hance declared in November 1980, "the problems have accelerated or reached a level of violence that is intolerable for the safety of our residents." One poll named "crime, violence, gangs, drugs" as the most important problems facing the city.

In order to meet these and other problems without raising property taxes, revenue innovations were introduced. Additional user fees, for example, helped, but cutbacks in state and federal allowances, along with uncertain sales tax returns during a recession, caused the city to observe established priorities. "It is all a matter of priorities," noted a City Council member in October 1981. The "present City Council perceives the role of city government [is] to provide a safe government and a clean environment, and an economically viable community." Mayor Hance, a self-professed Reagan Republican, deplored the city's dependence on federal money, but she continued to use her clout in Washington to obtain as much federal aid as possible.[1]

At the same time, Mayor Hance remained popular and no serious opposition emerged to challenge her. "Even in the face of constricting budgets and difficult decisions about program priorities, spending cuts and seeking new revenue sources for rapidly growing Phoenix, over 70 percent of Valley residents have a favorable impression of Mayor Hance," declared local pollster Earl de Berge. In the 1981 election campaign, Hance cited her support for crime prevention, water projects, better transportation, downtown redevelopment, and clean industry in Phoenix; also, she emphasized her support of "the principles of Charter—the council-manager form of government." Backed by the *Republic* and the *Gazette*, she easily won reelection to a fourth term in November 1981.

Calling her victory a "gratifying vote of confidence," Mayor Hance explained her lack of opposition this way: "Apparently I'm reflecting the interests of the majority of Phoenix. They know where I stand on the issues. So I guess I represent them to their satisfaction." Most City Council members also were reelected. Critics, however, continued to be heard; as one of them put it, "To the extent that the city is deteriorating, it is due to the fact that some of the present councilmen elected as independents have proven to be 'closet Charterites.'" In the 1981 election, the CGC endorsed Hance and most successful candidates for the City Council.

Critics noticed the low voter participation in the 1981 election. Even Mayor Hance called it a nonevent. What the mayor viewed as voter apathy, however, may have been citizen frustration. Many residents appeared satisfied with the system, but the polls indicated a strong preference for district representation on the City Council. According to critics, more identifiable government representation would stimulate more citizen interest in city elections. They maintained that a larger City Council and a district system of elections were needed to meet the varied problems of the increasing population. They complained about a lack of services in some city areas, and a lack of neighborhood concern on the part of City Council members elected at large. Minority leaders in south Phoenix believed specifically that inadequate representation helped explain the lack of adequate services in that part of the city.[2]

As the population of sprawling Phoenix soared, the failure of city hall to reach out to new as well as to older areas to meet their needs encouraged discontent. In October 1981, a *Gazette*-conducted poll revealed that 65 percent of those polled in Phoenix preferred a district system. In June 1982, hopeful proponents began circulating initiative petitions to provide residents the chance to vote in November on a plan to expand the City Council to eight members elected from wards with at-large voting for the mayor's position. Mayor Hance and the City Council had assigned the Citizens' Charter Review Committee the task of examining alternative methods of city government, but those in favor of change did not want to endure what they considered to be delaying tactics on the part of those opposed to change.

"We think it's the right time," noted Jim Weeks, a petition drive leader, "we think we can pull it off." Weeks and Phoenix lawyer Terry Goddard led the Committee for District Representation; they said the structural change would make the City Council more responsive to citizens' needs. Enough signatures were secured, and the initiative appeared as Proposition 200 in a December 1982 special election. Mayor Hance deplored it; the Citizens' Charter Revision Committee, along with local business organizations and the city's major newspapers, disliked it; and only one City Council member, Calvin Goode, approved of it. Nevertheless, the voters went with the proposal. The initiative won by a vote of 39,591 to 37,821, with 25.76 percent of the 303,881 registered voters casting ballots.[3]

The vote was close, but many observers noted that it was about time for change. Phoenix had outgrown at-large elections, which were acceptable when the city had less than 100,000 voters and covered only 17 square miles. In 1950 it was possible to know council members on a personal basis, but in 1982, with more than 800,000 residents in a city of 330 square miles, council members no longer adequately responded to neighborhood concerns. The at-large system made it difficult for voters to determine accountability for City Council decisions. According to district advocates, the time had come to wrest political power from special-interest groups and redistribute it to individual citizens and neighborhoods. Open up city hall and let democracy reign, they said. A district system would be not only more democratic but also less expensive, for candidates would not be dependent, as they were in at-large elections, upon large campaign contributions from special interests in order to be competitive.

Terry Goddard, who rapidly became the most dynamic spokes-

man for the district system, contended that the only way to dimin-
ish the influence traditional power groups held over the mayor
and the City Council was to adopt the district system. It would
help break up the elite hierarchy of businessmen and other special
interests who enjoyed unlimited access to city hall, and usher in
a new era of representative government to the benefit of all the
people. It had worked in other Sunbelt urban centers. Structural
changes had occurred in many cities of the new urban America in
recent years; indeed, Phoenix was the last city of its size in the
nation to drop at-large elections in favor of the district system.
Moreover, in Phoenix proponents insisted that elections would remain nonpartisan, the council-manager form of government would
not be altered, and the present civil service system protecting professional staff from political influence would not change.[4]

Opponents of the district system outspent proponents by a
three-to-one margin, with thousands of dollars contributed by
the city's largest financial institutions and two major utilities.
Opponents labeled the district effort a move to bring "wards and
Eastern-style politics to Phoenix." They pointed to the prominent
role played by city fire and police unions and other advocacy groups
in the election campaign, but this time change won approval. Support for the existing at-large system came mainly from traditional
Charter government strongholds in north central Phoenix, while
the district system was approved by most voters in all other areas
of the city. Voters in growing Phoenix had turned down similar
measures in 1967 and 1975, but in 1982, as Jim Weeks put it, "We
had the right proposal at the right time."[5]

Mayor Hance chose not to run under the new system. In May
1983 she announced she would not seek election to a fifth term.
Terry Goddard, the leader of the district system movement, noted,
"It's the end of an era. We're embarking on some new directions,
clearly." At the same time, the City Council voted to adopt a
city-drawn map that divided Phoenix into eight new districts and
split south Phoenix in two. By election eve, two mayoral hope-
fuls and fifty-one City Council candidates had qualified for a place
on the ballot. During the campaign most of the attention focused
on the mayoral candidates, Terry Goddard and Pete Dunn. Dunn
received the support of most of those groups and individuals who
had opposed the district system, and Goddard wasted no time
in labeling him the "establishment" candidate. Goddard stressed
his theme of openness in government, and he charged that Dunn

would serve at city hall as a "doorman" for the business elite and other special interest groups.[6]

In campaign debates there was little disagreement between the candidates on the need for improved transportation and water systems, downtown redevelopment, Phoenix Mountains preservation, less crime, and more economic development. The Phoenix Metropolitan Chamber of Commerce, the major newspapers, and other "establishment" forces endorsed Dunn, a successful businessman and former state legislator. They claimed that he offered Phoenix voters "a superior breadth of experience, a greater maturity of judgement and more potential for positive leadership" than his opponent, thirty-six-year-old attorney and political upstart Terry Goddard. In October, Mayor Hance endorsed Dunn. She praised the conservative Republican for his "experienced, mature and skilled leadership" while denouncing liberal Democrat Goddard for attacking the city hall establishment. "The Old Guard is attempting to pass the baton to a new person," Goddard noted, adding, "It gives a lot of credibility to what I've been saying."

Ambitious and pragmatic, Goddard modified his stance on the issues when necessary while emphasizing his "access to city hall for all the people" theme. He appealed to citizens who felt shut out of city hall, neighborhood groups that saw their interests ignored, and virtually the entire minority community. Minorities felt totally neglected; as Alfredo Gutierrez put it regarding members of the power structure in Phoenix: "Hispanics have been totally out— when they do talk to us, it's like they're addressing ambassadors from a foreign country." Goddard also began listing the "powerful few" he felt had special access to city government. Most of the names were on Dunn's campaign contribution statement filed with the city clerk. Heading Goddard's list of power brokers was millionaire builder Charles Keating, Jr., president of Continental Homes. Keating, his associates, and their relatives contributed $20,000 to Dunn, and another $60,000 to eight City Council candidates, one in each district. *Republic* columnist Tom Fitzpatrick called Keating "the Daddy Warbucks of Phoenix politics." Wealthy developers and other "fat cats" dominated Goddard's list.[7]

Both candidates favored continued growth and prosperity, but Goddard spent more time on "quality of life" issues, while Dunn took the traditional "whatever's good for business is good for Phoenix" approach. Goddard wanted the city to develop, but he offered hope of new leadership and vision. In emphasizing better planning for the city and more openness in government, he represented the feeling in Phoenix that the status quo must go; indeed, Goddard called Dunn "the henchman of the status quo."

On November 2, citizens seeking a more responsive government voted to change the status quo at city hall. The charismatic Goddard soundly defeated Dunn by more than ten thousand votes, capturing a majority in five of the city's eight districts; 46.3 percent of the city's registered voters turned out for the election. Incumbent Calvin Goode was the lone City Council member who received a majority of votes and won reelection. A December runoff election decided the other seven council seats; only three incumbents won. Like Goddard, all the successful City Council candidates promoted more openness in government. "I'm very confident it is a group I can work with," stated the new mayor.[8]

Asked why Goddard had won, Dunn replied: "He succeeded in making his issues the important ones. He got the message across I was the representative of the rich and the status quo." Goddard admitted that his charge that Dunn was the designated candidate of the city's power elite was effective, especially after he cited as evidence Dunn's acceptance of $20,000 in donations from developer Charles Keating, Keating's associates, and their relatives. That emphasis, he said, "helped to bring into focus some things I've talked about since the beginning of the campaign . . . that a few people are very powerful in this city, and the vast majority have no role at all in city government."

The new mayor and the new City Council, consisting of Calvin Goode, William Parks, Duane Pell, Barry Starr, John B. Nelson, Howard Adams, Ed Korrick, and Mary Rose Wilcox, called for more public access to city hall and more citizen participation in government. They agreed to hold Council sessions at times convenient for the public, to establish offices and hold forums in each district, and to assign staff assistants to handle the anticipated flood of complaints and requests from district residents. At the same time, Goddard promised that the actions of his administration would "dispel any lingering doubts that he is anti-business. . . . I was frequently chastised during the campaign for being anti-business," he recalled, but "what I was trying to do was to open the city to all citizens, not replace one small clique with another clique." No special favors to a powerful few, but access for all. "I'm not excluding anybody," he declared.[9]

Although critics remained, most observers agreed that the new

Terry Goddard, Mayor of Phoenix, 1984–. City of Phoenix Public Information Office.

district system was a success. Some lamented "the trend toward a city government run by politicians rather than by drafted civic leaders," but no organized opposition to the system emerged. Even many former opponents became "born-again districters." Voters also approved of Mayor Goddard and the City Council, and in November 1985 they easily won reelection; one candidate, Paul

Johnson, replaced Barry Starr, who chose not to run again, on the City Council. Since he had built bridges to the business community during his first term, no opposition candidate from that element appeared to challenge Goddard. "My perception is that I've done a good job for the business climate of this city and that business leaders have appreciated that," the mayor noted. "I think we've accomplished some pretty impressive things together."

As examples Goddard cited the formation of the Phoenix Economic Growth Corporation, a public/private entity designed to draw industry to the city and to encourage the expansion of existing enterprises, and his cooperative work with the business-dominated Phoenix Community Alliance in trying to revitalize downtown. "It doesn't take a lot of intelligence to know it would take a major catastrophe to defeat him," declared Phoenix Metropolitan Chamber of Commerce executive Jim Haynes in July 1985. Goddard was "most proud of what we've done in opening up City Hall and the district system." His emphasis on "quality of life" issues also was welcome. Polls clearly indicated his popularity, and he turned down a strong plea that he run for governor of Arizona in 1986.[10]

A progressive city, however, costs money, and as federal and state aid decreased, it became necessary to cut services or raise taxes. Some retrenchment occurred, and sales taxes and user fees rose in Phoenix in July 1986, as city officials pledged to continue their drive to improve the overall quality of life in the nation's ninth largest urban center. Not everybody appreciated the increases in taxes and fees, including the Phoenix Metropolitan Chamber of Commerce, but Mayor Goddard and the City Council balked at more spending cuts and pushed for more money. "If Phoenix is to progress in the future, we need more revenue, it's that simple," Goddard asserted. City Manager Marvin Andrews agreed.

Providing some solace was the fact that the property tax rate remained at $1.63 per $100 assessed valuation. To ensure citizen involvement in the future, the City Council appointed the Citizens' Tax Fairness Commission. If Phoenix hoped to compete successfully with other ambitious cities, it needed funds to support "quality of life" projects and programs. Economic prosperity was essential, and additional sources of revenue became imperative in the 1980s if the Arizona capital expected to provide adequate services for all of its people and stay in the race for urban growth and status.[11]

In June 1987, Mayor Goddard announced his candidacy for re-election, and among his goals he listed the need for tax increases or new taxes. "The alternative to higher taxes is deep cuts in city services," he asserted, adding, "Citizens would find that unacceptable." While vowing to continue the fight against crime and pollution, he endorsed downtown revitalization and neighborhood planning. In addition, he urged citizens to back "programs to support the arts and protect our historic resources." Goddard's election to a third term seemed assured, noted political observers; no major opposition was evident, and polls indicated that 85 percent of the public supported him. "A politician can't do better than that," declared Councilman Howard Adams. "Phoenix is literally a new challenge every day, and I love that," Goddard said. "I think we've made tremendous progress in both trying to open up the city government process and increase the quality of life quotient in Phoenix."

Other Sunbelt cities experienced the same kind of economic and political evolution that Phoenix did during the years following World War II. In the postwar period, growth-oriented business elites became the driving force in community decision making as groups similar to the CGC emerged in many Sunbelt urban centers. Devoted to a business approach to city government and dedicated to the support of selected candidates in at-large elections, they remained in power for many years. But as the decades passed and the cities grew larger, other groups demanded a share of the power. A movement to decentralize political power spread. As John Naisbett pointed out in his popular 1982 book *Megatrends*, "The failure of centralized, top-down solutions has been accompanied by a huge upsurge in grassroots political activity everywhere in the United States. . . . Some twenty million Americans are now organized around issues of local concern. Neighborhood groups are becoming powerful and demanding greater participation in decision-making." Phoenix may have been late to make structural changes, but the success of the new district system and the new openness and access to city hall for all the people in the 1980s set a political tone in line with most of the rest of the new urban America.[12]

In the 1980s, despite difficult periods reflecting the impact of national recessions, Phoenix economic development continued apace. During the decade political leaders talked about managed growth, but none of them dismissed growth as a desirable goal. Prosperity reports like the following continued to appear.

> Another year in the Valley. Another 90,000-or-so additional residents, 70,000 new jobs, 53,000 new housing units. Nothing special—just fast growth during 1985–86, growth just slower than the record setting 1984. And 1986? Slower rapid growth yet. Maybe 85,000 more people, 50,000 more jobs, and 45,000 housing units.[13]

Maricopa County accounted for nearly two-thirds of the population, employment, and income in Arizona during the period. Economists pointed to the phenomenal growth performance of the Valley of the Sun and called it "the envy of much of the country." From the beginning of 1980 to the middle of 1985, over twelve thousand new businesses were formed. That figure represented a growth rate of nearly 40 percent. That meant "almost four in ten businesses operating in the greater Phoenix area were not in business five and one-half years ago," noted a February 1986 Phoenix Metropolitan Chamber of Commerce report.[14]

Service-related categories were far out in front, with over five thousand new businesses (41.3 percent of all new businesses created). Small concerns were in the great majority in Phoenix, but employment concentrated in the medium-to-large companies. The 174,000 jobs created in the Phoenix metropolitan area between January 1980 and July 1985 represented a 27.1 percent increase, and most of them were in the service-related sectors, followed by construction and manufacturing. In this respect, metropolitan Phoenix drove the state's economy; in 1987 a study reported that the area generated seven of every ten new jobs in Arizona. That impressive statistic helped the state retain its status as first in the nation in new job creation. Metropolitan Phoenix's job and economic growth from 1983 to 1987 was so good that *Inc.* magazine ranked it number one in the nation.[15]

While gaining stature as a service center, Phoenix tried to retain its reputation as a hub of high technology. The competition for "footloose" industries proved to be fierce. Phoenix lost a number of new enterprises to other ambitious cities, but increased effort brought some success. By 1986 metropolitan Phoenix contained 80 percent of Arizona's high-tech jobs; one out of every two manufacturing jobs in the area was high tech. Area plants specialized in aerospace, computers, and electronics. By 1987 valley companies held military contracts worth over $7 billion. As in the past, observers agreed the valley had many of the factors usually cited as magnets for high-technology firms, including "quality of life, a favorable business climate, a young and well-educated work force and high per capita defense spending." Moreover, noted a Valley National Bank economist in 1985, "Through the state's recent commitment to expanding and upgrading engineering and research programs at Arizona's universities, an academic setting appropriate to high technology companies is burgeoning."

Improvements were needed, for the competition was increasing. When Phoenix lost Microelectronics and Computer Technology, a consortium of fifteen high-tech firms, to Austin, Texas, in 1983, local promoters realized they needed to offer more incentives if they expected to land the biggest prizes. "We must pursue a more aggressive strategy," declared Mayor Goddard. The Fantus Company, a nationally recognized economic development consulting firm, added in 1985, "Phoenix can no longer take effortless growth for granted." Continued economic development required "a concerted effort of existing business, governmental agencies, and Phoenix citizens." Moreover, the firm urged Phoenix leaders to try to attract more corporate headquarters; Phoenix's image as a "branch plant town" too often proved detrimental to the local economy and the quality of life. Consultants also urged that more emphasis be placed on both "the spirit of entrepreneurialism" and more venture capital to encourage the growth of more locally based corporate headquarters.[16]

Luxury resorts continued to boost the tourist trade. The Camelback Inn, along with the Arizona Biltmore, the Wigwam, and the Pointe at Squaw Peak, consistently won top ratings in national listings; in 1984, for example, the four valley resorts were among only twelve in the nation to receive the Mobil Corporation's prestigious five-star rating. "It's remarkable," a Mobil executive declared. "Whatever it takes to build and maintain an ultra luxury resort, it's obvious that Phoenix has it. These aren't fly-by-night, willy-nilly operations—they take a tremendous investment of capital and attention." Resort and commercial hotels increased in number, even during times of recession, as the seductive climate worked its magic.

Observers warned that the area would fall behind its competition without more financial support for promotion, and some local officials listened; for example, the Phoenix Economic Development Corporation made the growth of tourism one of its major goals. Moreover, the actual economic value of winter residents became better known in the 1980s. In a report, researchers stated that during the 1985–86 winter season, 190,000 Phoenix metropolitan area "snowbirds" (length of stay one or more months) injected $381 million into the local economy. Critics complained about the strain they put on public services, especially in heavily congested areas, but the economic value of their presence was clear. In the future, as the nation ages, more growth can be expected in this sector. One reporter noted, "Every winter that plunges below normal temperatures brings ten thousand new recruits to Phoenix."[17]

Less growth continued to be the outlook for agriculture in the Valley of the Sun. Relentless pressure on farmers caused them to sell their land to residential and commercial developers who were intent on expanding suburbia. The future of anything in their way seemed in jeopardy; even the existence of Luke Air Force Base, west of Phoenix, appeared to be in danger in the 1980s until it was pointed out that each year the installation generated "over 800 million dollars of spending in the local economy and sustained approximately 4000 jobs." Farmers, however, generated far less of a contribution; thus, they represented a barrier to development. Water use considerations and escalating energy expenditures also hindered farmers, but many of them became more efficient.

Still, inflated land values and the rising costs of farming provided an incentive for many farmers to sell their land to developers. Glendale and Peoria to the northwest of Phoenix, Chandler and Gilbert to the southeast, and other outlying farm towns increasingly were transformed by growth. Many farmers, to the delight of residents tired of inhaling insecticides and pesticides, moved their operations farther out in the desert; some retired as instant millionaires. At the same time, Maricopa County farmers who remained active were better off than their counterparts elsewhere in the country; indeed, in 1985 Maricopa County produced about 40 percent of the state's agricultural income and ranked among the top ten revenue-producing agricultural counties nationwide.[18]

Phoenix's attractions helped the city break records in the 1980s in the number of new subdivisions and shopping centers. Urban sprawl and infill occurred as residential and commercial growth tried to meet the demands of rapid population gains. Construction boomed, and builders from elsewhere flocked to Phoenix and other valley cities to join the action. Every year Phoenix ranked among the top five in the nation in housing starts; from 1983 to 1985, the number of subdivisions in the area jumped from 786 to 1,011. Single-family homes, townhouses, apartments, and other residences went up quickly. Home costs ran the gamut, but the typical price of a 1,500-square-foot home in Phoenix remained at $75,000 in 1986. The same home sold for $150,000 in San Francisco, $130,000 in Los Angeles, and $90,000 in Dallas. In some parts of the Phoenix metropolitan area, however, home prices could match similar places elsewhere; for example, in 1986 a house in the town of Paradise Valley, a very-low-density enclave for the wealthy located between Phoenix and Scottsdale, could easily cost several million dollars.[19]

The sprawling city seemed endless. Commercial and residential dispersal reminded critics of cancer spreading, but most residents loved it. "When the Phoenix bird really began to rise, it took off like a rocket," noted Mayor Hance in 1982. "We exploded in area ... now spreading over almost 350 square miles. Some planners have reacted negatively to what they see as 'urban sprawl.' If that term is translated to 'compatible, low-density neighborhoods,' it explains one reason why we now have more than 800,000 residents." Hance supported downtown redevelopment and infill in Phoenix, but she also recognized the appeal of deconcentration.

Many urban experts called Phoenix a city of the future, an excellent example of the new urban America where vast, low-density urban areas offered many commercial and residential centers rather than one dominating downtown core. It was a place where several downtowns existed, a suburbanized, multicentered metropolis. The "anticity" form in the new urban America emphasized escape from the rigid, tyrannical structure of the older, industrial metropolis. The multicentered metropolis reflected modern America's preference for job mobility, private automobiles, detached houses, convenience shopping, and other aspects of the perceived good life. "It's not that people are abandoning the city; it's that they're inventing a new and better kind of city," observed Gary Driggs, a Phoenix savings and loan executive.

The spreading "anticity" disturbed others, however, and they called for directed growth or even no growth. Some would have celebrated the erection of a large wall around the valley to keep newcomers out, as long as they were in; indeed, the "last settler" solution had its supporters. As Edward Abbey, who wrote an article entitled "The Blob Comes to Arizona," put it, allowing that his presence was itself a contradiction:

I was among the first of the displaced refugees, after the War, to give up the swarming East. And so when Arizona began to grow, as they call it, it was as much my fault as anyone else's. Like the man and his wife who moved from Des Moines into Phoenix last night, each of us wants to be the last to arrive. Each wants to be the final immigrant.

Abbey and other critics warned of the "cancer of growth." In his work, Abbey railed against the "near-sighted greedy crew who seek to completely Californicate what still survives of the Great American Desert." He likened Arizona's rapid growth to "a mad amoeba . . . egged on by the Chamber of Commerce." He suggested that society put "the growth maniacs under medical care." He described Phoenix as "the blob that is eating Arizona."

During the 1980s, residents of north Phoenix, north Scottsdale, Carefree, and Cave Creek, where massive development was occurring, protested what they considered to be the destruction of the desert's character. While builders declared "development in the desert is inevitable," dissenters spray-painted "Save Our Desert" and "Desert Rape" on real-estate and road signs. As Geoffrey Platts, a local poet and environmental activist, put it, "A sign is no thing of beauty but is lifeless and inanimate. Our desert, on the other hand, is a living, vibrant being." Lush golf courses, for example, horrified Platts: "There isn't a positive thing about destroying the desert for the sake of those green nightmares." The sheer numbers of migrants, who moved to the valley because of its lures, changed the nature of the place and lessened its attractions, cried the critics. Those who had resided in the area for years noticed the changes, but the new migrants who were creating them came from such "urban messes" that metropolitan Phoenix still looked good.[20]

As new subdivisions and shopping centers appeared, annexation continued, albeit at a slower pace. Surrounding cities often confronted Phoenix over expansion, and "annexation wars" resulted. The capital city held its own, and remained one of the largest urban centers in the nation in geographical area. By 1987, it contained a total of 389.8 square miles. The city, among the fastest growing in the country, retained its ranking as the ninth largest in the United States, with a population of 915,961 in 1987. The metropolitan

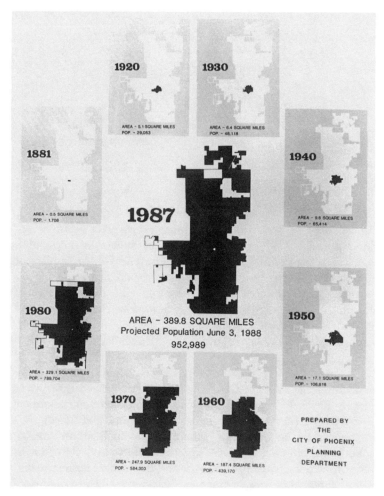

Annexation growth, 1881–1987. City of Phoenix Planning Department.

area, totaling 1,911,612 in 1987, continued to be the growth leader among the top fifty metropolitan areas in the nation; demographers expected it to exceed 3.2 million by the year 2000. Number one in the Southwest, Phoenix represented the great growth of the new urban America.[21]

Despite critics who objected to more downtowns, the Phoenix

Table 9. Ten Leading Cities in the United States, 1980

Ranking	City	Population in 1980
1	New York	7,017,639
2	Chicago	3,005,072
3	Los Angeles	2,968,579
4	Philadelphia	1,688,210
5	Houston	1,598,138
6	Detroit	1,203,369
7	Dallas	904,599
8	San Diego	875,538
9	Phoenix	789,704
10	San Antonio	785,927

SOURCE: U.S. Census of Population, 1980.

Concept 2000 urban village plan, adopted in 1979, was incorporated into a city General Plan, approved in October 1985. Each village, according to the plan, "would become relatively self-sufficient in providing living, working and recreational opportunities for residents," and the city "would encourage the concentration of shopping, employment and services located in the village core." Shopping malls centered a number of the contemplated nine villages, and they were envisioned as magnetic hubs of future development.

The urban village concept sounded good when it was incorporated into the Phoenix General Plan, but it proved difficult to pursue. Recently approved tax increases supported massive new freeway construction that promised to cut into and disrupt old neighborhoods as well as to extend uncontained urban sprawl. In addition, promoters persisted in their efforts to develop downtown into "a metropolitan hub rather than just another urban village core." Moreover, some viewed the ongoing construction of high-rise buildings along Central Avenue from Jackson Street north to Camelback Road as part of a process combining the CBD and the UBD into one "supercore." Such development jeopardized Phoenix's plans for two separate cores for two small villages in the Central Avenue corridor.

"What is occurring in concrete is quite different from what is being planned on paper," asserted the *Gazette* in November 1986. An ASU planning professor noted, "There's a huge gap between the concept of urban villages and getting even a portion of people to live according to the concept." People's lifestyles, stated another observer, appeared to be "metropolitan rather than village in scope and inconsistent with the premises of the urban village concept." Phoenix residents lived, worked, and played in different parts of the valley, and cities like Phoenix might very well be "too complex in the way people behave in urban space to make urban villages a viable concept." In a poll taken in late 1986, less than one-third of Phoenix residents were familiar with the city's urban village concept, and only about one-fourth knew the name of their own village.

Those who promoted the plan failed to appreciate the city as a unit anchored by one dynamic downtown. Unlike many boosters who remained wedded to redevelopment and the idea of downtown Phoenix as the heart of the metropolitan area, urban village advocates preferred a plan that encouraged "independent, and even competitive, development of separate sections of the city." Bemused observers noted that the plan represented a radical departure from land-use policies designed to unify the city.

Disagreement over the future form of Phoenix was not, of course, unusual. Various elements involved in promoting the city and themselves often disagreed over direction. Dismissing the critics, city planners remained convinced that the concept would work; as one of them put it, "It is just a matter of time until the villages take on a character of their own." Phoenix planning director Rick Counts insisted that the village plan had given the city a focus and framework for orderly growth through the year 2000.[22]

Downtown Phoenix was listed as one of the nine urban villages in the General Plan, but the drive to enhance its status as the vital center of the city continued. "Downtown is everybody's neighborhood—an asset for all Phoenix," asserted Mayor Goddard in 1986. It "provides our City's symbol," he insisted. "In the past few years, we have taken unprecedented steps to make downtown Phoenix a place people want to work, want to relax and, most recently, want to live." Not everybody possessed Goddard's "new faith and enthusiasm about downtown Phoenix," but enough area civic and business interests shared Goddard's views for the revitalization of downtown to go forward. Despite inadequate funding and other problems some progress was made.

Critics described downtown Phoenix as "dirty, dismal, depressing, and dangerous." For many years it had stagnated while explosive growth elsewhere in the city attracted interest. A bad image, a growing homeless population, expensive land, difficulty in assembling large project sites from several property owners, and limited automobile access and parking, among other problems, curtailed construction in the CBD, but promoters kept the faith.

As commercial development boomed along the prestigious North Central Avenue and East Camelback Road corridors during the decade, the CBD stepped up its struggle for survival. In 1980, the Central Phoenix Redevelopment Agency (CPRA) issued a visionary plan for the future of the "Valley Center," an area bounded by Seventh Street and Seventh Avenue, McDowell Road and the railroad tracks. It contained the original townsite of Phoenix, which had remained the downtown core. The downtown area continued as a governmental, legal, and financial center as well as a cultural and convention center comprising the Phoenix Civic Plaza complex and two major hotels, the Hyatt Regency and the Phoenix Hilton (formerly the Adams). A large work force occupied the many core office buildings during the day, but little activity occurred at night. Downtown retail and residential facilities failed to materialize during the early 1980s, but they boomed in the outlying areas. Downtown Phoenix did not become a "people place." The fear of crime and the presence of the homeless in the core area dampened the enthusiasm of many potential residents.

Despite their disappointment, Phoenix officials and downtown interests remained hopeful. Finally, despite the lack of public support, the City Council in 1984 authorized the development of a retail marketplace called Square One and of Renaissance Park, the first new downtown residential housing complex in forty years. In addition, the Council boosted the arts downtown when it purchased and promised to renovate the old Palace West Theater (formerly the Orpheum), and when it underwrote Civic Plaza performances of the Phoenix Symphony Orchestra. Moreover, efforts to locate a domed stadium downtown escalated.

"We have only begun to tap the Phoenix sports potential," Goddard remarked in 1985. "We are the largest market in the nation without an NFL team and without major league baseball. I believe professional football and baseball will contribute a great deal to our community and we should continue efforts to attract them." Wanting Phoenix to be a big-league city, the mayor and the City Council formed the Professional Sports Advisory Committee to examine "the need for a major sports facility and make recommendations on location and methods of financing." A domed stadium, it was said, would do wonders for downtown redevelopment. Finally,

The old and the new in downtown Phoenix, 1985. The city plans to preserve the Palace West Theater. Dutton Collection, Arizona Historical Foundation, Hayden Library, Arizona State University.

after public airings of "conflict of interest" charges regarding locations and land speculation that involved several prominent downtown property owners, a downtown site for the facility was chosen in 1986. Funding, however, proved to be a problem, and a year later construction had not started at the site, bounded by Fourth and Thirteenth avenues and Jefferson and Jackson streets.

A few visionaries speculated that a new stadium and a revitalized Union Station nearby might "spur rejuvenation of the warehouse district." One writer offered the following scenario: "The year: 1990. After an exciting baseball game at Phoenix's new domed stadium, you hop on a trolley and head over to Union Station and the warehouse district to stroll through the art galleries, grab a bite to eat, and boogie the night away. You might even live there in a loft apartment." Union Station, placed on the National Register of Historic Places in 1985, represented potential not yet realized.

Among the skyscrapers of downtown Phoenix, pieces of history remained. Weak historic preservation ordinances were passed in the 1980s to protect designated buildings from "development pressures that could replace them with bigger, newer, much plainer structures." The "charming old structures are a precious commodity in this city of glass boxes," a reporter declared in 1987. "Besides providing an aesthetic rush, they remind us that Phoenix does have a history." An attitude of indifference prevailed among many citizens, and a number of significant structures were lost, but there were those who displayed a genuine concern. Charles Driscoll, Phoenix's historic preservation officer, observed:

> There are people coming here from all over the country who expect to see, in a downtown area, some roots, some distinction. Once these unique buildings are gone, they're gone forever and you're stuck with a kind of bland, faceless environment where you have to look around and say, "Where am I? In Los Angeles or Dayton or where?" Because a glass skyscraper looks pretty much like any other glass skyscraper.

In 1986 Renaissance Park opened its condominium units and construction began on Renaissance Square, the first high-rise office building to go up in downtown Phoenix in twelve years. Opposite Renaissance Square, work commenced on an underground garage, to be capped by a refurbished Patriots Square, whose centerpiece would be, declared an official, "a laser beam aimed at the heavens." The City Council approved tax abatements and other incentives for developers to build a hotel, office, and retail complex on what local planners called the Superblock, a key part of the Phoenix Community Alliance's vision for downtown. The Alliance, a group of CBD boosters, called it "a trendy six-square-block downtown Phoenix mall that will upstage all but a handful of the nation's rebuilt city centers." Bounded by Van Buren and Fillmore, Third and Fifth streets, the mixed-use Superblock could cost as much as $500 million. "It is intended," a reporter stated in 1986, "to rival Horton Plaza in San Diego, Faneuil Hall in Boston or Harborplace in Baltimore." Promoters expected the Superblock to be one of the downtown area's saviors; as one of them put it: "What we need more of are the fun things people can do, the retail, the restaurants. We want to make a quality pedestrian environment to welcome visitors to the city."

Thanks to a few completed projects and some impressive plans,

Downtown Phoenix, c. 1987. Photograph by Bob Rink.

downtown Phoenix in early 1987 appeared to be making gains, but it still had a long way to go; indeed, insufficient public and private support, financial and otherwise, remained a major obstacle. Unconvinced critics continued to declare it would never be the exciting "people place" envisioned by its promoters.[23]

In the 1980s, prospects for a better freeway system in Phoenix and the valley appeared brighter than at any time in the past. Better late than never, declared boosters who looked to the future. Construction of new freeways was under way, but by 1985 the nation's ninth largest city still had only forty-two miles of freeways, ranking it last among major urban centers. At that time, no loop existed around the city, nor did any direct route across the valley in any direction. People and cars multiplied, as did plans for freeway construction. Business and civic leaders considered freeways necessary for continued growth. Without them, an observer noted, "new business will not arrive, job opportunities will be lost, delivery costs for goods and services will increase, and residents will wallow in traffic jams and choke on polluted air."

The Arizona Legislature raised gasoline taxes in 1981 and again in 1983 to finance freeway construction in urban areas, but efforts continued to fall short. Some gains occurred, however. The Papago

Inner Loop, for example, was scheduled to open in 1988. That part of Interstate 10 designed to run through central Phoenix, the Inner Loop underwent design changes putting it underground between Third Avenue and Third Street with a deck park on top. And since it was part of the last link of the interstate system in Arizona, the federal government agreed to help fund it.

Unlike the Papago, the 150 miles of metropolitan area freeways that business and civic leaders wanted constructed in the next two decades lacked adequate financial support. Without federal funding, freeway boosters turned to state and local revenue sources. "We're late, but we still have a chance," promoters asserted. "Transportation is the most serious problem facing Phoenix and the Valley of the Sun," noted the *Gazette* in late 1983. Some supporters called for more gas taxes, but critics noted they always fell short. In October 1984 a proposal by the Phoenix Metropolitan Chamber of Commerce to pay for freeways and roads with a valley wide half-cent sales tax attracted interest. "After careful analysis we concluded that the only way to make up for 2 1/2 decades of neglect was the one-half cent sales tax," noted Chamber president Bob Robb. The increase would raise $5.8 billion over the next twenty years. "Valley residents are shouting for a better transportation system. . . . it is time to bring that system into being," the *Gazette* declared.

Although critics fought Proposition 300, most public and private interests supported the proposal; for example, poll takers announced that Maricopa County residents favored it by a three-to-one margin. In the Arizona Legislature, Phoenician Burton Barr and other freeway proponents spearheaded a successful drive to adopt the sales tax proposal and make it part of a transportation package placed before the voters in a special election in October 1985. Led by Residents for Safe and Efficient Transportation, a massive, million-dollar pro-freeway promotion campaign proved effective. "Traffic congestion will get worse (even if the freeways are built), but congestion will get much, much worse without them," warned Mayor Goddard. "The freeway plan attempts to anticipate our growth and do something about it," he added. "Without it, we will end up in an unlivable situation in twenty years."

In metropolitan Phoenix little opposition to the $5.8 billion, twenty-year plan emerged, and as Proposition 300 it easily won approval from Maricopa County voters; in return, they were promised a 233-mile network of freeways, as well as mass-transit

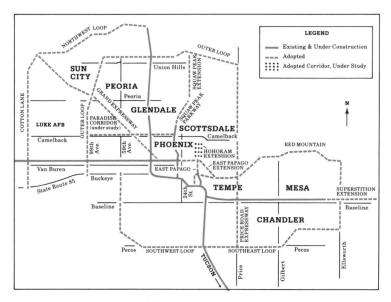

Freeway plans, c. 1985. Maricopa Association of Governments.

improvements, all proposed in the Maricopa County Association of Government's Regional Transportation Plan, adopted several months before the election. More than half the freeways, it said, would be completed within ten years.

Ecstatic over their victory, Proposition 300 proponents noted that the entire metropolitan area contained only seventy miles of freeway, with an additional sixteen miles in varying stages of construction. Statistically, the valley was as bad as Phoenix; it ranked last in the number of freeway miles among the seventy-five largest metropolitan areas in the nation. Freeways already in use included the Black Canyon (I-17), the Maricopa (I-17), the Papago (I-10), the Superstition, and the Hohokam (I-10). The sales tax increase meant 233 more freeway miles, and supporters looked forward to steady progress. Planned freeways included the fifty-nine-mile Outer Loop, an extension of the Superstition Freeway, the East Papago Freeway, the Hohokam Expressway, the Paradise Parkway, improvements to Grand Avenue, and extension of the Phoenix-financed Squaw Peak Parkway and several other loops on the outskirts of the valley.[24] (See map above.)

Once the general plan was approved, sensitive issues such as

freeway sitings, land acquisition, and design features created dissension among officials and neighborhood residents and groups,
causing uncertainties and delays. Neighbor vs. neighbor confron-
tations emerged over such issues. Problems of relocation and "freeway next door" stories multiplied. The removal of thousands of
homes and the displacement of long-time residents caused instability and angry protests; on one occasion an unhappy crowd
mobbed the City Council over a freeway alignment decision. Practically everybody agreed a need existed for more freeways, parkways, and expressways, but no one wanted one running through
his backyard or along the street out front.

While problems accompanied progress in the game of "freeway
catch-up," there was money to be made. All the transportation
projects greatly benefited contractors and provided thousands of
jobs. Land speculators and developers made millions in residential
and commercial real estate along freeway extensions, new freeways, and proposed freeway routes. Freeway properties rose in
price and popularity; by January 1987, for example, at least seventeen new hotels were being planned or built along completed parts
of the freeway system.[25]

Freeways, parkways, and expressways were important, but
other transportation arteries needed attention. One frustrated
motorist, complaining about the traffic in his neighborhood, noted,
"Not many supermarkets are located on freeways." It could be a
problem getting around in heavy traffic on arterial streets that
needed to be widened and improved, as countless Phoenicians
attested. Funds from voter-approved bonds, state gasoline taxes,
and the Arizona State Lottery helped Phoenix build and repair
streets throughout the period, and more left-turn signals and other
upgrades helped keep auto accident figures down, but it proved
difficult to keep ahead of the population explosion. Public transportation also needed attention, and some gains in that critical
area occurred. The 1985 transportation plan approved by voters
not only added to the freeway network but also took an important
step toward a workable transit system. It called for a Regional
Public Transportation Authority to use some of the $5.8 billion in
sales tax over the next twenty years for mass transit planning and
development.

Critics remained unconvinced that mass transit would go far
in helping to solve the valley's transportation problems. In 1987,
the use of public transportation in Phoenix was still dismally low.

Phoenix ranked at the bottom of a list of twenty peer cities in bus ridership. Bus travel remained a subsidized service, offering a means of transportation to poor and minority riders. As a Phoenix City Council member stated, bus riders are a "relatively small group and not a relatively influential group." The bus system "has always been for someone else to use."

Residents complained about polluted air as well as traffic congestion, but pollution, too, failed to get them out of their automobiles. Experts made it clear that another benefit of mass transit was the reduction of polluting carbon monoxide. "If we get people to ride the buses, we're going to reduce our pollution," noted a local planner. Throughout the 1980s, the Arizona capital developed a reputation for bad air; in February 1987 critics were still declaring that Phoenix had "the worst carbon monoxide pollution of any city in the nation." State inaction caused Maricopa County to miss several federal air-quality deadlines for reduction of carbon monoxide and ozone, two traffic-related pollutants. Found in violation of the 1970 Clean Air Act, metropolitan Phoenix faced heavy Environmental Protection Agency (EPA) penalties, including the loss of millions of dollars in federal highway funds. State officials promised to strengthen Maricopa County's motor vehicle emission-control system, but delays bothered clean air advocates. Critics also pushed for mass transit and other measures to reduce auto use, and they asserted that particulate (dust) standards were being violated wherever development encroached upon the desert.

The Arizona Legislature finally passed a tougher vehicle emissions-control bill in April 1986, but it did not solve the problems. Local critics and EPA officials continued to call for more stringent measures to reduce the amount of automobile travel and dirty, unhealthy air in metropolitan Phoenix. "We need stronger measures," insisted public interest lawyer David Baron. "There is a crying need for the state and Phoenix-area governments to take this problem seriously. It's a matter of public health, not just a matter of seeing South Mountain." He also reminded promoters of the growing image problem: "If people see Phoenix as becoming another Los Angeles, it may very well defeat the kinds of economic growth people are hoping for." In June 1987, legislators strengthened and broadened the auto-emissions system, and noted the need for studies and testing of other anti-pollution strategies, such as alternative fuels, winter daylight-saving time, and light rail transportation.[26]

Sky Harbor International Airport remained a leader in the Phoenix transportation picture, despite complaints of noise pollution from nearby Tempe. Expansion, largely financed by revenue bonds and federal grants, increasingly allowed it to meet the needs of record-breaking air traffic in the area, and it retained its ranking as one of the busiest airports in the nation. One economist estimated that Sky Harbor contributed $4.5 billion to the economy in 1983.

Airport expansion continued to tear up Hispanic barrios and displaced thousands of people, but "progress" advocates worried little about them. Most of those displaced relocated to west side neighborhoods. Many were relieved to get away from the noise, jet-exhaust pollution, and other unwelcome hazards, but social problems continued to plague people involved in such moves. Often experiencing a forced removal from family members, friends, churches, and schools, they suffered as others suffered when tall buildings, new freeways, and/or other intrusions arrived in residential neighborhoods.

A few critics called for a regional airport away from the heart of the city, but most city officials and business leaders thought Sky Harbor's central location a major asset. As Mayor Goddard put it, "I don't think a regional airport makes a lot of sense when we've got a very, very good bird in the hand that's one of the most popular destination airports in the country." Talk of a regional airport persisted among many valley leaders, however; some suggested a location between Phoenix and Tucson. At the end of 1986, the Valley of the Sun contained fifteen civilian and three military airports, and an advisory committee recommended that four of them be expanded and that two new airports be added. They all had a long way to go, of course, to post the record fourteen million passengers that passed through Sky Harbor in 1986. From one million in 1962 to fourteen million in 1986 to a forecast twenty-eight million in 2000—such figures, not unusual in the rapidly growing Valley of the Sun, impressed observers.[27]

The debate over water quantity and quality in the Valley of the Sun persisted in the 1980s. Many observers continued to declare that no water shortage existed, only an allocation problem. The culprit, they declared, was agriculture. In 1985, farmers still used 89 percent of Arizona's water, yet accounted for only 2 percent of its personal income, while the cities used 7 percent of the water and produced 95 percent of the income. By reducing the amount of water consumed by agriculture, most, if not all, of the groundwater depletion would be eliminated while the population continued to expand.

The 1980 Arizona Groundwater Management Act had come into being to resolve the groundwater depletion problem, and Central Arizona Project water from the Colorado River was expected to allow replenishment of the groundwater by providing farmers with another source. Critics viewed the CAP as another "massive agribusiness handout," and they placed valley farmers among the fattest of "Arizona's Welfare Queens." The state did not need more water projects, they pleaded; it needed less agriculture. Retiring Arizona farmland would be far less costly for taxpayers and water users, most of whom were urban dwellers, than huge water projects designed to subsidize agricultural interests. Urban Arizonans, it was said, were paying for water projects that helped farmers grow cotton and other market-glutted crops. As one critic put it in March 1987, "Agriculture is a dead industry in Arizona, kept alive only by government subsidies paid to grow surplus, water-intensive crops, such as cotton. Eliminate the subsidies, and Arizona could begin to solve her water problems." Observers estimated that cotton growers in Arizona received more than $100 million in subsidies in 1986; one stated, "A simple shift from cotton farming to urban use could provide enough water in Phoenix to handle a population the size of New York's." [28]

Other observers viewed the situation differently. Since the Arizona Groundwater Management Act cuts into pumping to correct groundwater overdrafts through requiring that by 2025 there be a balance in metropolitan Phoenix between well production and natural recharge, promoters insisted that the CAP and other water projects are necessary. The Phoenix area will be permitted to pump out only as much groundwater as can be replaced by either nature or man-made mechanisms; the CAP and other water projects should, it is said by supporters, prevent shortages. Moreover, advocates noted that future development of metropolitan land beyond the Salt River Project service area would intensify the need for additional supplies of water and water-storage systems. And those who recalled the dry times of earlier years reminded others that droughts as well as floods were always possible. As former Phoenix mayor and Arizona governor Jack Williams declared in February 1987, criticizing environmentalists and others who opposed new dams and other water projects: "Somewhere along the line, there is going to be another drought, and this drought will bring meetings to call for projects that are defeated by the zealots."

Phoenix and Arizona officials approved of the CAP and the water projects; indeed, the feeling that there can never be enough water in reserve in the desert remained compelling, and thus they encouraged expansion as well as increased efficiency in city and state water systems. For example, the reuse of treated wastewater effluent offered Phoenix substantial opportunities for more fully utilizing existing water resources. Phoenix and other valley cities also purchased "water farms" in the 1980s, acquiring agricultural lands throughout the state for their water rights in order to help ensure a future supply.[29]

In the 1980s, the push for voluntary water conservation intensified. Per capita consumption dropped as public education programs expanded and the price of water increased. Cynics allowed that pricing probably was the key, especially in the future, but politics precluded radical changes in that direction.

The quality as well as the quantity of water available interested valley residents. As in the case of polluted air, many Phoenix promoters thought that critics exaggerated the problem of polluted water, but concerned individuals and groups let it be known that they considered it serious enough to warrant corrective action. Wells polluted with TCE and other chemicals threatened the water supply of parts of the metropolitan area. In 1980, a Phoenix landfill had the distinction of numbering among the country's 115 worst hazardous waste dumps, and in 1982 numerous well closings brought added attention to the issue of toxicity. As in so many other areas, explosive growth was partly responsible; "more people create a greater concentration of pollutants," stated one observer. Toxic wastes had been polluting the groundwater for decades. "Legally and illegally," a reporter noted, "they've been dumped in riverbeds, landfills, wells, and the desert—eventually seeping into the groundwater." Critics became more aware of the problem in the 1980s, and some progress was made.

The sites contained high levels of toxic industrial solvents, pesticides, nitrates, and other chemicals. Many wells located near high-tech plants have been closed because of the presence of the toxic industrial solvent TCE. For example, Motorola for years used TCE in manufacturing its electronics components; in recent years it has spent millions of dollars investigating the extent of TCE pollution around its facilities. The cleanup of the TCE, a reporter

wrote in August 1984, "which has not yet begun, will take several
years and cost millions more dollars." At that time, neither the
state nor the city had made a firm commitment to support adequate hazardous-waste controls. A state official predicted it would
"take time to learn and interpret hazardous-waste regulations, to
build enforcement programs and to educate industries." Some accused legislators of being too "reasonable" and too influenced by
the state's industrial, farming, and mining lobbies. Moreover, as
in the case of air pollution, the EPA showed concern and set guide-
lines, but local environmental activists complained about the slow-
ness of federal and local authorities to enforce EPA standards.[30]

While air and water pollution threatened the good life in Phoenix, hordes of newcomers joined in the area's cultural and social
life. Religion remained a prominent factor in valley life, according
to surveys. Church attendance was high, and many valley residents participated in church-related cultural and social activities.
Much of the activity occurred in the suburbs. In Phoenix, both the
population and the churches continued to move away from the city
core. "Many great old churches are moving to greener pastures in
the suburbs," lamented the Rev. Lawrence Hinshaw of the Central
United Methodist Church in 1984. Hinshaw's church, engulfed by
the expanding inner city, decided to stay; as the clergyman put it,
"We believe the church needs a great voice in the central city."

At the same time, according to one observer, "In an area like
Phoenix, with a luxuriant climate and rootless people, leisure becomes an important part of a person's lifestyle. What this means is
that religion may not be as influential as in a more settled community." All told, however, churches had a difficult time keeping up
with growth. Parking lots jammed with cars and churches crowded
with people reflected the massive growth of Phoenix. As one min-
ister put it, "We don't really notice those folks who move out here
and don't start going to church. Growth is incredible out here. You
don't have to beat the bushes to find people because the church
just grows with the area." Membership in a congregation filled a
variety of spiritual and secular needs; it also denoted a reverence
for tradition and a wish to perpetuate the familiar in an unfamiliar
society.[31]

Despite austerity budgets, the public schools and the community colleges remained crowded, with record enrollments. In the
fall of 1986, 72,250 students registered at nine valley campuses;
Mesa Community College led the way with 18,881, but courses

at most of the schools had to be dropped for lack of operating funds. The Maricopa County community college system, the third largest in the nation, sent many students on to Arizona State University. While achieving a national reputation as an athletic power and a party school, ASU also managed to improve its academic reputation during the 1980s. Out of several scandals came change. Changes in the administration of the institution early in the decade brought an emphasis on academic excellence as well as athletic prestige. Although most of the publicity centered on the development of the engineering, business, and public administration programs, a general upgrading of the university occurred. It achieved substantial progress toward meeting the charge of the Board of Regents to "continue development as a major research university, with special emphasis on programs needed in the state's major urban area and . . . to be competitive with the best public universities in the nation."

To better meet the higher education needs of the valley's growing population, in 1984 the university dedicated a 300-acre west side branch campus; ASU West planners expected it to accommodate several thousand students by the end of the decade. For many years, ASU held classes throughout the valley, including downtown Phoenix.

The student body passed the forty thousand mark in the 1980s, but funding to meet the demands of both growth and quality often fell short. Continued public and private support was deemed essential if ASU hoped to achieve excellence, but recent budget cuts had threatened to retard progress. Many civic and business leaders, as well as educators, expressed alarm over the lack of adequate funding for education, especially higher education. Mayor Goddard denounced it, and Phoenix 40 members agreed in March 1987 that "this is not the time to turn back or tread water." As one member declared, the last message the state needs to present to the nation's business community is that "Arizona is losing its interest in higher education."[32]

ASU remained a major part of Arizona's cultural network. Cultural programs and projects emanating from the school enhanced the local and regional scene; Grady Gammage Center for the Performing Arts remained a leading dispenser. At the same time, Symphony Hall, part of the Phoenix Civic Plaza complex downtown, the Scottsdale Center for the Arts, and several other facilities offered quality programs. In general, critics claimed that Phoenix cultural life during the 1980s was undergoing a transition. Certainly it lagged behind the demographic and economic growth of the area. "Phoenix has to realize that it goofed," a critic declared in 1984. "In its tremendous drive to make a metropolis, it left the arts out. Now it has to play catch-up."

COMPAS (Combined Metropolitan Phoenix Arts and Sciences) and other local booster organizations helped, but the lack of major sources of private money presented a problem. Generous patrons the caliber of Robert and Katherine "Kax" Herberger, who donated millions to the planned Herberger Theatre Center and other cultural institutions, were rare. As a supporter of the Phoenix Symphony Orchestra put it in 1986, "In the East there is plenty of 'old money,' which has resulted in sizable endowments for such symphonies as the Philadelphia Orchestra and the New York Philharmonic." Also, in Phoenix, "We have people who still give money to the Cleveland Symphony but who don't give any to the Phoenix Symphony." Meager governmental and corporate support for the arts during the 1980s did not make progress any easier; in 1983, for example, Arizona ranked forty-third among the fifty states in its per capita spending for the arts, and in corporate giving, lamented an observer, "Phoenix is just way behind."

Under Terry Goddard, the city became more involved. In 1983 the Phoenix Symphony, trying to achieve major status as a professional orchestra, ran into financial problems. An austerity program kept the orchestra going until it reached a crisis state in 1984. In that year, Mayor Goddard and the City Council issued an emergency grant of $650,000 to allow the orchestra to survive. Conductor Theo Alcantara and the professional musicians under his direction made great artistic strides during the decade, but financial problems continued to plague them. Whether or not the Phoenix Symphony would continue as "the jewel in the Valley's cultural crown" remained to be seen in early 1987. A lack of community support persisted, but a public education program was underway. David R. Johns, Symphony Association president in 1986, noting that the orchestra and other cultural amenities "are prime factors in attracting industry and residents to the Valley," called for more community support. "The symphony is one of the key cultural indicators in the city and the state," he said. "It is also a way of promoting our community, and making people aware that there is more in Phoenix than just cactus."

In 1985, Mayor Goddard and the City Council appointed a

Phoenix Arts Commission to administer modest grants (financed partly with Arizona State Lottery money) to local cultural organizations, and in 1986 a "percent-for-arts" city ordinance was approved; it set aside as much as 1 percent of the construction costs of municipal buildings to be used for art projects for those facilities. Goddard, impressed with the success of similar ordinances in Seattle, Portland, and other cities, proved to be a strong leader in promoting the cultural development of Phoenix and the valley.

Goddard and his supporters called for more taxes to nurture and improve Phoenix's quality of life. "A great city does not come free," he declared. "I believe Phoenix has reached a size and stage in its development where we cannot afford not to think beyond tradition, beyond streets, sewers, traffic lights and police protection." In January 1987, Arizona received a $1.5 million grant from the New York-based National Arts Stabilization Fund (NASF), an organization financed by the Ford, Mellon, and Rockefeller foundations. The Phoenix-based Flinn Foundation, Arizona's largest grantmaking organization, had worked for more than two years to convince NASF to select the state as a project area. The Flinn Foundation and the new Arizona Arts Stabilization Committee each pledged another $1.5 million, making $4.5 million available in the future for the state's art economy. The plan is designed to strengthen the financial position and managerial skills of Arizona's major performing and visual arts organizations. Eligible Phoenix groups should benefit in the future; as one participant exclaimed, "The impact of this unheard-of infusion of funds into Arizona's arts organizations is so exciting it sends chills up my spine!"[33]

Concerned citizens supported movements to "save the parks" and "save the preserve." Encanto Park, for example, underwent considerable improvement during the 1980s, and the Phoenix Zoo and the Desert Botanical Garden in Papago Park expanded. The battle to keep developers away from the Phoenix Mountain Preserve also persisted. "Phoenix does indeed have a soul, an identity," declared a supporter of the preserve, and those who agreed insisted that the wilderness park be left undeveloped. Acquisition deals to complete the preserve, and the issue of open or limited access to it, remained controversial. Trades were increasingly viewed with suspicion until December 1986, when several support groups, led by the Mountain Preserve Trust, promoted Proposition 100, a citizens' initiative that closed a loophole in previous policy that allowed the City Council to trade or lease mountain land until January 1989;

the new amendment prohibited the Council from trading or leasing any land in the preserve unless voters approved it.

No organized opposition emerged, and the vote was three-to-one in favor of the proposition, a clear reflection of how residents felt about their "urban wilderness." The future of the 23,500-acre Phoenix Mountain Preserve, which included South Mountain as well as the Phoenix Mountains on the north side of the city, appeared to be safe from developers for the time being, but wary preservationists vowed to remain vigilant in protecting their beloved mountain land from possible harmful incursion.[34]

With a demographic rate of growth several times the national average, and minimal levels of human services to meet the problems of those who failed to succeed, the Valley of the Sun showed some alarming trends throughout the decade. Critics declared a policy of "benign neglect and indifference" in the state took its toll in human terms. In fact, in a national study measuring aid to the poor, Phoenix was found to be one of the worst places to live in the nation. It continued as a national leader in divorce, suicide, substance abuse, and mental illness, but relief for the victims of rampant growth and limited social services fell short. Those without roots or other sources of support in the Phoenix area often experienced a difficult time adjusting to their new environment, and many of them joined the homeless in the streets and shelters of Phoenix. The homeless in the city reached several thousand during the decade.

Unwanted and largely ignored in Phoenix, the homeless constructed makeshift camps downtown and along the Salt River. When the police broke up the camps in 1983, advocates of the homeless loudly disapproved and called for more constructive action. The situation focused national attention on the homeless problem in Phoenix and embarrassed local leaders. It also prompted the establishment in 1984 of Central Arizona Shelter Services (CASS), a public-private partnership organized to provide facilities and services for the growing number of homeless in the city. Mayor Goddard and the City Council cooperated with other government entities and private interests in finding a more humane response to the need.[35]

During the 1980s minority percentages of the total population changed little. In 1986, the figures were 17 percent Hispanic; 5 percent black; 1 percent Indian. At the same time, more members of minority groups, many of them professional and business people, moved into the middle class. The positive effects of civil rights awareness and of economic growth and prosperity made it easier for individual members to benefit from new economic and political opportunities, but progress for minority groups within the larger Phoenix population remained slow.

Educational and employment gains for individuals were noted during the decade, and structural changes in the city's political system allowed for more minority group representation. Since the change to the district system in 1983, south Phoenix and much of west Phoenix had elected minority group members to the City Council. A Hispanic, Mary Rose Wilcox, represented District 7, where the majority of the city's Hispanic population lived, and Calvin Goode represented District 8, where the majority of the city's blacks resided. Hispanic and black members of the Arizona Legislature from south and west Phoenix, including Alfredo Gutierrez and Art Hamilton, continued to make their presence felt in that body.

The southern section of the city continued to contain a wide range of socioeconomic neighborhoods. South of the Salt River, the population in 1986 was approximately one-third white, one-third black, and one-third Hispanic. The most racially balanced part of the city, the area south of the river contained a variety of housing ranging from shacks to mansions. As the 1980s progressed, developers as well as residents began thinking about its future. One resident called it "a gemstone in the rough." A builder called it the city's "last frontier," a section still retaining large tracts of developable land. Many residents fought hard during the decade to keep what they considered to be unwanted industrial, commercial, and residential development out of the area.

At the same time, poorer residents often looked to the jobs such development could provide for minority group members. The low-density area provided a pleasant, upscale, rural lifestyle for those who could afford it, but for those who resided in substandard housing in the poorer neighborhoods, general development meant economic opportunities and a more prosperous future for the area. As one black leader asserted, it was time to "move south Phoenix forward" and "take advantage of the growth and opportunity that the rest of the city enjoys." For too long, the section had been Phoenix's "dumping ground" for sewer plants, major landfills, and other undesirable projects. The conflict over the future of south Phoenix below the Salt River promised to persist; observers hoped that the residents, developers, and politicians involved would eventually work out a plan beneficial to all concerned.[36]

South Phoenix, both south and north of the Salt River, and parts of central Phoenix contained some neighborhoods with conditions as bad as any in the country. For example, the predominantly minority low-income neighborhoods in the area bounded by McDowell Road, Broadway Road, Thirty-fifth Avenue, and Forty-eighth Street were plagued with the problems of substandard housing, decaying schools, poverty, and unemployment. Observers referred to them as "low-density slums." They helped support the view of critics that Phoenix increasingly "resembled many other cities with a minority-populated, impoverished core surrounded by affluent white enclaves." Especially burdened were neighborhoods such as the barrio bordered by Roosevelt and Van Buren, Seventh and Sixteenth streets. In that area, noted reporter Andy Zipser in 1983:

> "For Rent" signs are everywhere, some posted on homes that are merely tired and untidy, others that verge on collapse. A few of the houses are only memories, marked by gravestone pilings or a rectangle of foundation, broken glass glittering like sequins on the broken ground. The dirt alleys that bisect each block turn to mud at just a kiss of rain. Graffiti is omnipresent, the distinctive, diamond-shaped letters sprayed on trash-containers, telephone poles, stop signs, buildings that have been abandoned and buildings that are still occupied.[37]

During the decade, members of minority groups who could afford it dispersed throughout the city, but not without difficulty. Hispanics found it easier than blacks to relocate in predominantly Anglo neighborhoods; for blacks, it often remained frustrating. Some progress was made, but never enough. "Racism is not as overt, not as blatant as it was," Phoenix television reporter Evelyn Thompson noted in 1982. "When I first came here in 1971, a real estate agent said to me, 'Blacks don't live north of Thomas Road. I'm not going to show you any apartments in that area because nobody will rent to you.'" Unfortunately, the practice of steering blacks to "appropriate" neighborhoods persisted throughout the 1980s. In 1987, according to a study by the Equal Opportunity Department of the city of Phoenix, housing discrimination remained a problem and continued to encourage segregated living patterns.

Blacks and other minority group members shared some of the

prosperity of growth in booming Phoenix, especially those individuals who took advantage of their opportunities and made gains in education, employment, and housing, but expectations often fell short. As one observer pointed out, "Educational opportunities for blacks in the Valley have improved considerably, but they still are not proportionately represented in the professional, scientific and technological areas of advanced studies."

Black organizations helped center attention on the need for change. Black leader Clovis Campbell stated, "Job discrimination is not as open as it used to be in the Phoenix area, but it is still here." The change was brought about, he declared, not because of "any substantial change in the basic belief of white businessmen, but because of the efforts of such affirmative-action groups as the NAACP." Cutbacks in federal and local financial aid hurt, however. "A lot of programs that were begun during the Great Society have been cut back," stated Junius Bowman, head of the Phoenix Urban League, in 1985. "There used to be a great and conscious promotion of economic development for blacks. Some of that is happening but not with such intensity as before." [38]

Chicanos por la Causa (CPLC) and other organizations continued to serve the Hispanic community during the 1980s. CPLC and its affiliates remained partly self-sustaining, but also depended upon federal grants and private grants and donations. "The Reagan administration's cutbacks have drastically affected us, which means we've had to turn more and more to foundations and corporations for help," declared Peter Garcia, new director of CPLC, in 1984.

CPLC continued to offer the Hispanic community a wide range of basic economic and social programs and projects, as well as to serve as a training school for Hispanic community leaders. "Some very outstanding people have come out of CPLC," Frank Hidalgo, a director of community relations at ASU, noted in 1984. As Phoenix developer Tom Espinosa, former executive director of CPLC, put it, "We need to develop a cadre of leadership that feeds into the community—a cadre composed of successful Chicano individuals who will donate their time and effort back into CPLC and the Hispanic culture." Espinosa served as a role model for many young Hispanics. His Espinosa Development Corporation demonstrated that success was possible for the ambitious and talented Chicano. "Chicanos from south Phoenix can be successful," he said. In 1985, Espinosa became the only Hispanic member of the Phoenix 40. [39]

The American Indian population in the Valley of the Sun numbered about twenty thousand in 1986, with over half of them living in Phoenix. Indians in the city occupied various rungs on the economic ladder. Upward mobility proved difficult, however, especially in the private sector, and many of them needed help. The Phoenix Indian Center, Southwest Indian Development, Inc., and other organizations remained active during the decade, but financial cutbacks made it more difficult to supply needed services. The city of Phoenix tried to respond with what resources it could muster. By the 1980s, LEAP had become the city's Human Resources Department, and despite inadequate resources, that agency and its community advisory committees continued to respond to the problems of low-income groups, including poor urban Indians.

With a sizable number of Indians in the city and more arriving each year from the reservations of Arizona and elsewhere in the Southwest, public and private social agencies proved essential. One young Indian woman called the Phoenix Indian Center "a lifesaver." At the Center, "they teach you how to make it in the world outside the reservation. Things like how to act and dress for an interview, alcohol abuse programs and how to get around in the city. Many Indians fail because they don't know how to adjust to their new surroundings." Through the federally funded job training programs administered by the Center, Indians found work.

In 1985, the Center serviced nearly nine hundred people who were making the move from the Indian reservations to the metropolitan Phoenix area. "We try to make the transition of the reservation Indian into the urban setting an easier one," noted Nadine Telayumptewa, an education specialist at the Center. Besides offering such services as employment and training programs, individual and family counseling, child and elderly welfare projects, and legal aid, the Center tried to foster a sense of ethnic identity and cultural awareness among urban Indians; for example, each year it helped promote Native American Recognition Week.

Off-reservation Indians residing in urban centers such as Phoenix continued to qualify for fewer programs and projects than reservation Indians. The Phoenix Indian Medical Center, according to critics, paid more attention to the health needs of nearby Salt River Indian Reservation residents than it did to Phoenix Indians in need of health care. In March 1986, for example, two hundred Phoenix Indians protested and forced reconsideration of service cuts to urban Indians at the medical center. Federal cuts during the decade threatened the future of the Phoenix Indian School. The 515-student boarding school already suffered from an undesirable reputation resulting from attacks on the poor quality of its academic programs and the abusive nature of its social atmosphere. The institution, one critic noted in 1985, served as a "dumping ground for large numbers of problem students." With declining enrollment, more schools being built on the reservations, and federal funds diminishing, the need for the Phoenix school was increasingly questioned.

In 1986, when the federal government decided to close the school, the city of Phoenix insisted it should become a large public park. "Phoenix is in need of more Encantos," cried an observer. "If this property falls into private hands, the city of Phoenix will lose an opportunity that will never come again." Private interests, of course, insisted they should get an opportunity to develop the land. The Interior Department wanted to give it to a Florida corporation in exchange for swampland that the department could add to Florida's Everglades. The Indians "must get their share," asserted Donald Antone, president of the Inter-Tribal Council of Arizona. The debate seemed endless; finally, in March 1987, Arizona's senior representative in Washington, Morris Udall, introduced legislation that would delay the planned closure of Phoenix Indian School and require the Interior Department to take into careful account the interests of all concerned in any sale of the campus.[40]

From 1980 to 1985, greater Phoenix grew faster than any other metropolitan area of its size in the nation. During that period, the population increased by nearly 22 percent (328,904 new residents). "It's not going to stop," declared a local observer in July 1986, "we're still building all over the place. There's still room for more growth." And most of the growth in recent years had occurred in the major suburban population centers; indeed, it became clear by 1985 that, for the first time, Phoenix had less than half the county's population. Evolving from towns to cities since World War II, the suburban centers continued to retain a sense of identity, but each of them expanded in similar ways. Under the push of more people, automobiles, housing tracts, shopping centers, office buildings, and industrial parks, the urbanization of the sprawling metropolitan area persisted, as the figures from the Maricopa County 1985 census clearly indicate.[41]

Growth remained critical to the economy of the expanding cities

Table 10. Population of Phoenix and Neighboring
Communities, 1980 and 1985

City	1980	1985
Phoenix	789,704	881,640
Mesa	152,453	239,587
Tempe	106,920	132,942
Glendale	97,172	122,392
Scottsdale	88,622	108,447
Chandler	29,673	63,817
Peoria	12,307	27,598
Gilbert	5,717	12,102
Paradise Valley	11,085	11,510
Avondale	8,168	9,704
Guadalupe	4,506	4,609
Goodyear	2,747	4,598
Tolleson	4,433	4,438
Surprise	3,723	4,020
Wickenburg	3,535	3,925
Buckeye	3,434	3,779
El Mirage	4,307	3,908
Youngtown	2,254	2,287
Gila Bend	1,585	1,999
Unincorporated	176,917	193,136
Maricopa County	1,509,262	1,837,956

SOURCE: U.S. Census of Population, 1980–85.

but, as in Phoenix, increasing attention turned to "quality of life"
issues. In early 1987, a *Republic* poll showed that 72 percent of
Maricopa County residents thought the valley was growing too
quickly. "It's not at all like it was 10 years ago," noted a Mesa developer. "People are a lot more sensitive to environmental issues."
In 1986 Peggy Morgan and other neighborhood activists in Mesa
waged a successful campaign for design review in that city similar
to that employed in Tempe, Chandler, and other valley cities to help
promote attractive and quality construction. The vote against "ugly
development" was three-to-one. Mesa Planning Director Wayne
Balmer stated that the citizens' demand for design review was a result of the city's rapid growth and a change in residents' attitudes
toward development. "It took us from 1878 to 1975 to get our first
100,000 people, and only nine years to get our second 100,000." In
the rush to accommodate the need for new housing, the City Council "at times has approved projects that were sparsely landscaped
and of low-quality construction. Many residents are fed up with
such projects."

Most of the time, however, Mesa boosters promoted industrial, commercial, and residential growth with a passion. Companies like Motorola, Talley Industries, and McDonnell-Douglas operated in Mesa, the massive Fiesta Mall attracted customers from throughout the area, and sprawling new subdivisions radiated from the Superstition Freeway as it passed out of Tempe through the city. New high-rise office buildings, hotels, and "retirement havens" laced the landscape of Arizona's third largest city. Schools and churches multiplied. Mesa bought "water farms," built community centers, and pursued downtown redevelopment. Newcomers attended Mesa Symphony Orchestra performances, and Mesa Community College enrolled nearly twenty thousand students.

At the same time, according to critics, Mesa suffered from peculiar image problems. In February 1985, the Chicago-based Fantus Company submitted a report on Mesa's economic development potential. The city's "'nice place to raise a family' reputation translates into conservative and boring to some," the report declared. And "coupled with the strong presence of Mormons in the community, Mesa is perceived as offering very little to the young, fast-paced engineer or electronics executive." Perplexed local leaders responded. "We've always prided ourselves in our schools, our parks, and our big, wide streets," a Mesa Chamber of Commerce official asserted. "We never thought that a young, upwardly mobile electronics executive might equate all these values as being boring."

When developers suggested "jazzing up" downtown Mesa to make it more of a "people place," reactions varied. One City Council member opined: "I am very much in favor of Mesa being a home-and-family kind of place." Another City Council member noted: "We want to maintain the family atmosphere, but we also don't want to be known as the yawn capital of central Arizona. I get annoyed when people say we roll up the sidewalks at 10 p.m., but it's true. And Mesa's getting large enough so people should not have to go into Phoenix or Scottsdale anymore." Most residents appreciated Mesa and felt no need to change its image. "Make Mesa the city of traditional values," urged promoters.[42]

In the 1980s, Tempe acquired a reputation as a city where planning was taken seriously. Quality development made it one of the most desirable places to live in the valley. Builders had to meet high construction standards, and it showed. "Even some convenience markets in south Tempe look like they've been 'designed,'"

Arizona State University in Tempe, 1965. The Herb and Dorothy Mc-Laughlin Photographic Collection.

a reporter observed in 1986. "Tempe's small signs and billboards stand in sharp contrast to their hideous counterparts in Mesa." At times high standards proved to be costly; Tempe lost Fiesta Mall to Mesa because of developer discontent. "Doing business in Tempe was too difficult," stated a builder representative. "That was one of the factors that tipped things in Mesa's favor."

Tempe also led east valley cities in downtown redevelopment. Although Superstition Freeway access encouraged widespread development in Tempe, Old Town, located next to Arizona State University, evolved into an attractive "people place" in the 1980s. Locked in on all sides, Tempe's general growth became more intense, but the city's general plan underwent updating to ensure quality. While most other valley cities expanded into the desert, Tempe concentrated on infill. ASU remained the principal industry in Tempe, and it helped the city attract several new high-tech companies. People in search of a center of higher education and cultural opportunities sought residence in Tempe. At the same time, problems existed in Arizona's fourth largest city; for example, Tempe carried on a decade-long battle with Phoenix over noise emanating from busy, nearby Sky Harbor International Airport.[43]

While Tempe was filling up, Chandler's cotton fields and citrus trees were giving way to electronics plants and planned communities. Motorola, Intel, Honeywell, General Instruments, and other high-tech companies located in the city and helped make it another valley boom town of the 1980s. Williams Air Force Base continued to boost the economy of both Mesa and Chandler, and plans to renovate the San Marcos Hotel in Chandler assured a future for that famous landmark as a focal point. As in other valley cities, Chandler leaders and citizens supported Proposition 300 to provide more freeways. They talked of "six-lane street patterns going in where cows once lined up on their way back to milking barns." A Chandler official, talking about the proposed freeway system that promised to connect Interstate 10 to Power Road east of Chandler, proclaimed: "I can see those cars just flying down that Southwest loop."

"Land that sold for $20,000 an acre in 1980 can now command between $70,000 and $90,000," a reporter declared in 1987. The rural lifestyle and wide open spaces that had characterized Chandler fast disappeared in the 1980s as its population doubled. For years people had been reluctant to say they lived in Chandler, for in the valley it was synonymous with "Hicksville," but it was rapidly changing. The familiar problems of growth appeared in Chandler, but promoters assured newcomers that all was well. For example, it was said that the water supply was more than adequate to meet the city's growth. As a Chandler Chamber of Commerce executive put it, "most people don't know that a square mile of new housing development uses only 25 percent of the water required to grow a square mile of cotton." As "more of Chandler's land is taken out of agricultural production, more water is freed up." Moreover, he stated that Chandler did not take its seeming abundance of water for granted; it was proud of its water conservation program and its modern wastewater treatment plant. Chandler still lagged behind in restaurants, movie theaters, and other amenities, however, and according to one observer in 1986, much of the city resembled "a war zone" with "hundreds of half-built houses surrounding roads that are being torn up and widened."

Growth from Mesa and Chandler began spilling over into Gilbert in the 1980s. Many predicted Gilbert would be a valley boom town of the 1990s. Those who had moved to the town to escape the

McDowell and Scottsdale roads in 1958 (top) *and 1970* (bottom). *The Herb and Dorothy McLaughlin Photographic Collection.*

"cancer of growth" prepared to defend their rural way of life. With freeway access and local promoters to contend with, the "horse and garden set" left their mini-ranches and mini-farms to do battle against builders intent on developing the area. Gilbert, observers pointed out during the decade, "is a town at a crossroads."[44]

Many observers hailed Scottsdale as "the class act in the Valley of the Sun." Expensive and exclusive, it also experienced rapid growth and development. No longer reflecting its image as "The West's Most Western Town," a billing cultivated in the 1950s and 1960s, Scottsdale during the 1970s and 1980s remained a famous winter resort and emerged as a popular residential and commercial suburban city. McCormick Ranch, Gainey Ranch, and other planned subdivisions offering "designer" golf courses and lakeside living lured affluent residents, as did the fashionable shops and art galleries in several new shopping centers.

Scottsdale claimed to be the "Arts Capital of the Southwest," and its many cultural attractions appealed to artists and celebrities; for example, its Cowboy and Indian art shows drew enthusiastic crowds. The Scottsdale Center for the Arts, sponsored by the 2200-member Scottsdale Arts Center Association, offered residents and visitors quality programs, and tourists flocked to Frank Lloyd Wright's Taliesin West architectural studios, Paolo Soleri's Cosanti Foundation, and other landmarks. The annual Parada del Sol Rodeo and the recently relocated Phoenix Open Golf Tournament brought added attention to the sixth largest city in Arizona, as did world-famous Arabian horse shows and classic car auctions. Cactus League baseball flourished in Scottsdale, where the San Francisco Giants held spring training. Loyal fans turned out to watch the Giants play the Oakland A's from Phoenix, the Chicago Cubs from Mesa, the Milwaukee Brewers from Chandler, and the Seattle Mariners from Tempe.

Along with Tempe, Scottsdale engaged in serious planning. In 1965 city officials and citizens joined together to form the Scottsdale Town Enrichment Program (STEP). STEP committees and city officials boosted bond issues and federal aid, and supported projects that benefited Scottsdale, including a civic center complex, quality downtown redevelopment, and the Indian Bend Wash project, a flood-control and greenbelt system of fishing lakes, golf courses, tennis courts, biking and jogging trails, picnic areas, swimming pools, softball diamonds, wildlife areas, and the nation's first urban campground. STEP committees also supported a num-

Scottsdale in the 1950s. The Herb and Dorothy McLaughlin Photographic Collection.

ber of other desirable measures, such as sign and hillside control ordinances. "The mountains should be left natural for our kids and our grandchildren," declared Scottsdale Mayor Herb Drinkwater in 1984. Restrictive but fair building codes and zoning laws fit Scottsdale's image, and developers observed them; they proved good for business and they helped make the city a good place to live.[45]

Northwest valley cities such as Glendale and Peoria lagged behind east side communities in growth and development, but they boomed more than ever in the 1980s. Glendale, the fifth largest city in Arizona, led the way. It remained an active trading center for agricultural production, but its farm town image was slowly changing. Massive planned communities like Arrowhead Ranch (sixty model homes, thirty-three lakes, two Arnold Palmer golf courses) promised to attract upscale residents to Glendale, especially after Proposition 300 assured freeway access in the future. Downtown redevelopment, however, proved slow; as in several other valley cities, older barrios and neighborhoods resisted removal and relocation.

Affordable land and the prospect of new freeways drew residential subdivisions, shopping centers, and office and industrial parks to Glendale during the decade. In order to attract industry, Glendale in 1984 offered a $20,000 bounty to the first person nationwide who was able to convince a company to locate a 100,000-square foot or larger plant in the city; a new Sperry Space Systems Division plant soon appeared. In 1987, the city hired a full-time marketing director to lure new firms to the area. Grand Avenue, the historic route from Phoenix, underwent improvements as transportation became a priority item. Nearby Luke Air Force Base, Metrocenter, and Black Canyon Freeway corridor electronics plants also attracted growth to the area. Glendale boosters called the city "a budding center of higher education, with Glendale Community College, American Graduate School of International Management, and the embryo west side campus of ASU."

As Glendale evolved during the 1980s, a new city hall and a new municipal airport came into being, and local officials successfully promoted a percent-for-art ordinance. "Art is a way to express our sheer joy in civilization," Glendale Mayor George Renner stated upon passage of the legislation. "Certainly in our city, growing as rapidly as we are and with a fair amount of public investment ahead of us, it's appropriate that our new facilities be pleasing, be attractive, be more than just bricks and mortar. It's important to make art part of the growth process."

In the 1980s, the small farming community of Peoria seemed to disappear under the relentless pressure of urbanization. Farmers found it difficult to resist $35,000 an acre for their land, so they sold to developers. Office buildings went up downtown and housing subdivisions replaced cotton fields. Promoters looked forward to new freeways opening up Peoria to industrial development. By 1985, four hundred newcomers a month were settling in Peoria. City infrastructure improvements were made, but they lagged behind growth. Unincorporated Sun City and Sun City West also continued to grow rapidly, impacting on nearby Peoria.

Smaller west side towns such as Goodyear, Tolleson, and Avondale looked upon the completion of Interstate 10 and other highways and freeways as the key to future development. In the meantime, they served as bedroom communities. One subdivision advertised: "ROOM TO BREATHE—COUNTRY LIVING MINUTES FROM PHOENIX—ONE ACRE MINI-RANCHES— HORSE PRIVILEGES AND BRIDLE PATH." Promoters of the west valley expected to benefit from waves of growth similar to those that already had hit the east valley, and critics, mindful of the past, hoped that development in that area would be planned to properly meet boom town needs and aspirations.[46]

East Valley Partnership, West Valley Alliance, Phoenix Together, and other booster organizations were all quick to oppose "balkanization" and "parochialism" in the metropolitan area, but they wanted their territory to get its share. The territorial imperative at work, an observer noted. The cities making up the parts of the metropolitan whole wanted to cooperate in solving common problems such as transportation, pollution, and water, but they preferred to compete in many areas, such as economic growth and cultural and social development. Like Phoenix promoters, the boosters of neighboring cities bragged about the "entrepreneurial verve" and the "attractive amenities" in their communities. The cities competed for everything from sports facilities to educational institutions in order to offer unique advantages to residents and businesses. For the most part, metropolitan pluralism prevailed in the Valley of the Sun.

Metropolitan pluralism was not unique to the Valley of the Sun. Despite the presence of cooperation in the new urban America, fragmentation and competition has been the tendency in recent years. Efforts to sell the entire metropolis on common goals have failed in Phoenix, as elsewhere. Little progress has been made in strengthening historically weak Maricopa County government or regional organizations like the voluntary Maricopa Association of Governments. Local control and local identity, rather than "metropolitan centralization," has been the trend. The concern for suburban cities as well as city neighborhoods has been overriding. The leadership of Phoenix, the core city in the valley, could not overcome the desire of individual centers to pursue their own destiny. Moreover, cities of the East Valley Partnership and other alliances often failed to cooperate with each other.

Everybody in Phoenix talked about the need for cooperation, and everybody wanted to do his own thing. In the metropolitan area, as in Phoenix itself, the local or neighborhood interest largely defined the public interest, frustrating those who wanted to deal with the common concerns of the various municipalities. Discussion about the need for more cooperation, along with other vital issues, promises to persist in the Valley of the Sun, and in the future the major problem facing Phoenix will continue to be the rapidly evolving conflict between the area's two most cherished values—growth and the good life. Growth seems to be inevitable; the quality of life does not.

The statistics are as frightening as they are impressive. Forecasters predict that metropolitan Phoenix's population of 1.8 million in 1985 will grow to 3.2 million by the year 2000. The addition of 1.4 million more residents during that period means a 77 percent increase in population, an imposing figure. It means that Phoenix will remain among the fastest growing of the nation's thirty major metropolitan areas. The Valley of the Sun will become the nation's eleventh largest metropolitan region by 2000, up from thirty-first in 1970 and twenty-second in 1985. In the face of such massive growth, the great challenge confronting Phoenix and its neighboring cities now and in the future is to handle that growth in ways that will improve life in the Southwest metropolis rather than harm it.[47]

NOTES TO CHAPTERS

Chapter 1. Phoenix and the Urban Experience

1. Bradford Luckingham, *The Urban Southwest: A Profile History of Albuquerque, El Paso, Phoenix and Tucson* (El Paso: Texas Western Press, University of Texas, El Paso, 1982); Bradford Luckingham, "The Urban Dimension of Western History," in Michael P. Malone, ed., *Historians and the American West* (Lincoln: University of Nebraska Press, 1983), 324–43.

2. Bradford Luckingham, "Urban Development in Arizona: The Rise of Phoenix," *Journal of Arizona History*, 22 (Summer 1981), 197–234. For boosters on other urban frontiers, see Charles N. Glaab, "The Historian and the American Urban Tradition," *Wisconsin Magazine of History*, 66 (Autumn 1963), 13–25; Daniel J. Boorstin, *The Americans: The National Experience* (New York: Random House, 1965); Earl Pomeroy, *The Pacific Slope: A History of California, Oregon, Washington, Idaho, Utah and Nevada* (New York: Knopf, 1966); Raymond A. Mohl, *The New City: Urban America in the Industrial Age, 1860–1920* (Arlington Heights, Ill.: Harlan Davidson, 1985).

3. Luckingham, *The Urban Southwest*. For the importance of railroad promotion on other urban frontiers, see Charles N. Glaab, "Historical Perspective on Urban Development Schemes," in Leo F. Schnore, ed., *Social Science and the City: A Survey of Urban Research* (New York: Praeger, 1968), 197–219; William Silag, "Gateway to the Grasslands: Sioux City and the Missouri River Frontier," *Western Historical Quarterly*, 14 (October 1983), 396–414; John W. Reps, *Cities of the American West: A History of Frontier Urban Planning* (Princeton: Princeton University Press, 1979).

4. On Los Angeles, see John H. Bauer, "Los Angeles County in the Health

Rush, 1870–1900," *California Historical Society Quarterly*, 31 (Spring 1952), 13–21; Oscar O. Winther, "The Use of Climate as a Means of Promoting Migration to Southern California," *Mississippi Valley Historical Review*, 33 (December 1947), 411–23.

5. On the frontier entrepreneur, see William D. Angel, Jr., "To Make a City: Entrepreneurship on the Sunbelt Frontier," in David C. Perry and Alfred J. Watkins, eds., *The Rise of the Sunbelt Cities* (Beverly Hills: Sage, 1977), 109–28; Kenneth W. Wheeler, *To Wear a City's Crown: The Beginnings of Urban Growth in Texas, 1836–1865* (Cambridge, Mass.: Harvard University Press, 1968); Charles Glaab and A. Theodore Brown, *A History of Urban America*, 3rd ed. (New York: Macmillan, 1983).

6. Harry Welch, "The Wonderful Roosevelt Dam and the Salt River Valley of Arizona," *National Irrigation Journal*, 2 (August 1910), 10–11. On the hydraulic West, see Donald Worster, "New West, True West: Interpreting the Region's History," *Western Historical Quarterly*, 18 (April 1987), 141–56; Donald Worster, *Rivers of Empire: Water, Aridity, and the Growth of the American West* (New York: Pantheon, 1985). See also Walter Prescott Webb, "The American West: Perpetual Mirage," *Harper's Magazine*, 214 (May 1957), 25–31; Howard J. Nelson, "The Southern California Experience," in Carl Hodges, ed., *Urbanization in the Arid Lands* (Lubbock: Texas Tech, 1974), 247–62. For the similarities in western urban development, see Lawrence A. Larsen, *The Urban West at the End of the Frontier* (Lawrence: Regents Press of Kansas, 1978).

7. Luckingham, *The Urban Southwest*. On the West, see Mark S. Foster, "The Model T, the Hard Sell, and Los Angeles's Urban Growth: The Decentralization of Los Angeles During the 1920's," *Pacific Historical Review*, 44 (November 1975), 459–84; Sam Bass Warner, Jr., *The Urban Wilderness: A History of the American City* (New York: Harper & Row, 1972); Jon C. Teaford, *The Twentieth-Century American City* (Baltimore: Johns Hopkins University Press, 1986).

8. Bradford Luckingham, "The American Southwest: An Urban View," *Western Historical Quarterly*, 15 (July 1984), 261–80; Mario T. Garcia, *Desert Immigrants: The Mexicans of El Paso, 1880–1920* (New Haven: Yale University Press, 1981). For similar experiences in the West, see Albert Camarillo, *Chicanos in a Changing Society: From Mexican Pueblos to American Barrios in Santa Barbara and Southern California, 1848–1920* (Cambridge, Mass.: Harvard University Press, 1979); Richard Griswold del Castillo, *The Los Angeles Barrio, 1850–1890: A Social History* (Berkeley: University of California Press, 1980); Ricardo Romo, *East Los Angeles: History of a Barrio* (Austin: University of Texas Press, 1983); Lawrence B. de Graaf, "The City of Black Angels: Emergence of the Los Angeles Ghetto, 1890–1930," *Pacific Historical Review*, 39 (August 1970), 323–52.

9. Luckingham, *The Urban Southwest*. On the West, see Gerald D. Nash, *The American West in the Twentieth Century: A Short History of an Urban Oasis* (Englewood Cliffs, N.J.: Prentice-Hall, 1973); Carl Abbott, *Urban America in the Modern Age: 1920 to the Present* (Arlington Heights, Ill.: Harlan Davidson, 1987).

10. Luckingham, *The Urban Southwest*. On the West, see Gerald D. Nash, *The American West Transformed: The Impact of the Second World War* (Blooming-

ton: Indiana University Press, 1985); Mark I. Gefland, *A Nation of Cities: The Federal Government and Urban America, 1933–1965* (New York: Oxford University Press, 1975); Roger Lotchin, *The Martial Metropolis: United States Cities in War and Peace* (New York: Praeger, 1984); Carl Abbott, *The New Urban America: Growth and Politics in Sunbelt Cities* (Chapel Hill: University of North Carolina Press, 1981); Richard M. Bernard and Bradley R. Rice, eds., *Sunbelt Cities: Politics and Growth Since World War II* (Austin: University of Texas Press, 1983).

11. Bradford Luckingham, "Phoenix: The Desert Metropolis," in Bernard and Rice, *Sunbelt Cities*, 307–27. On the West, see Nash, *The American West in the Twentieth Century*; Daniel J. Elazar, *The Metropolitan Frontier: A Perspective on Change in American Society* (Morristown, N.J.: Heath, 1973); Bernard L. Weinstein and Robert E. Firestine, *Regional Growth and Decline in the United States: The Rise of the Sunbelt and the Decline of the Northeast* (New York: Pantheon, 1978); Zane L. Miller and Patricia M. Melvin, *The Urbanization of Modern America* (New York: Harcourt Brace Jovanovich, 1987).

12. Webb, "Perpetual Mirage," 25–31; Nash, *The American West in the Twentieth Century*; Richard Louv, *America II: The Book That Captures America in the Act of Creating the Future* (New York: Penguin, 1983); Teaford, *The Twentieth-Century American City*, 156.

13. Bernard and Rice, *Sunbelt Cities*; Abbott, *The New Urban America*; Angel, "Entrepreneurship," 109–27; Ray Arsenault, "The End of the Long Hot Summer: The Air-Conditioner and Southern Culture," *Journal of Southern History*, 50 (November 1984), 597–626; Carrie Sears Bell, "The Rio Salado Story," *Phoenix*, 19 (November 1984), 97–108; Louv, *America II*; Peter Wiley and Robert Gottlieb, *Empires in the Sun: The Rise of the New American West* (New York: G. P. Putnam's Sons, 1982); Teaford, *The Twentieth-Century American City*; Peter O. Muller, *Contemporary Suburban America* (Englewood Cliffs, N.J.: Prentice Hall, 1981); William Sharpe and Leonard Wallock, eds., *Visions of the Modern City* (Baltimore: Johns Hopkins University Press, 1986).

14. Bernard and Rice, *Sunbelt Cities*, 11–26; Franklin J. James, *et al.*, *Minorities in the Sunbelt* (New York: Oxford University Press, 1984), 135–39.

Chapter 2. The Emergent Years, 1867–1889

1. Herbert R. Patrick, *The Ancient Canal Systems and Pueblos of the Salt River, Arizona* (Phoenix: Phoenix Printing Company, 1903); Jeffrey Cook, "Patterns of Desert Urbanization: The Evolution of Metropolitan Phoenix," in Gideon Golaney, ed., *Urban Planning for Arid Zones: American Experiences and Directions* (New York: Praeger, 1978), 205–08; Geoffrey Padraic Mawn, "Phoenix, Arizona: Central City of the Southwest, 1870–1920" (Ph.D. dissertation, Arizona State University, 1979), 2–3; Michael H. Bartlett, Thomas M. Kolaz, and David A. Gregory, *Archaeology in the City: A Hohokam Village in Phoenix, Arizona* (Tucson: University of Arizona Press, 1986), 17–34.

2. John Francis Bannon, *The Spanish Borderlands Frontier, 1513–1821* (New York: Holt, Rinehart and Winston, 1970); David J. Weber, *The Mexican Frontier, 1821–1846: The American Southwest Under Mexico* (Albuquerque: University of New Mexico Press, 1982); Bradford Luckingham, *The Urban Southwest* (El

Paso: Texas Western Press, University of Texas, El Paso, 1982). See also Marc Simmons, *Albuquerque: A Narrative History* (Albuquerque: University of New Mexico Press, 1982); C. L. Sonnichsen, *Pass of the North: Four Centuries on the Rio Grande*, 2 vols. (El Paso: Texas Western Press, University of Texas, El Paso, 1980); C. L. Sonnichsen, *Tucson: The Life and Times of an American City* (Norman: University of Oklahoma Press, 1982).

3. Earl Zarbin, *The Swilling Legacy* (Phoenix: Salt River Project, 1979), 7–12; Geoffrey P. Mawn, "John William (Jack) Swilling: A Reevaluation" (typescript, Hayden Library, Arizona State University, 1978), 10–21; Edward H. Peplow, Jr., ed., *The Taming of the Salt* (Phoenix: Salt River Project, 1979), 11–19; Thomas Edwin Farish, *History of Arizona*, vol. II (San Francisco: Filmer Brothers Electrotype Company, 1915), 251–57.

4. Geoffrey P. Mawn, "Promoters, Speculators, and the Selection of the Phoenix Townsite," *Arizona and the West*, 19 (Fall 1977), 214–15; Karen Lynn Smith, "From Town to City: A History of Phoenix, 1870–1912" (M.A. thesis, University of California, Santa Barbara, 1978), 7–13; Farish, *History of Arizona*, vol. II, 251–67.

5. *Arizona Republic*, February 24, 1981; James M. Barney, "Phoenix, a History of Its Pioneer Days and People," *Arizona Historical Review*, 5 (January 1933), 264–68; Mawn,"Phoenix Townsite," 215–18; Farish, *History of Arizona*, vol. VI, 162–78; Smith, "From Town to City," 13–16.

6. *Arizona Republic*, February 24, 1981; Peplow, *The Taming of the Salt*, 25–32; Farish, *History of Arizona*, vol. VI, 162–78; Smith, "From Town to City," 16–19.

7. *Arizona Republic*, February 24, 1981; Barney, "Phoenix," 269–76; Mawn, "Phoenix Townsite," 222–26; Farish, *History of Arizona*, vol. VI, 162–78; Smith, "From Town to City," 13–19.

8. Mawn, "Phoenix Townsite," 221–23; Naomi Zunker, "The Birth of Maricopa County" (typescript, Hayden Library, Arizona State University, 1982), 5–6; Luckingham, *The Urban Southwest*, 32.

9. (Prescott) *Arizona Miner*, April 1 and May 20, 1871; Zunker, "Maricopa County," 7–15; Mawn, "Phoenix Townsite," 221–22.

10. Peplow, *The Taming of the Salt*, 29–32; John W. Reps, *Cities of the American West: A History of Frontier Urban Planning* (Princeton: Princeton University Press, 1979), 8–10, 631, 668.

11. *Arizona Miner*, March 4, 1871. On boom towns, see Gunther Barth, *Instant Cities: Urbanization and the Rise of San Francisco and Denver* (New York: Oxford University Press, 1975).

12. *Arizona Miner*, March 4 and June 3, 1871; John T. Alsap, "Resources of the Salt River Valley, 1872," *Arizona Historical Review*, 3 (July 1936), 50–54; Barney, "Phoenix," 270–84; Smith, "From Town to City," 19–22; G. Wesley Johnson, Jr., *Phoenix: Valley of the Sun* (Tulsa: Continental Heritage Press, 1982), 31.

13. *Salt River Herald*, March 2, 1878; Mawn, "Central City," 41–51; Blaine Lamb, "Jews in Early Phoenix, 1870–1920," *Journal of Arizona History*, 18 (Autumn 1977), 299–302.

14. *Salt River Herald*, March 2 and April 12, 1878; *Phoenix Herald*, April 23, 1879; Mawn, "Central City," 50–54, 66–67; David F. Myrick, *Railroads of*

Arizona, vol. II (San Diego: Howell-North Books, 1981), 481–94; Bernard M. Boyle, ed., *Materials in the Architecture of Arizona, 1870–1920* (Tempe: Arizona State University College of Architecture, 1976), 2–4.

15. Charles S. Sargent, "Towns of the Salt River Valley, 1870–1930," *Historical Geography*, 5 (Fall 1975), 3; Blaine P. Lamb, "Historical Overview of Tempe, Arizona, 1870–1930" (typescript, Hayden Library, Arizona State University, 1981), 2; Johnson, *Valley of the Sun*, 32–34. On Mormon town building, see Thomas G. Alexander and James B. Allen, *Mormons and Gentiles: A History of Salt Lake City* (Boulder, Colo.: Pruett, 1984).

16. *Salt River Herald*, August 10, 1878; *Phoenix Herald*, April 16, 1879, September 4 and 6, 1880, February 28 and May 4, 1881; *Arizona Gazette*, January 12, 15, 22, and 24, February 25, 1881; *Arizona Republic*, February 24, 1981; "Act to Incorporate the City of Phoenix, Arizona, February 25, 1881," *Acts and Resolutions of the Eleventh Legislative Assembly of the Territory of Arizona* (Prescott: Arizona Miner, 1881), 105–16.

17. Peplow, *The Taming of the Salt*, 25–28; Patrick Hamilton, *The Resources of Arizona* (San Francisco: A. L. Bancroft & Co., 1883), 29. On the booster spirit in the American West, see Bradford Luckingham, "The City in the Westward Movement: A Bibliographical Note," *Western Historical Quarterly*, 5 (July 1974), 295–306.

18. *Arizona Gazette*, May 9, 14, and 28, June 16, July 22, 1881; *Arizona Republic*, February 24, 1981; Mawn, "Central City," 74–80; Smith, "From Town to City," 42–43; Stephen D. Rockstroh, "An Analysis of Phoenix Municipal Administration, 1881–1952" (M.A. thesis, Arizona State University, 1952), 24–35.

19. *Arizona Gazette*, January 1, May 4, August 16, 1883, May 27, 1885, April 22, August 6 and 12, September 27, 1886; Rockstroh, "Municipal Administration," 35–37; James Barney, *A Historical Sketch of the Volunteer Fire Department of Phoenix, Arizona* (Phoenix: n.p., 1954), 18–24.

20. *Arizona Gazette*, June 25, 1883; *Phoenix Herald*, April 5, 1887; Mawn, "Central City," 77–78.

21. Mawn, "Central City," 80–81; Merwin L. Murphy, "W. J. Murphy and the Arizona Canal Company," *Journal of Arizona History*, 23 (Summer 1982), 139.

22. Murphy, "Arizona Canal," 139–70; Mawn, "Central City," 81–94; Peplow, *The Taming of the Salt*, 37–44; Merwin L. Murphy, *W. J. and the Valley* (Alhambra, Calif.: By the Author, 1975), 5–51.

23. *Arizona Gazette*, June 1, 1885; Mawn, "Central City," 107–14; Murphy, *W. J. and the Valley*, 103–15.

24. Myrick, *Railroads of Arizona*, vol. II, 481–501; Mawn, "Central City," 103–07; Charles N. Glaab, "Urban Development Schemes," in Leo F. Schnore, ed., *Social Science and the City* (New York: Praeger, 1968), 197–219.

25. *Arizona Gazette*, July 3 and 5, 1887; Myrick, *Railroads of Arizona*, vol. II, 501–12.

26. *Arizona Gazette*, April 28, 1889; *Meyer's Business Directory of the City of Phoenix, Arizona* (Phoenix: A. Leonard Meyer, 1888), 3–7; *Phoenix City Directory, 1892* (Phoenix: Phoenix Directory Company, 1892), 19; Smith, "From Town to City," 44–45; Mawn, "Central City," 114–17; Charles S. Sargent, "Evolution

of Metro Phoenix," in James W. Elmore, ed., *A Guide to the Architecture of Metro Phoenix* (Phoenix: Phoenix Publishing, 1983), 9–10.

27. Richard E. Lynch, "The Relationship of Streetcars to Real Estate Promotion in Phoenix, 1887–1925" (typescript, Hayden Library, Arizona State University, 1973), 5–12; William O. Hendricks, *M. H. Sherman: A Pioneer Developer of the Pacific Southwest* (Corona del Mar, Calif.: Castle Press, 1973), 3–8; Laurence J. Fleming, *Ride a Mile and Smile the While: A History of the Phoenix Street Railway, 1887–1948* (Phoenix: Swaine Publications, 1977), 1–7; Lawrence A. Larsen, *The Urban West at the End of the Frontier* (Lawrence: Regents Press of Kansas, 1978), 69–88.

28. Lamb, "Jews in Early Phoenix," 302–09; Floyd S. Fierman, *Some Early Jewish Settlers on the Southwest Frontier* (El Paso: Texas Western Press, 1960); Robert A. Levinson, *The Jews in the California Gold Rush* (New York: Praeger, 1978); Blaine Lamb, "Jewish Pioneers in Arizona, 1850–1920" (Ph.D. dissertation, Arizona State University, 1982).

29. *Arizona Gazette*, September 15, 1881; *Phoenix Herald*, September 16, 1881; Shirley J. Roberts, "Minority Group Poverty in Phoenix: A Socio-Economic Survey," *Journal of Arizona History*, 14 (Winter 1973), 349–51; James M. Barney, "Famous 'Indian' Ordinance," *The Sheriff*, 13 (June 1954), 77.

30. Roberts, "Minority Group Poverty," 351–52; Phoenix Chamber of Commerce, *Resources of the Salt River Valley* (Phoenix: Phoenix Directory Company, 1891), 8; Bradford Luckingham, "The Southwestern Urban Frontier, 1880–1930," *Journal of the West*, 18 (July 1979), 46–48.

31. *Arizona Gazette*, February 26, 1886; Roberts, "Minority Group Poverty," 250–51; Gary P. Tipton, "Men out of China: Origins of the Chinese Colony in Phoenix," *Journal of Arizona History*, 18 (Autumn 1977), 341–56; Bradford Luckingham, "Immigrant Life in San Francisco," *Journal of the West*, 12 (October 1973), 601–02.

32. John A. Black, *The Land of Sunshine and Silver, Health and Prosperity; The Place for Ideal Homes* (Tucson: Republican Book & Job Print, 1890), 64–66; Smith, "From Town to City," 52–56; *Phoenix City Directory, 1892* (Phoenix: Phoenix Directory Company, 1892), 19; Bradford Luckingham, "The Urban Dimension of Western History," in Michael P. Malone, ed., *Historians and the American West* (Lincoln: University of Nebraska Press, 1983), 326–27.

33. Luckingham, *The Urban Southwest*, 24–25.

34. *Arizona Miner*, December 19, 1888, January 9, 1889; Karen Lynn Ehrlich, "Arizona's Territorial Capital Moves to Phoenix," *Arizona and the West*, 23 (Fall 1981), 239–40; Margaret Finnerty, "Arizona's Capital: The Politics of Relocation," *History Forum*, 3 (Spring 1981), 29–30.

35. *Arizona Miner*, January 9 and 13, 1889; *Phoenix Herald*, December 8, 1888; Finnerty, "Arizona's Capital," 30–32; Larsen, *The Urban West*, 69–88.

36. *Arizona Miner*, December 12 and 26, 1888, January 2 and 30, 1889; *Phoenix Herald*, January 24, 1889; Ehrlich, "Capital Moves to Phoenix," 240; Luckingham, *The Urban Southwest*, 24–25; Lynch, "Streetcars," 9.

37. *Arizona Miner*, January 30, 1889; *Phoenix Herald*, January 26, 1889; George H. Kelly, comp., *Legislative History, Arizona, 1864–1912* (Phoenix: The Manufacturing Stationers, Inc., 1926), 132–35; Ehrlich, "Capital Moves to Phoenix," 241; Finnerty, "Arizona's Capital," 32–34.

38. *Phoenix Herald*, January 29, 1889; Finnerty, "Arizona's Capital," 30–31, 35–36; Luckingham, *The Urban Southwest*, 25.

39. *Phoenix Herald*, June 7, 1889; Lynch, "Streetcars," 9–10; Mawn, "Central City," 124–25; Stephen C. Shadegg, *Miss Lulu's Legacy* (Tempe: Arizona State University, 1984), 8–9.

40. *Phoenix Herald*, January 2, 1890; E. S. Gill, "Phoenix, Arizona," *California Illustrated Magazine*, 3 (June 1892), 247; Luckingham, *The Urban Southwest*, 30. For a description of Denver in the 1880s, see Lyle W. Dorsett, *The Queen City: A History of Denver* (Boulder, Colo.: Pruett, 1977).

Chapter 3. Arizona Capital, 1890–1913

1. David Myrick, *Railroads of Arizona*, vol. II (San Diego: Howell-North Books, 1981), 515–19; Geoffrey Mawn, "Phoenix . . . Central City of the Southwest" (Ph.D. dissertation, Arizona State University, 1979), 149–51; G. A. Neeff, "The Santa Fe, Prescott and Phoenix Railroad," *Southwest Illustrated Magazine*, 2 (February 1896), 5–6.

2. *Phoenix Herald*, February 8, 1895; *Arizona Republican*, March 1, 1895; Neeff, "The Santa Fe, Prescott and Phoenix Railroad," 3–10; Mawn, "Central City," 151–64; Bradford Luckingham, "Urban Development in Arizona: The Rise of Phoenix," *Journal of Arizona History*, 22 (Summer 1981), 198; William S. Greever, "Railway Development in the Southwest," *New Mexico Historical Review*, 32 (April 1957), 168–72.

3. *Arizona Republican*, December 8 and 25, 1891, February 10, 1895; *Arizona Gazette*, February 4, 1894; *The Salt River Valley, Arizona: Questions Answered and Current Comment That May Be Found Interesting to the Homeseeker and Investor* (Phoenix: Republican Book & Job Print, 1894), 21–22; Clark M. Carr, "The Salt River Valley, Arizona," *Southwest Illustrated Magazine*, 1 (June 1895), 107–11.

4. Myrick, *Railroads of Arizona*, vol. II, 519–22, 570–76; Mawn, "Central City," 292–302; Bradford Luckingham, *The Urban Southwest* (El Paso: Texas Western Press, University of Texas, El Paso, 1982), 33–40.

5. Karen Lynn Smith, "The Campaign for Water in Central Arizona, 1890–1903," *Arizona and the West*, 23 (Summer 1981), 127–48; Karen Lynn Smith, *The Magnificent Experiment: Building the Salt River Reclamation Project, 1890–1917* (Tucson: University of Arizona Press, 1986), 1–69; Mawn, "Central City," 219–41; Earl Zarbin, *Roosevelt Dam: A History to 1911* (Phoenix: Salt River Project, 1984), 19–61.

6. Edward H. Peplow, Jr., ed., *The Taming of the Salt* (Phoenix: Salt River Project, 1979), 66–70; Mawn, "Central City," 233–35; Smith, *Magnificent Experiment*, 16–17.

7. Smith, "The Campaign for Water," 127–48; Smith, *Magnificent Experiment*, 25–48; Mawn, "Central City," 231–41; Zarbin, *Roosevelt Dam*, 43–75.

8. Peplow, *The Taming of the Salt*, 84–87; Smith, *Magnificent Experiment, passim*; Mawn, "Central City," 242–61; Zarbin, *Roosevelt Dam*, 101–11, *passim*.

9. Smith, "The Campaign for Water," 127–48; Smith, *Magnificent Experiment*, 70–124, *passim*; Zarbin, *Roosevelt Dam*, 75–247; The Editors, "Water for Phoenix: The Building of the Roosevelt Dam," *Journal of Arizona History*, 18

(Autumn 1977), 279–94; H. L. Meredith, "Reclamation in the Salt River Valley, 1902–1917," *Journal of the West*, 7 (January 1968), 76–83; Earl Zarbin, *Salt River Project: Four Steps Forward, 1902–1910* (Phoenix: Salt River Project, 1986), *passim*.

10. Harry Welch, "The Wonderful Roosevelt Dam of the Salt River Valley of Arizona," *National Irrigation Journal*, 2 (August 1910), 10–12; C. J. Blanchard, "The Call of the West: Homes Are Being Made for Millions of People in the Arid West," *National Geographic*, 20 (May 1909), 425–27; Ernest Douglas, "What Capital Is Doing in the Salt River Valley," *Arizona: The New State Magazine*, 1 (December 1910), 1–2; Mawn, "Central City," 288–91; Luckingham, *The Urban Southwest*, 41–42.

11. Luckingham, "The Rise of Phoenix," 204–05; *Arizona Gazette*, February 4, 1894, January 2, 1900; *The Salt River Valley, Arizona: Questions Answered and Current Comment*, 29; Joseph Stocker, "Crossroads of the Cow Country," *Arizona Highways* (June 1950), 17; Bradford Luckingham, "The American Southwest: An Urban View," *Western Historical Quarterly*, 15 (July 1984), 265–69.

12. Carr, "Salt River Valley, Arizona," 107–11; *Phoenix Directory for the Year 1895* (Phoenix: Phoenix Directory Company, 1895), *passim*; *Phoenix Directory for 1899–1900* (Phoenix: Phoenix Directory Company, 1899–1900), *passim*; Roberta Kagan, "Phoenix at the Turn of the Century" (typescript, Hayden Library, Arizona State University, 1981), 4–19.

13. Phoenix and Maricopa County Board of Trade, *Arizona, Maricopa County* (Phoenix: Phoenix Directory Company, 1901), 47–56; *Phoenix City and Maricopa County Directory, 1905–06* (Phoenix: Phoenix Directory Company, 1906), *passim*; *Phoenix City and Salt River Valley Directory, 1913* (Phoenix: Arizona Directory Company, 1913), *passim*; Mawn, "Central City," 348–54; Shirley J. Roberts, "Minority Group Poverty in Phoenix," *Journal of Arizona History*, 14 (Winter 1973), 353–54.

14. Richard E. Lynch, "The Relationship of Streetcars to Real Estate Promotion in Phoenix" (typescript, Hayden Library, Arizona State University, 1973), 12–17; Laurence J. Fleming, *Ride a Mile and Smile the While: A History of the Phoenix Street Railway* (Phoenix: Swaine Publications, 1977), 9–38.

15. Thomas H. Peterson, "The Automobile Comes to Territorial Arizona," *Journal of Arizona History*, 15 (Autumn 1974), 249–68; Mawn, "Central City," 308–10; Daniel C. Davis, "Phoenix, Arizona, 1907–1913," (typescript, Hayden Library, Arizona State University, 1976), 10–12; Karen L. Smith, "From Town to City: A History of Phoenix, 1870–1912" (M.A. thesis, University of California, Santa Barbara, 1978), 122–38, 154–55; Sylvia Loughlin, "Iron Springs: Timeless Summer Resort," *Journal of Arizona History*, 22 (Summer 1981), 235–54; Phoenix Planning Department, *City of Phoenix Annexation Areas* (Phoenix: The Department, 1974), *passim*.

16. *Phoenix City and Salt River Valley Directory, 1913*, 46–54; Mawn, "Central City," 308–19, 361–85; "Phoenix, Arizona, 1907–1913," 15–17; Smith, "From Town to City," 156–58.

17. *The Salt River Valley, Arizona: Questions Answered and Current Comment*, 3–5; *Phoenix Directory for the Year 1895*, 18–19; *Phoenix City and Maricopa County Directory, 1905–06*, 30–34; *Phoenix City and Salt River Valley Directory, 1913*, 46–54; Mawn, "Central City," 280–84; G. Wesley Johnson, *Phoenix: Valley*

of the Sun (Tulsa: Continental Heritage Press, 1982), 52–53; Luckingham, *The Urban Southwest*, 26.

18. Gaylord M. McGrath, "The Evolution of Resorts and Guest Ranches in Greater Phoenix" (typescript, Hayden Library, Arizona State University, 1973), 3–6; Mawn, "Central City," 284–86.

19. Aimee Lykes, "Phoenix Women in the Development of Public Policy: Territorial Beginnings" (typescript, Hayden Library, Arizona State University, 1982), 9–12, 29; Mawn, "Central City," 287–88; Luckingham, *The Urban Southwest*, 43–44.

20. McGrath, "Resorts," 4–8; *Arizona State Business Directory, 1911–12* (Denver: Gazetteer Publishing Company, 1912), 362; *Phoenix City and Salt River Valley Directory, 1913*, 40–43; Mawn, "Central City," 173–74, 374.

21. Blaine Lamb, "Jews in Early Phoenix, 1870–1920," *Journal of Arizona History*, 18 (Autumn 1977), 302–17.

22. *Phoenix Herald*, February 18 and 19, 1896; Roberts, "Minority Group Poverty," 351–54; Robert A. Trennert, "'And the Sword Will Give Way to the Spelling-Book': Establishing the Phoenix Indian School," *Journal of Arizona History*, 23 (Spring 1982), 35–58; Robert A. Trennert, "'Peaceably if They Will, Forcibly if They Must': The Phoenix Indian School, 1890–1901," *Journal of Arizona History*, 20 (Autumn 1979), 297–322.

23. Lamb, "Jews in Early Phoenix," 299–318; Phyliss Cancilla Martinelli, "Italy in Phoenix," *Journal of Arizona History*, 18 (Autumn 1977), 319–40; Roberts, "Minority Group Poverty," 353; Albert D. Beasley, *Phoenix, Arizona* (Phoenix: Phoenix Printing Company, 1910), 14; James E. Officer, *Arizona's Hispanic Perspective* (Phoenix: Arizona Academy, 1981), 95–99; *Phoenix City and Salt River Valley Directory, 1913*, 49–51.

24. *Arizona Republican*, June 23, 1890, March 9 and 11, 1910; Roberts, "Minority Group Poverty," 351–54; Gary P. Tipton, "Men out of China," *Journal of Arizona History*, 18 (Autumn 1977), 345–56; Booker T. Washington, "The Race Problem in Arizona," *The Independent*, 71 (October 1911), 909–13.

25. Geoffrey Mawn, "The Growth of Minority Population in Greater Phoenix" (typescript, Arizona Historical Foundation, Hayden Library, Arizona State University, n.d.), *passim*; Mawn, "Central City," 347–48; "History of Blacks in Phoenix Notes" (Geoffrey P. Mawn files, Arizona Historical Foundation, Hayden Library, Arizona State University); Roberts, "Minority Group Poverty," 353.

26. Mary E. Gill and John S. Goff, "Joseph H. Kibbey and School Segregation in Arizona," *Journal of Arizona History*, 21 (Winter 1980), 411–22; Richard E. Harris, "First Families," *Black Heritage in Arizona*, 1 (November 1976), 35; "Blacks in Phoenix Notes" (Mawn files).

27. *Arizona Republican*, September 20, 23, and 24, 1911; "Blacks in Phoenix Notes" (Mawn files).

28. *Arizona Republican*, October 12 and 13, 1913; *Arizona Gazette*, February 3, 1914; Joseph C. Smith, "The Phoenix Drive for Municipal Reform and Charter Government, 1911–1915" (typescript, Hayden Library, Arizona State University, 1975), *passim*; Mark Passolt, "Phoenix, 1914–1919" (typescript, Hayden Library, Arizona State University, 1976), 8–9; Mawn, "Central City," 419–30; Smith, "From Town to City," 166–77.

Chapter 4. Urban Oasis, 1914–1929

1. *Arizona Gazette*, March 16, 1915; *Arizona Republican*, March 20, 1915; Geoffrey Mawn, "Phoenix . . . Central City of the Southwest" (Ph.D. dissertation, Arizona State University, 1979), 430–31; Stephen D. Rockstroh, "An Analysis of Phoenix Municipal Administration, 1881–1952" (M.A. thesis, Arizona State University, 1952), 63–68.

2. Joseph C. Smith, "The Phoenix Drive for Municipal Reform and Charter Government, 1911–1915" (typescript, Hayden Library, Arizona State University, 1975), 4–8; Mawn, "Central City," 430–42; Rockstroh, "Municipal Administration," 6–9, 68–76.

3. *Arizona Gazette*, February 25, 1915; *Arizona Republican*, March 16, April 16, 1915; Smith, "Charter Government," 23–26; Mawn, "Central City," 443–47; Rockstroh, "Municipal Administration," 76–79.

4. *Arizona Republican*, April 15 and 16, 1915; Smith, "Charter Government," 25–29; Mawn, "Central City," 446–47; Rockstroh, "Municipal Administration," 78–79; Michael J. Kotlanger, "Phoenix, Arizona, 1920–1940" (Ph.D. dissertation, Arizona State University, 1983), 481–87; Leonard D. White, *The City Manager* (Chicago: Star Press, 1927), 219–20. For the national experience of commission-city manager governments, see Bradley Robert Rice, *Progressive Cities: The Commission Government Movement in America, 1901–1920* (Austin: University of Texas Press, 1977), 100–11.

5. *Arizona Republican*, February 20, 1919, January 1, 1920; A. George Daws, ed., *The Commercial History of Maricopa County* (Phoenix: Daws Publishing Company, 1919), *passim*; *Phoenix City and Salt River Valley Directory, 1920* (Los Angeles: Henry G. Langley, 1920), 58–60, *passim*; Mawn, "Central City," 489–96; Joseph H. McGowan, *History of Extra-Long Staple Cottons* (El Paso: Texas Western Press, 1961), 143–58, 171–85.

6. Sidney P. Osborn, *Arizona Blue Book, 1917* (Phoenix: H. H. McNeil Co., 1917), 16–18; Beulah Austin, "The Progress of the Salt River Valley During the Past Twenty Years" (typescript, Hayden Library, Arizona State University, 1920), 6–9; Kotlanger, "Phoenix, 1920–1940," 56–57.

7. Kotlanger, "Phoenix, 1920–1940," 57–61; McGowan, *Cottons*, 162–68; Herbert B. Peterson, "A Twentieth Century Journey to Cibola: Tragedy of the *Bracero* in Maricopa County, 1917–1921" (M.A. thesis, Arizona State University, 1975), *passim*; Herbert B. Peterson, "Twentieth Century Search for Cibola: Post-World War I Mexican Labor Exploitation in Arizona," in Manuel P. Servin, ed., *An Awakened Minority: The Mexican-Americans* (Beverly Hills: Sage, 1974), 113–30.

8. *Arizona Republican*, December 28, 1924, December 30, 1928; *Phoenix City and Salt River Valley Directory, 1925* (Los Angeles: Arizona Directory Company, 1925), *passim*; *Phoenix City and Salt River Valley Directory, 1930* (Los Angeles: Arizona Directory Company, 1930), *passim*; Kotlanger, "Phoenix, 1920–1940," 61–70; Carol Ann Muller, "The Cattle Industry in Maricopa County" (typescript, Hayden Library, Arizona State University, 1981), 21–26; R. L. Matlock and S. P. Clark, "Production Costs and Returns from Major Salt River Valley Crops, 1928–1930," *University of Arizona College of Agriculture Bulletin*, 146 (March 1934), *passim*.

9. Kotlanger, "Phoenix, 1920–1940," 23–27, 70–71; Karen Lynn Smith, *The Magnificent Experiment: Building the Salt River Reclamation Project, 1890–1917* (Tucson: University of Arizona Press, 1986), 92–157; Paul Mandel, "Carl Trumbull Hayden: Arizona's First Congressman, 1912–1926" (M.A. thesis, Arizona State University, 1980), 31–33; Stephen C. Shadegg, *Century One: One Hundred Years of Water Development in the Salt River Valley* (Phoenix: Salt River Project, 1969), 35–36.

10. Bradford Luckingham, "Urban Development in Arizona: The Rise of Phoenix," *Journal of Arizona History*, 22 (Summer 1981), 204–05.

11. *Arizona Republican*, December 27, 1925, December 29, 1929; *Phoenix City and Salt River Valley Directory, 1930, passim*; Anthony E. Chapelle, "Phoenix, 1920–1925" (typescript, Hayden Library, Arizona State University, 1976), 30–33; Manya Winsted, "The Encanto-Palmcroft Area," *Phoenix*, 8 (April 1973), 37–39, 86; Charles S. Sargent, "Evolution of Metro Phoenix," in James W. Elmore, ed., *A Guide to the Architecture of Metro Phoenix* (Phoenix: Phoenix Publishing, 1983), 17–18; Kotlanger, "Phoenix, 1920–1940," 91–128; Goldie Weisberg, "Panorama: Phoenix, Arizona," *American Mercury*, 4 (May 1929), 99–100.

12. Luckingham, "The Rise of Phoenix," 206–08; G. Wesley Johnson, *Phoenix: Valley of the Sun* (Tulsa: Continental Heritage Press, 1982), 95–96; Kotlanger, "Phoenix, 1920–1940," 310–13, 343–46.

13. *Arizona Republican*, October 15, 1920, November 24, 1929; Mawn, "Central City," 519–20; Luckingham, "The Rise of Phoenix," 206.

14. *Arizona Republican*, January 26, 1919, December 28, 1924; Luckingham, "The Rise of Phoenix," 206; Kotlanger, "Phoenix, 1920–1940," 155–71; Sam Leopold, "The Impact of the Automobile in Phoenix in the 1920s" (typescript, Hayden Library, Arizona State University, 1976), 18–19; Charles C. Colley, "Carl T. Hayden—Phoenician," *Journal of Arizona History*, 18 (Autumn 1977), 247–57.

15. *Arizona Gazette*, June 16 and October 1, 1923, November 8, 1924; *Arizona Republican*, October 15 and 16, 1926; Kotlanger, "Phoenix, 1920–1940," 188–96; David Myrick, *Railroads of Arizona*, vol. II (San Diego: Howell-North Books, 1981), 781–802; William S. Greever, "Railway Development in the Southwest," *New Mexico Historical Review*, 32 (April 1957), 185–86.

16. *Arizona Republican*, November 11, 1928, September 23, 1929; Kotlanger, "Phoenix, 1920–1940," 196–204; Ruth M. Reinhold, *Sky Pioneering: Arizona in Aviation History* (Tucson: University of Arizona Press, 1982), 86–91, 109–12.

17. Luckingham, "The Rise of Phoenix," 208; Kotlanger, "Phoenix, 1920–1940," 224–26; Stephen C. Shadegg, *Miss Lulu's Legacy* (Tempe: Arizona State University, 1984), 26–35; Ruth Miller, "A History of Desert Mission" (typescript, Hayden Library, Arizona State University, 1940), 4–28; Weisberg, "Panorama," 97.

18. Bradford Luckingham, *The Urban Southwest* (El Paso: Texas Western Press, 1982), 58–60; Kotlanger, "Phoenix, 1920–1940," 226–48; Gaylord M. McGrath, "The Evolution of Resorts and Guest Ranches in Greater Phoenix" (typescript, Hayden Library, Arizona State University, 1973), 8–12; *Phoenix City and Salt River Valley Directory, 1930, passim*; Johnson, *Valley of the Sun*, 98–100.

19. Luckingham, *The Urban Southwest*, 60–62; Kotlanger, "Phoenix, 1920–1940," 294–303; *Phoenix City and Salt River Valley Directory, 1916* (Phoenix: Arizona Directory Company, 1916), 20–21; *Phoenix City and Salt River Valley Directory, 1930,* 14–15; H. W. Lawrence, "A History of the Phoenix Union High School System, 1895–1948" (M.A. thesis, Arizona State University, 1949), 23–29, 55–56.

20. Mabel Hughes Blue, "A History of the Phoenix College at Phoenix, Arizona, 1920–1948" (M.A. thesis, Arizona State University, 1948), 10–13, 58–60; Johnson, *Valley of the Sun,* 90–95.

21. Edith S. Kitt, "Motoring in Arizona in 1914," *Journal of Arizona History,* 11 (Spring 1970), 34–35; *Phoenix City and Salt River Valley Directory, 1916,* 20–26; *Phoenix City and Salt River Valley Directory, 1930,* 14–15; Blaine Lamb, "Jews in Early Phoenix, 1870–1920," *Journal of Arizona History,* 18 (Autumn 1977), 311–15.

22. Kotlanger, "Phoenix, 1920–1940," 271–84, 332–54; *Phoenix City and Salt River Valley Directory, 1916,* 24–25; *Phoenix City and Salt River Valley Directory, 1930,* 10–12.

23. *Arizona Republican,* March 15, 1929, May 16, 1965; Bradford Luckingham, "The Urban Dimension of Western History," in Michael P. Malone, ed., *Historians and the American West* (Lincoln: University of Nebraska Press, 1983), 326–27; G. Wesley Johnson, Jr., "Dwight Heard in Phoenix: The Early Years," *Journal of Arizona History,* 18 (Autumn 1977), 259–78; Bonnie F. Hughes, "Dwight B. Heard: Arizona's Economic and Cultural Pioneer" (typescript, Hayden Library, Arizona State University, 1977), 2–21.

24. *Arizona Republican,* December 29, 1929, February 24, 1930; Kotlanger, "Phoenix, 1920–1940," 271–72, 352–72; Edward H. Peplow, Jr., "Down by the Riverside," *Phoenix* (November 1983), 117–18, 121, 132; *Phoenix City and Salt River Valley Directory, 1930,* 10–15; Weisberg, "Panorama," 100–01.

25. Luckingham, *The Urban Southwest,* 57–58; Weisberg, "Panorama," 100.

26. *Arizona Gazette,* October 28, 1918; *Arizona Republican,* January 21, 23, and 30, 1919, September 8, 1920, November 30, 1922, February 29, 1924, May 4, June 14, and July 10, 1928; *Phoenix City and Salt River Valley Directory, 1930,* 14–15; Mawn, "Central City," 549–51; Kotlanger, "Phoenix, 1920–1940," 512–26; Thomas A. Hvidsten, "Prostitution in Phoenix 1889–1920" (typescript, Hayden Library, Arizona State University, 1973), 12–23.

27. Luckingham, "The Rise of Phoenix," 204–06; Kotlanger, "Phoenix, 1920–1940," 396–98; *Phoenix City and Salt River Valley Directory, 1920,* 3.

28. Kotlanger, "Phoenix, 1920–1940," 404–06; Weisberg, "Panorama," 97–98; *Phoenix City and Salt River Valley Directory, 1920,* 3.

29. Kotlanger, "Phoenix, 1920–1940," 400–04; Weisberg, "Panorama," 98.

30. Kotlanger, "Phoenix, 1920–1940," 443; Emmett McLoughlin, *People's Padre: An Autobiography* (Boston: Beacon, 1954), 37–38; Interview with Adam Diaz, October 25, 1977 (Arizona Collection, Hayden Library, Arizona State University).

31. James McBride, "The Liga Protectora Latina: A Mexican-American Benevolent Society in Arizona," *Journal of the West,* 19 (October 1975), 82–90; Kotlanger, "Phoenix, 1920–1940," 431–33; Mary Ruth Titcomb, "Americanization and Mexicans in the Southwest: A History of Phoenix's Friendly House,

1920–1983" (M.A. thesis, University of California, Santa Barbara, 1983), *passim.*

32. *Arizona Republican,* April 10 and June 10, 1918; Titcomb, "Friendly House, 1920–1983," 435–37. See also Albert Camarillo, *Chicanos in a Changing Society: From Mexican Pueblos to American Barrios in Santa Barbara and Southern California, 1848–1920* (Cambridge, Mass.: Harvard University Press, 1979), 225–27.

33. Kotlanger, "Phoenix, 1920–1940," 410–18; Gary P. Tipton, "Men out of China: Origins of the Chinese Colony in Phoenix," *Journal of Arizona History,* 18 (Autumn 1977), 348–56; Susie Sato, "Before Pearl Harbor: Early Japanese Settlers in Arizona," *Journal of Arizona History,* 14 (Winter 1973), 317–34.

34. Kotlanger, "Phoenix, 1920–1940," 444–49, 458–62; Shirley J. Roberts, "Minority Group Poverty in Phoenix," *Journal of Arizona History,* 14 (Winter 1973), 352; Chapelle, "Phoenix, 1920–1925," 59; "History of Blacks in Phoenix Notes" (Geoffrey P. Mawn files, Arizona Historical Foundation, Hayden Library, Arizona State University).

35. J. Morris Richard, *Birth of Arizona* (Phoenix: West Publishing Company, 1940), 24; Kotlanger, "Phoenix, 1920–1940," 296–97; W. A. Robinson, "The Progress of Integration in the Public Schools," *Journal of Negro Education,* 25 (Fall 1956), 371–72; W. A. Robinson, "Segregation and Integration in Our Phoenix Schools," in Greater Phoenix Council for Civic Unity, ed., *To Secure These Rights* (Phoenix: The Council, 1961), 19–25.

36. *Arizona Republican,* December 29, 1929; Harris, "First Families," 6; Richard E. Harris, *The First 100 Years: A History of Arizona's Blacks* (Apache Junction: Relmo, 1983), 51.

37. Luckingham, *The Urban Southwest,* 62; *Phoenix City and Salt River Valley Directory, 1930,* 13–14.

Chapter 5. Decline and Recovery, 1929–1940

1. Bradford Luckingham, *The Urban Southwest* (El Paso: Texas Western Press, 1982), 62; Jay Edward Niebur, "The Social and Economic Effect of the Great Depression on Phoenix, Arizona, 1929–1934" (M.A. thesis, Arizona State University, 1967), 2–15.

2. Niebur, "Great Depression," 15–18; Leonard J. Arrington, "Arizona in the Great Depression Years," *Arizona Review,* 17 (December 1968), 11–19.

3. Niebur, "Great Depression," 44–45, 75–76; William H. Jervey, Jr., "When the Banks Closed: Arizona's Bank Holiday of 1933," *Arizona and the West,* 10 (Summer 1968), 127–52.

4. Luckingham, *The Urban Southwest,* 67; Michael J. Kotlanger, "Phoenix, Arizona, 1920–1940" (Ph.D. dissertation, Arizona State University, 1983), 254–60; Niebur, "Great Depression," 46–74.

5. Arrington, "Arizona," 11–19; Niebur, "Great Depression," 46–74; Kotlanger, "Phoenix, 1920–1940," *passim.* The *Arizona Republican* became the *Arizona Republic* in November 1930.

6. *Arizona Republic,* March 19, 1933, December 26, 1934; Niebur, "Great Depression," 72–84; Jan Christian and Virginia Coulter, "The New Deal in Phoenix" (typescript, Hayden Library, Arizona State University, 1977), *passim.*

7. Luckingham, *The Urban Southwest*, 68; Don C. Reading, "A Statistical Analysis of New Deal Economic Programs in the Forty-Eight States, 1933–1939" (Ph.D. dissertation, Utah State University, 1972), 155–56; Office of Government Reports, Statistical Section, Report no. 10, Volume 1—County Data: "Arizona" (Washington, D.C.: U.S. Government Printing Office, 1940).

8. Kotlanger, "Phoenix, 1920–1940," *passim*; Christian and Coulter, "The New Deal," *passim*; Arrington, "Arizona," 11–19; Arthur G. Horton, *An Economic, Political and Social Survey of Phoenix and the Valley of the Sun* (Tempe: Southside Progress, 1941), 145; WPA Arizona, *Summary of Inventory of Physical Accomplishments by the Works Progress Administration, 1935–1940* (Phoenix: Works Progress Administration, 1940), 14–23, 48–50.

9. *Arizona Republic*, November 17, 1940; Horton, *Survey of Phoenix, passim*; Charles S. Sargent, "Arizona's Urban Frontier: Myths and Realities," in Charles S. Sargent, ed., *The Conflict Between Frontier Values and Land Use Control in Greater Phoenix* (Tempe: Arizona State University, 1976), 16–17; Bert Fireman, "Urbanization and Home Comfort," in William R. Noyes, ed., *Progress in Arizona* (Tucson: University of Arizona Press, 1973), 3–4; Bob Cunningham, "The Box That Broke the Barrier: The Swamp Cooler Comes to Southern Arizona," *Journal of Arizona History*, 26 (Summer 1985), 163–74.

10. Horton, *Survey of Phoenix*, 181; Ray Sancho, "Southwest Builder: A Profile of Del Webb" (typescript, Hayden Library, Arizona State University, 1980), 7–16.

11. Horton, *Survey of Phoenix*, 174; Carl Bimson, "Thirty Years of Progress in Arizona Home Financing," *Arizona Review of Business and Public Administration*, 12 (February 1963), 1–4, 10; Keith Monroe, "Bank Knight in Arizona," *American Magazine* (November 1945), 24–25, 116–22; Larry Schweikart, *A History of Banking in Arizona* (Tucson: University of Arizona Press, 1982), 83–106.

12. *Arizona Republic*, November 11, 1935, December 20, 1940; Kotlanger, "Phoenix, 1920–1940," *passim*; Christian and Coulter, "The New Deal," *passim*; Ruth M. Reinhold, *Sky Pioneering* (Tucson: University of Arizona Press, 1982), 190–97.

13. Reed W. Teeples and Richard E. Lynch, "Salt River Project," *Arizona Waterline*, 3 (Spring 1983), 8–9; Courtland L. Smith, *The Salt River Project* (Tucson: University of Arizona Press, 1972), 15–18.

14. Kotlanger, "Phoenix, 1920–1940," 27–48; Horton, *Survey of Phoenix*, 65–78.

15. *Arizona Republic*, November 26, 1936, November 20, 1938; Horton, *Survey of Phoenix*, 145.

16. *Arizona Republic*, November 18, 1934, November 17, 1940; Horton, *Survey of Phoenix*, 134–36.

17. *Arizona Republic*, November 17, 1940; Charles S. Stevenson, *We Met at Camelback* (Kingsport, Tenn.: Croft, 1968), 206–31; Richard Barnett and Joseph Garai, *Where the States Stand on Civil Rights* (New York: Bold Face Books, 1962), 18; Horton, *Survey of Phoenix*, 134–36; Kotlanger, "Phoenix, 1920–1940," 243–49; Gaylord M. McGrath, "The Evolution of Resorts and Guest Ranches in Greater Phoenix" (typescript, Hayden Library, Arizona State University, 1973), 12–14.

18. *Phoenix City and Salt River Valley Directory, 1930* (Phoenix: Arizona

Directory Company, 1930), 935–37; *Phoenix City Directory, 1940* (Phoenix: Arizona Directory Company, 1940), 29–30; Horton, *Survey of Phoenix*, 253–54.

19. H. W. Lawrence, "A History of the Phoenix Union High School System, 1895–1948," (M.A. thesis, Arizona State University, 1949), 55–68; Mabel H. Blue, "A History of the Phoenix College at Phoenix, Arizona, 1920–1948" (M.A. thesis, Arizona State University, 1948), 31–35; Kotlanger, "Phoenix, 1920–1940," 303–06.

20. Horton, *Survey of Phoenix*, 255–60; Kotlanger, "Phoenix, 1920–1940," 286–89; Daniel August Hall, "Federal Patronage of Art in Arizona from 1933 to 1943" (M.A. thesis, Arizona State University, 1974), 65–102, 157–61.

21. *Arizona Republic*, November 17, 1940; Kotlanger, "Phoenix, 1920–1940," 314–20; A. Francis Cane, "A Survey of Municipal Recreation in Phoenix, Arizona" (M.A. thesis, Arizona State University, 1944), 23–25.

22. *Arizona Republic*, November 17, 1934, November 22, 1936, November 20, 1938, November 17, 1940; Kotlanger, "Phoenix, 1920–1940," 381–85.

23. *Arizona Republic*, April 29, 1940; Kotlanger, "Phoenix, 1920–1940," 512–31; G. Wesley Johnson, *Phoenix: Valley of the Sun* (Tulsa: Continental Heritage Press, 1982), 108; Kel M. Fox, "Foreman of the Jury: Sidelights on the Trial of Winnie Ruth Judd," *Journal of Arizona History*, 26 (Autumn 1985), 295–306; Horton, *Survey of Phoenix*, 230–31, 241–44; W. D. Chesterfield to Joseph S. Jenckes, "Report, November 14, 1935" (typescript, Fred Wilson Papers, Arizona Collection, Hayden Library, Arizona State University), 1–23.

24. Shirley J. Roberts, "Minority Group Poverty in Phoenix," *Journal of Arizona History*, 14 (Winter 1973), 356.

25. Roberts, "Minority Group Poverty," 355–58; Kotlanger, "Phoenix, 1920–1940," 444–48.

26. Richard E. Harris, *The First 100 Years: A History of Arizona's Blacks* (Apache Junction: Relmo, 1983), 53–57; Alton Thomas, "Minority Housing in Phoenix," in Greater Phoenix Council for Civic Unity, ed., *To Secure These Rights* (Phoenix: The Council, 1961), 9; Roberts, "Minority Group Poverty," 357–58; Kotlanger, "Phoenix, 1920–1940," 447–48; Mattie Hackett, "A Survey of Living Conditions of Girls in the Negro Schools of Phoenix, Arizona" (M.A. thesis, Arizona State University, 1939), 17, 43.

27. *Arizona Republic*, April 17, 1931; Harris, *The First 100 Years*, 56–57; Kotlanger, "Phoenix, 1920–1940," 449–50, 462–63.

28. Emmett McLoughlin, *People's Padre* (Boston: Beacon, 1954), 34–57.

29. McLoughlin, *People's Padre*, 55–58; Kotlanger, "Phoenix, 1920–1940," 136–39.

30. Kotlanger, "Phoenix, 1920–1940," 432–37, 442–44; Raymond Johnson Flores, "The Socio-Economic Status Trends of the Mexican People Residing in Arizona" (M.A. thesis, Arizona State University, 1951), 55–58, 91–93; Mary R. Titcomb, "Americanization and Mexicans in the Southwest: A History of Phoenix's Friendly House, 1920–1983" (M.A. thesis, University of California, Santa Barbara, 1983), 41–42.

31. *Arizona Republic*, September 17, 1935; Titcomb, "Friendly House, 1920–1983," 41–57.

32. Roberts, "Minority Group Poverty," 358–59; Kotlanger, "Phoenix, 1920–1940," 403–06; Barnett and Garai, *Where the States Stand on Civil Rights*, 18–20.

33. Gary P. Tipton, "Men out of China: Origins of the Chinese Colony in Phoenix," *Journal of Arizona History*, 18 (Autumn 1977), 352–53; Chesterfield to Jenckes, "Report, November 14, 1935," 7; *Phoenix City Directory, 1940*, 32; Vivian Chang Wei, "The Chinese Community in Phoenix, Arizona" (M.A. thesis, Arizona State University, 1970), 44–45; Michael H. Bernstein, "Geographical Perspectives on Skid Row in Phoenix, Arizona" (M.A. thesis, Arizona State University, 1972), 60–61.

34. Susie Sato, "Before Pearl Harbor: Early Japanese Settlers in Arizona," *Journal of Arizona History*, 14 (Winter 1973), 317–34; Jack August, "The Anti-Japanese Crusade in Arizona's Salt River Valley, 1934–35," *Arizona and the West*, 21 (Summer 1979), 113–36; Yoshiju Kimura, *Arizona Sunset* (Phoenix: Nipy, 1980), *passim*. Not until the Walter-McCarran Act of 1952 were Japanese immigrants allowed to petition for United States citizenship.

35. Bradford Luckingham, "Urban Development in Arizona: The Rise of Phoenix," *Journal of Arizona History*, 22 (Summer 1981), 204–05, 229–30; Blaine Lamb, "Historical Overview of Tempe, Arizona, 1870–1930" (typescript, Hayden Library, Arizona State University, 1981), 1–11.

36. Luckingham, *The Urban Southwest*, 24–25; James H. McClintock, *Arizona, Maricopa: A Land of Plenty, Under Smiling Skies* (Phoenix: Manufacturing Stationers, 1901), 57–58.

37. Lamb, "Tempe, Arizona," 10–18; Herbert B. Peterson, "A Twentieth Century Journey to Cibola: Tragedy of the *Bracero* in Maricopa County, 1917–1921" (M.A. thesis, Arizona State University, 1975), *passim*.

38. Kotlanger, "Phoenix, 1920–1940," 308–10; Horton, *Survey of Phoenix*, 182–83; Ernest Hopkins and Alfred Thomas, Jr., *The Arizona State University Story* (Tempe: Arizona State University, 1960), 215–39.

39. *Arizona Gazette*, September 28, 1893; *Phoenix City and Salt River Valley Directory, 1930*, 1167; Holland Melvin, "A History of Mesa" (M.A. thesis, University of Arizona, 1933), 26–29, 40–73; Linda Laird and Robert Jones, *City of Mesa Historical Survey* (Mesa: City of Mesa, 1984), 37–54.

40. *Arizona Republican*, April 1, 1908, November 6, 1911, February 20, 1919; *Arizona Republic*, November 20, 1938, November 17, 1940; *Phoenix City and Salt River Valley Directory, 1920* (Los Angeles: Arizona Directory Company, 1920), 553; Sato, "Before Pearl Harbor," 317–34; August, "Anti-Japanese Crusade," 112–36.

41. Richard E. Lynch, *Winfield Scott: A Biography of Scottsdale's Founder* (Scottsdale: City of Scottsdale, 1978), 95–136; Patricia Myers McElfresh, *Scottsdale: Jewel in the Desert* (Woodland Hills, Calif.: Continental Heritage Press, 1984), 13–47.

42. *Arizona Republican*, May 5 and 17, 1912, March 28, 1926; Sylvia Lee Bender-Lamb, "Chandler, Arizona: Landscape as a Product of Land Speculation" (M.A. thesis, Arizona State University, 1983), 19–56, 66–78, 101–16; Robert Conway Stevens, *A History of Chandler, Arizona, 1912–1953* (Tucson: University of Arizona, 1954), 14–76.

43. Charles S. Sargent, "Towns of the Salt River Valley, 1870–1930," *Historical Geography*, 5 (Fall 1973), 3–8; Luckingham, *The Urban Southwest*, *passim*.

Chapter 6. The Boom Years, 1941–1960

1. *Arizona Republic*, January 15 and 22, June 7 and 24, August 11 and 16, 1941; Edward H. Peplow, Jr., "The Thunderbirds," *Phoenix* (May 1976), 36–39; G. W. Charlesworth, "Brief History of Luke Air Field (typescript, Luke Air Force Base Library, 1945), 2–12; Susan M. Smith, "Litchfield Park and Vicinity" (M.A. thesis, University of Arizona, 1948), 94–101.

2. *Arizona Republic*, December 3, 1978; David Myrick, *Railroads of Arizona*, vol. II (San Diego: Howell-North Books, 1981), 808–14.

3. *Arizona Republic*, July 28, 1941, November 22 and 28, 1942, March 4 and December 21, 1943, January 4, 1944, December 3, 1978; Smith, "Litchfield Park," 101–13; Connie J. May, "Corporate Growth in Phoenix, 1940–1977" (typescript, Hayden Library, Arizona State University, 1978), 2–6.

4. *Arizona Republic*, November 27, 28, and 30, 1942, February 26, 1943, December 3, 1978.

5. *Arizona Republic*, October 25, November 30, December 1, 2, 11, 17, and 19, 1942; Record of Commission, City of Phoenix, 20 (May 27, 1942–March 14, 1944).

6. *Arizona Republic*, February 18 and November 16, 1943, December 22, 1944, January 10, 1947, March 11, June 1, and October 18, 1948; Leonard E. Goodall, "Phoenix: Reformers at Work," in Leonard E. Goodall, ed., *Urban Politics in the Southwest* (Tempe: Arizona State University, 1967), 113–16.

7. Stephen D. Rockstroh, "An Analysis of Phoenix Municipal Administration, 1881–1952," (M.A. thesis, Arizona State University, 1952), 85–116; Goodall, "Phoenix," 113–16; Paul Kelso, "Phoenix Charter Arises Anew," *National Municipal Review* (April 1949), 176–77; Brent Whiting Brown, "An Analysis of the Phoenix Charter Government Committee as a Political Entity" (M.A. thesis, Arizona State University, 1968), 15–22; Michael Konig, "Toward Metropolis Status: Charter Government and the Rise of Phoenix, Arizona, 1945–1960" (Ph.D. dissertation, Arizona State University, 1983), 24–30; Russell Pulliam, *Gene Pulliam, Last of the Newspaper Titans* (Ottowa, Ill.: Jameson Books, 1984), 133.

8. Goodall, "Phoenix," 114–17; Kelso, "Phoenix Charter," 177–80; Brown, "Charter Government Committee," 22–29.

9. *Arizona Republic*, January 1 and November 11, 15, 16, 17, 24, and 30, 1948, March 3, April 9, and June 25, 1949; *Phoenix Gazette*, July 6, 1949; Goodall, "Phoenix," 114–18; Kelso, "Phoenix Charter," 179–80; Paul Kelso, "Phoenix Makes New Start," *National Municipal Review* (September 1950), 383–85; Brown, "Charter Government Committee," 29–33; Konig, "Phoenix, Arizona, 1945–1960," 35–55.

10. *Arizona Republic*, October 25 and November 1, 6, 7, and 19, 1949, January 4, 1950; Kelso, "Phoenix Makes New Start," 383–85; Konig, "Phoenix, Arizona, 1945–1960," 62–72; Brown, "Charter Government Committee," 44–56.

11. Kelso, "Phoenix Makes New Start," 384–85; Konig, "Phoenix, Arizona, 1945–1960," 73–76; Pulliam, *Gene Pulliam*, 130–37.

12. Fern Stewart, "The Pioneering Rosenzweigs: A Jewel of a Family," *Phoenix*, 17 (October 1982), 90–97; Brown, "Charter Government Committee," 44–56; Goodall, "Phoenix," 118–26; Konig, "Phoenix, Arizona, 1945–1960," *pas-*

sim; G. Wesley Johnson, "Generation of Elites and Social Change in Phoenix," in Jessie L. Embry and Howard A. Christy, eds., *Community Development in the American West* (Salt Lake City: University of Utah Press, 1985), 94–98; Bradford Luckingham, *The Urban Southwest* (El Paso: Texas Western Press, 1982), 88–89; Richard M. Bernard and Bradley R. Rice, eds., *Sunbelt Cities* (Austin: University of Texas Press, 1983), *passim*.

13. Paul Kelso, "Efficiency Pays off: Citizen Action over Past Decade Has Brought Good Government with Competent Officials to Phoenix," *National Civic Review* (September 1959), 408–13; Charles A. Esser, "Phoenix Votes $70 Million in Bonds for Long Range Capital Improvement Plan," *Western City*, 33 (July 1957), 30–33; Paul Kelso, *A Decade of Council-Manager Government in Phoenix, Arizona* (Tucson: University of Arizona Press, 1960), *passim*; Konig, "Phoenix, Arizona, 1945–1960," *passim*.

14. *Arizona Republic*, March 11, 1956, February 11, 1962; Charles T. Colley, "Carl T. Hayden—Phoenician," *Journal of Arizona History*, 18 (Autumn 1977), 293–94; Tom McKnight, *Manufacturing in Arizona* (Berkeley: University of California Press, 1962), 325–30, *passim*; Michael Konig, "Postwar Phoenix, Arizona: Banking and Boosterism," *Journal of the West*, 23 (April 1984), 72–76; Courtland L. Smith, *The Salt River Project* (Tucson: University of Arizona Press, 1972), 18–22; Larry Schweikart, *A History of Banking in Arizona* (Tucson: University of Arizona Press, 1982), 107–31; Carl Bimson, *Transformation in the Desert: The Story of Arizona's Valley National Bank* (New York: Newcomen Society, 1962), 20–26; William Reilly, *Arizona Public Service Company: Power, People, and Progress* (New York: Newcomen Society, 1970), 8–11.

15. *Arizona Republic*, November 16, 1948, May 22 and December 14, 1954, March 11, 1956, January 4, 1958, January 1, 1960; McKnight, *Manufacturing*, 312–40.

16. John Shirer, "The Motorola Research Laboratory in Phoenix," *Arizona Business and Economic Review*, 2 (February 1953), 2–3; Daniel E. Noble, "Motorola Expands in Phoenix," *Arizona Business and Economic Review*, 3 (June 1954), 1–2.

17. *Arizona Republic*, March 11, 1956, January 1, 1961; *Phoenix City Directory, 1960* (Phoenix: Phoenix Directory Company, 1960), 2–11; Knight, *Manufacturing*, 312–40; Konig, "Phoenix, 1945–1960," 196–216; Luckingham, *The Urban Southwest*, 82–83; Hiram S. Davis, "New Manufacturing Plants Strengthen the Phoenix Economy," *Arizona Business and Economic Review*, 6 (February 1957), 1–2.

18. Bradford Luckingham, "Urban Development in Arizona," *Journal of Arizona History*, 22 (Summer 1981), 219–20; Knight, *Manufacturing*, 312–40; Konig, "Phoenix, 1945–1960," 196–216; "Why the Big Boom in the Desert State?" *U.S. News & World Report* (October 11, 1957), 76–81; "Arizona: Thriving Oasis," *Time* (February 15, 1960), 28–35; "Phoenix Rises and Soars: 'Miracle' in Arizona," *Newsweek* (January 4, 1960), 45–49; Royal Alderman, "Phoenix Big Six in Electronics and What They Are Doing," *Western Electronic News* (June 1959), 26–32; Royal Alderman, "Phoenix Revisited: Electronic Boom Keeps Booming," *Western Electronic News* (June 1959), 16–24.

19. *Arizona Republic*, August 16, December 10 and 20, 1955, January 1, February 1, and March 11, 1956; "Disinterested Outsiders Say Phoenix Best

Publicized City in U.S.—Here's Why," *Phoenix Action* (February 1950), 4–5; W. Eugene Hollon, *The Southwest: Old and New* (New York: Knopf, 1961), 343–47; Michael Konig, "Phoenix in the 1950s: Urban Growth in the Sunbelt," *Arizona and the West*, 24 (Spring 1982), 24–31; Luckingham, "Urban Development in Arizona," 219–20.

20. Kelso, "Efficiency Pays off," 411–12; Kelso, *Council-Manager Government*, *passim*; Konig, "Phoenix, Arizona, 1945–1960," *passim*.

21. Margaret Finnerty, "The Labor Movement in Phoenix, 1940–1950" (typescript, Hayden Library, Arizona State University, 1978), 9–22; Clifford Sturges Newell, "The Right to Work Law in Arizona" (M.A. thesis, Arizona State University, 1977), *passim*; Michael S. Wade, *The Bitter Issue* (Tucson: Arizona Historical Society, 1976), *passim*.

22. *Arizona Republic*, March 11, 1956, February 1, 1958, December 24, 1960, February 11, 1962; Mark Adams and Gertrude Adams, *A Report on Politics in El Paso* (Cambridge, Mass.: Harvard University Press, 1963), sec. V, 26–27.

23. *Arizona Republic*, March 11, 1956, February 11, 1962; Sharon Thomas Cropsey, "The Impact of Urbanization on the Beef and Dairy Cattle Industries of Maricopa County" (M.A. thesis, Arizona State University, 1975), *passim*; G. M. Hermanson, "Urbanization of Agricultural Lands in Maricopa County, Arizona, 1950–1980" (M.A. thesis, Arizona State University, 1968), *passim*.

24. *Arizona Republic*, November 21, 1954, March 11, 1956, February 11, 1962; Bert Fireman, "Urbanization and Home Comfort," in William R. Noyes, ed., *Progress in Arizona* (Tucson: University of Arizona, 1973), 3–4; Luckingham, "Urban Development in Arizona," 220–22; Sam Boal, "Sunniest City in the USA," *Holiday* (March 1954), 98–103. See also Raymond Arsenault, "The End of the Long Hot Summer: The Air Conditioner and Southern Culture," *Journal of Southern History*, 50 (November 1984), 597–626.

25. *Arizona Republic*, May 16, 1954, March 2, 1960; *Phoenix Gazette*, May 6, 1961; Neil Morgan, *Westward Tilt: The American West Today* (New York: Random House, 1961), 344–45, 354; Harold H. Martin, "The New Millionaires of Phoenix," *The Saturday Evening Post*, 234 (September 30, 1961), 25–30; Manya Winsted, "Pioneer Builder John F. Long Celebrates an Anniversary," *Phoenix*, 10 (February 1977), 47–49.

26. *Arizona Republic*, May 9 and December 8, 1955, March 11, 1956, March 26, April 1 and 30, 1959, March 21 and May 24, 1960, February 11, 1962; Konig, "Phoenix, Arizona, 1945–1960," 80–122; "Annexation Work Receives Tribute," *Phoenix Action* (July 1959), 7; City of Phoenix, *75th Anniversary Report* (Phoenix: City of Phoenix, 1960), 8; Pulliam, *Gene Pulliam*, 136–37; John D. Wenum, *Annexation as a Technique for Metropolitan Growth: The Case of Phoenix, Arizona* (Tempe: Arizona State University, 1970), *passim*.

27. *Arizona Republic*, March 6, 1946; John Shirer, "Business in Arizona, 1929–1951, as Reflected in Phoenix Department Store Sales," *Arizona Business and Economic Review*, 1 (March 1952), 1–6; Richard Anthony Sertich, "Comparative Analysis of Regional Shopping Centers in the Phoenix, Arizona Planning Area" (M.A. thesis, Arizona State University, 1980), *passim*.

28. Laurence J. Fleming, *Ride a Mile and Smile the While: A History of the Phoenix Street Railway* (Phoenix: Swaine Publications, 1977), 131–52; Konig, "Phoenix, Arizona, 1945–1960," 216–53; Joseph Stocker, "That's No Mirage,"

Phoenix Point West, 2 (January 1960), 20–21; J. M. Hunter, "The Challenge of the Mess We Live in," *Arizona Architect*, 4 (February 1961), 9–11.

29. *Arizona Republic*, March 11, 1956, February 11, 1962; Konig, "Phoenix, Arizona, 1945–1960," 253–83; Wilbur Smith, *A Major Street and Highway Plan for the Phoenix Urban Area and Maricopa County* (San Francisco: n.p., 1960), *passim*; W. S. Peters, "A Billion $ of Buildings in 5 Years," *Phoenix Point West*, 2 (July 1960), 20–21, 56–57.

30. *Arizona Republic*, July 5 and 15, 1951, June 2, 1952; Smith, *The Salt River Project*, 11–15; Stephen C. Shadegg, *Century One* (Phoenix: Salt River Project, 1969), 39–40; Reilly, *Arizona Public Service Company*, 8–32; Rich Johnson, *The Central Arizona Project, 1918–1968* (Tucson: University of Arizona Press, 1977), *passim*.

31. *Phoenix, Arizona Directory 1950* (Phoenix: Baldin & Mullin-Kille Company, 1950), 9–12; *Phoenix, Arizona Directory 1960* (Phoenix: Baldin & Mullin-Kille Company, 1960), 3–11; Ernest J. Hopkins and Alfred Thomas, Jr., *The Arizona State University Story* (Tempe: Arizona State University, 1960), 245–304; Michael W. Rubinoff, "Arizona State University . . . YES!," *Phoenix*, 8 (April 1973), 40–42, 44–45.

32. *Arizona Republic*, November 20, 1960, May 17, 1964, November 14, 1965; Konig, "Phoenix, Arizona, 1945–1960," 316–24; Paul Hughes, "The Big Three of Valley Entertainment," *Phoenix Point West*, 2 (November 1960), 27–29; A. B. Cutts, "The Shakespeare Festival, a Retrospective View," *Phoenix Point West*, 3 (March 1961), 56–57, 69–71.

33. Hughes, "Valley Entertainment," 27; Maggie Savoy, "Society in the Valley of the Sun," *Phoenix Point West*, 2 (February 1960), 16–19; Robert de Roos, "Arizona: Booming Youngster of the West," *National Geographic*, 123 (March 1963), 307; Joseph Stocker, "Mrs. Archer Linde, Beloved Impresario," *Phoenix*, 20 (January 1985), 94–96.

34. *Arizona Republic*, January 12, 1958, March 21, 1961; Desmond Muirhead, "The Arizona Landscape, a Critique," *Arizona Architect*, 2 (June 1959), 12–16; "Population Growth and Land Use, Maricopa County and Phoenix Area," *Arizona Architect*, 3 (March 1960), 21–27; Robert B. Whitaker, "Phoenix: City of Beautiful Parks," *Arizona Highways*, 40 (March 1964), 24–27; Konig, "Phoenix, Arizona, 1945–1960," 313–16; MacKaye, "Phoenix," 37; "Big Boom in the Desert States," *U.S. News & World Report* (October 11, 1957), 78–79; Leonard Arrington and George Jensen, "Comparison of Income Changes in the Western States, 1929–1960," *Western Economic Journal*, 1 (February 1963), 205–17. For the "barbecue culture" prevalent in the West, see Gerald D. Nash, *The American West in the Twentieth Century* (Englewood Cliffs, N. J.: Prentice-Hall, 1973), 226–28.

35. Joyotpaul Chaudhuri, *Urban Indians of Arizona: Phoenix, Tucson and Flagstaff* (Tucson: University of Arizona Press, 1973), 20–33; Anna Moore Shaw, *A Pima Past* (Tucson: University of Arizona Press, 1974), 152–53, 180–81, 189–90; *Hearings Before the United States Commission on Civil Rights, Phoenix, Arizona, February 3, 1962* (Washington D.C.: U.S. Government Printing Office, 1962), 12, 95–98; Shirley J. Roberts, "Minority Group Poverty in Phoenix," *Journal of Arizona History*, 14 (Winter 1973), 357–58.

36. Vivian Chang Wei, "The Chinese Community in Phoenix, Arizona" (M.A. thesis, Arizona State University, 1970), 45–57; *Hearings*, 125–26.

37. Yoshiju Kimura, *Arizona Sunset* (Phoenix: Nipy, 1980), 59–82; Shelly C. Dudley, "Japanese Relocation: Local Attitudes and Reactions," *History Forum*, 3 (Spring 1981), 5–20; Samuel T. Caruso, "After Pearl Harbor: Arizona's Response to the Gila River Relocation Center," *Journal of Arizona History*, 14 (Winter 1973), 335–45; Paul Bailey, *City of the Sun: The Japanese Concentration Camp at Poston, Arizona* (Los Angeles: Westernlore Press, 1970), *passim*; Roger Daniels, *Concentration Camps USA: Japanese Americans and World War II* (New York: Atheneum, 1971), 83–84.

38. James E. Officer, *Arizona's Hispanic Perspective* (Phoenix: Arizona Academy, 1981), 111–12; *Hearings*, 67–79, 86–95, *passim*; Raymond Johnson Flores, "The Socio-Economic Status Trends of the Mexican People Residing in Arizona" (M.A. thesis, Arizona State University, 1951), 42–59, 69–95; Jose Amaro Hernandez, *Mutual Aid for Survival: The Case of the Mexican-American* (Malabar, Fla.: Krieger, 1983), 49–51; Greater Phoenix Council for Civic Unity, *To Secure These Rights* (Phoenix: The Council, 1961), 14–16, 62–65, *passim*; Interview with Adam Diaz, October 25, 1977 (Arizona Collection, Hayden Library, Arizona State University); Mary R. Titcomb, "Americanization and Mexicans in the Southwest: A History of Phoenix's Friendly House, 1920–1983" (M.A. thesis, University of California, Santa Barbara, 1983), 54–74.

39. Emmett McLoughlin, *People's Padre* (Boston: Beacon, 1954), 101–14; Joseph Stocker, "The Ball and the Cross," *The Catholic World*, 165 (June 1947), 260–64; Barbara Lambesis, "Memorial Hospital History," *Arizona Medicine*, 33 (July 1976), 592–97.

40. Mattie Hackett, "A Survey of Living Conditions of Girls in the Negro Schools of Phoenix" (M.A. thesis, Arizona State University, 1939), 1–2, 43–50; Richard Newhall, "Losers into Winners: The Story of Carver High School," *Phoenix Point West*, 6 (September 1965), 27–29; Interview, William P. Mahoney, Jr., (Arizona Collection, Hayden Library, Arizona State University); Hayzel Burton Daniels, "A Black Magistrate's Struggles," in Anne Hodges Morgan and Rennard Strickland, eds., *Arizona Memories* (Tucson: University of Arizona Press, 1984), 335–38; W. A. Robinson, "The Progress of Integration in the Phoenix Schools," *Journal of Negro Education*, 25 (Fall 1956), 371–79; Greater Phoenix Council for Civic Unity, *To Secure These Rights*, 9–13, 17–46, *passim*; *Hearings*, 16–26, 34–68, 101–39, *passim*; Richard E. Harris, *The First 100 Years: A History of Arizona's Blacks* (Apache Junction: Relmo, 1983), 69–74, 81–98, 138–41, *passim*.

41. *Arizona Republic*, February 23, 1952; Milton Mackaye, "Phoenix," *Saturday Evening Post* (October 18, 1947), 37, 88–95; Roberts, "Minority Group Poverty," 355–60; Luckingham, "Urban Development in Arizona," 227–28.

Chapter 7. Sunbelt Center, 1960–1980

1. Richard M. Bernard and Bradley R. Rice, eds., *Sunbelt Cities* (Austin: University of Texas Press, 1983), 1–30; Carl Abbott, *The New Urban America* (Chapel Hill: University of North Carolina Press, 1981), *passim*; Bradford Luck-

ingham, *The Urban Southwest* (El Paso: Texas Western Press, 1982), 95–96; David C. Perry and Alfred J. Watkins, eds., *The Rise of the Sunbelt Cities* (Beverly Hills: Sage, 1977), 19–52, *passim*. For another individual city biography, see David G. McComb, *Houston: A History*, rev. ed. (Austin: University of Texas Press, 1981).

2. *Phoenix Gazette*, February 7, 1963, November 20, 1967, October 16, 1968, October 9 and 28, November 12, December 10, 1969; *Arizona Republic*, March 31, 1963, January 31 and June 12, 1964, June 4, 1965, November 12 and December 10, 1969; Leonard E. Goodall, "Phoenix: Reformers at Work," in Leonard E. Goodall, ed., *Urban Politics in the Southwest* (Tempe: Arizona State University, 1967), 114–26; Brent Whiting Brown, "An Analysis of the Phoenix Charter Government Committee as a Political Entity" (M.A. thesis, Arizona State University, 1968), 44–93; David L. Altheide and John S. Hall, "Phoenix: Crime and Politics in a New Federal City," in Anne Henry, Herbert Jacob, and Robert L. Lineberry, eds., *Crime in City Politics* (New York: Longman, Inc., 1984), 201–21; Barbara Cortright, "Leading Citizens—Where Do They Lead?" *Reveille*, 2 (July 1967), 18–21; John Louis Ruppel, Jr., "Urban Community Participation in Federal Grant Programs for the Phoenix Metropolitan Area" (M.A. thesis, Arizona State University, 1971), 75–94; Peter C. Boulay, "Milt Graham: Afterthoughts and Ambitions," *Phoenix*, 5 (March 1970), 37–40; "Phoenix: The Blemishes in Boomtown," *Business Week* (November 15, 1969), 148–49.

3. *Arizona Republic*, December 11, 1971; Pam Hait, "A Conversation with John Driggs," *Phoenix*, 9 (April 1974), 42–45, 110–11; Altheide and Hall, "Crime and Politics," 221–24, *passim*; John S. Hall, "Phoenix, Arizona," in Paul R. Dommel, ed., *Decentralizing Urban Policy: Case Studies in Community Development* (Washington, D.C.: The Brookings Institution, 1982), 47–83.

4. *Arizona Republic*, November 8 and December 12, 1973; *Phoenix Gazette*, November 8 and December 12, 1973; "Charter Government," *Phoenix*, 8 (August 1973), 98–99; Pam Hait, "A Look at Charter Government," *Phoenix*, 8 (October 1973), 21–23; Bruce D. Merrill, "Attitudes Toward Charter Government in Phoenix: A Behavioral Perspective," Arizona State University *Public Service Bulletin*, 12 (December 1973), 1–3.

5. *Arizona Republic*, October 28, November 1 and 5, December 10, 1975; *Phoenix Gazette*, November 5 and December 10, 1975; Pam Hait, "Her Honor, the Mayor," *Phoenix*, 9 (January 1976), 34–37; "Hance of Phoenix," *People Weekly*, 11 (March 19, 1979), 30; Altheide and Hall, "Crime and Politics," 227–37; Hall, "Phoenix, Arizona," 59–83.

6. *Arizona Republic*, September 27 and November 10, 1977, November 3, 1979; *Phoenix Gazette*, November 10, 1977, November 3, 1979; Altheide and Hall, "Crime and Politics," 227–37; John S. Hall, *Case Studies of the Impact of Federal Aid on Major Cities: City of Phoenix* (Washington, D.C.: The Urban Institute Press, 1979), 13–14, 66–67; Hall, "Phoenix, Arizona," 59–83; John S. Hall and Frank J. Sacton, "Fiscal Federalism and Arizona's Role," in Nicholas Henry, ed., *Toward Tax Reform* (Tempe: Arizona State University, 1979), 36–37; G. Wesley Johnson, *Phoenix: Valley of the Sun* (Tulsa: Continental Heritage Press, 1982), 155–64; Fenwick Anderson, "Bricks Without Straws: The Mirage of Competition in the Desert of Phoenix Daily Journalism Since 1947" (Ph.D. dissertation, University of Illinois, 1980), 331–33.

7. *Arizona Republic*, June 29, 1980; *Phoenix Gazette*, February 21, 1981; Phoenix Newspapers, Inc., *Inside Phoenix, 1978* (Phoenix: Phoenix Newspapers, Inc., 1978), 35; Charles M. Swaart, "What Makes Phoenix Grow?" *Phoenix Point West*, 7 (January 1966), 15–17; Edward H. Peplow, Jr., "Growth Patterns," *Phoenix*, 8 (August 1973), 73–74, 123, 132; "Valley Progress Report," *Phoenix*, 15 (August 1980), C3.

8. Connie J. May, "Corporate Growth in Phoenix" (typescript, Hayden Library, Arizona State University, 1978), 8–18; "Valley Progress Report," *Phoenix*, 13 (August 1978), 105–06; Phoenix Newspapers, Inc., *Inside Phoenix, 1979* (Phoenix: Phoenix Newspapers, Inc., 1979), *passim*.

9. *El Paso Times*, December 22 and 23, 1978; *Wall Street Journal*, September 18–21 and 25, October 1, 1979; *Arizona Republic*, October 29, 1978; Phoenix Newspapers, Inc., *Inside Phoenix, 1980* (Phoenix: Phoenix Newspapers, Inc., 1980), *passim*; Luckingham, *The Urban Southwest*, 96–98; "Greyhound Goes to Phoenix," *Business Week* (July 3, 1971), 59.

10. Marie Simington, *Metro Phoenix* (Phoenix: Phoenix Chamber of Commerce, 1977), 19–20; Johnson, *Valley of the Sun*, 129–30, 147; "Valley Progress Report," *Phoenix*, 14 (August 1979), 92–94; Western Savings, *Foresight Eighty* (Phoenix: Western Savings, 1980), 8–9.

11. *Arizona Republic*, May 26, October 29, November 13, 1980; Luckingham, *The Urban Southwest*, 98–99; G. M. Hermanson, "Urbanization of Agricultural Lands in Maricopa County, Arizona, 1950–1980" (M.A. thesis, Arizona State University, 1968), 67–82; Sharon T. Cropsey, "The Impact of Urbanization on the Beef and Dairy Cattle Industries of Maricopa County" (M.A. thesis, Arizona State University, 1975), 28–75.

12. Gaylord M. McGrath, "The Evolution of Resorts and Guest Ranches in Greater Phoenix" (typescript, Hayden Library, Arizona State University, 1973), 23–32; Hogan Smith, "The Changing Resort Scene," *Phoenix*, 5 (January 1968), 18–19, 65; "Marriott's Camelback Inn," *Arizona Highways*, 50 (April 1974), 5; "Valley Progress Report," *Phoenix*, 11 (1976), 77–78, 126; Neal R. Peirce, *The Mountain States of America* (New York: Norton, 1972), 236–40.

13. *New York Times*, February 24, 1970, April 5, 1975; Luckingham, *The Urban Southwest*, 102–07; Bradford Luckingham, "The American Southwest," *Western Historical Quarterly*, 15 (July 1984), 274–75; Valley National Bank, *Arizona Statistical Review*, 36 (September 1980), 13; *Inside Phoenix 1980, passim*.

14. *New York Times*, April 5, 1975, May 19, 1979; *Boston Globe*, May 18, 1980; *Arizona Republic*, May 20, 1979, October 12, 1980; *Phoenix Gazette*, February 24, 1981; Luckingham, *The Urban Southwest*, 107–13; Jeffrey Cook, "Patterns of Desert Urbanization: The Evolution of Metropolitan Phoenix," in Gideon Golaney, ed., *Urban Planning for Arid Zones: American Experiences and Directions* (New York: John Wiley & Sons, 1978), 221–28; Charles S. Sargent, *Planned Communities in Greater Phoenix* (Tempe: Arizona State University, 1973), 1–57; Jay Bashear, ed., *The Urban Challenge* (Phoenix: Phoenix Newspapers, Inc., 1978), 31–32; Richard Anthony Servitch, "Comparative Analysis of Regional Shopping Centers in Phoenix, Arizona Planning Area" (M.A. thesis, Arizona State University, 1980), 22–38, 61–122; *Phoenix Concept Plan 2000* (Phoenix: City of Phoenix, 1979), 19, *passim*.

15. Luckingham, *The Urban Southwest*, 107–10; Luckingham, "The Ameri-

can Southwest," 277–80; Bernard and Rice, *Sunbelt Cities*, 8–11; Phoenix City Clerk's Office, *Phoenix Annexation Manual* (Phoenix: City of Phoenix, 1972), 2; Robert William Hildebrand, "Metropolitan Area Government: Miami, Nashville, and Phoenix in Perspective" (M.A. thesis, Arizona State University, 1974), 73–82; Donna Culbertson, "Phoenix's Creative Annexations," *Nation's Cities*, 11 (July 1973), 18–20.

16. Robert C. Hook, "Phoenix Yesterday and Today," *Arizona Business Bulletin*, 13 (April 1966), 3–6; Peter Russell, "Downtown's Downturn: A Historical Geography of the Phoenix Central Business District, 1890–1986" (M.A. thesis, Arizona State University, 1986), 93–98, *passim*.

17. *Arizona Republic*, May 29–31, June 1–5, 1966.

18. *New York Times*, February 19, 1967; *Arizona Republic*, May 29–31, June 1–5, 1966, April 16, 1970, May 16 and June 22, 1971; Russell, "Downtown's Downtown," 101–28; Clemenc Anthony Ligocki, "Spatial Analysis of Automobile Parking in Downtown and Uptown Phoenix, Arizona" (M.A. thesis, Arizona State University, 1981), 34–42; Peter L. Sandberg, "How Ugly Is Phoenix? It's Pretty Ugly, Man . . . ," *Phoenix Point West*, 7 (March 1966), 29; "Annual Valley Progress Report," *Phoenix*, 8 (August 1973), 77–104; "Annual Valley Progress Report," *Phoenix*, 16 (August 1981), 106–11; Central Phoenix Redevelopment Agency, *Downtown Phoenix: A Vision of the Valley Center* (Phoenix: City of Phoenix, 1980), 4–5; Joe Kullman, "Sprucing up the Deuce," *Phoenix*, 19 (August 1979), 123–26, 205–06.

19. *Phoenix Gazette*, October 13, 1975; Luckingham, *The Urban Southwest*, 111–12; Richard Newhall, "The Long Wait at the Intersection," *Arizona* (January 15, 1967), 6–10; Pam Hait, "Transportation: One of the Most Complex Issues Facing the Valley Today," *Phoenix*, 8 (August 1973), 96–97; Pam Hait, "Transportation Update," *Phoenix*, 9 (August 1974), 50–51; Michael Konig, "Toward Metropolitan Status: Charter Government and the Rise of Phoenix, Arizona, 1945–1960" (Ph.D. dissertation, Arizona State University, 1983), 79. Russell Pulliam, *Gene Pulliam* (Ottowa, Ill.: Jameson Books, 1984), 283–87.

20. Leo Moore, "The People Moving Problem," *Phoenix*, 6 (May 1971), 17–21; Pam Hait, "The City's Ailing Bus System: An Expensive Problem," *Phoenix*, 8 (July 1973), 25–26; "You Can't Get Here from There," *Arizona* (May 22, 1977), 38–41; Ronald William Brooks, "Transportation (Availability) and Employability of the Urban Poor" (M.A. thesis, Arizona State University, 1974), 3–8, 32–35; Maricopa Association of Governments Transportation and Planning Office, *Guide for Regional Development and Transportation* (Phoenix: Maricopa County, 1980), IV-1 to IV-15.

21. *Phoenix Gazette*, May 7, 1966; *Arizona Republic*, March 9, 1969; James E. Cook, "Nobody Ever Finishes Building an Airport," *Arizona* (July 9, 1972), 12–17; Peggy De Marco, Sam LaTona, Ronnie A. Null, and Claude C. Vallieres, "The West Approach Land Acquisition Project: A Post-Relocation Study" (M.S.W. thesis, Arizona State University, 1979), 5–36, *passim*; "Annual Valley Progress Report," *Phoenix*, 15 (August 1981), 96–106.

22. Luckingham, *The Urban Southwest*, 99–102; Dean E. Mann, *The Politics of Water in Arizona* (Tucson: University of Arizona Press, 1963), 66, 253–56; Frank Welsh, *How to Create a Water Crisis* (Boulder, Colo.: Johnson Books,

1985), 8–25, *passim*; Doug MacEachern, "Agriculture: Essential Industry or Anachronistic Pursuit?" *Phoenix*, 15 (August 1980), C13–C14.

23. *Arizona Republic*, October 29 and November 23, 1980; *Phoenix Gazette*, November 29, December 1 and 13, 1980; Paul Bracken and Herman Kahn, *A Summary of Arizona Tomorrow* (New York: Arizona Tomorrow, 1979), 15–17; Luckingham, *The Urban Southwest*, 99–101.

24. Luckingham, "The American Southwest," 275; David B. Scoular, *The First Decade: A History of Events at Grady Gammage Memorial Auditorium* (Tempe: Arizona State University, 1976), 1–9.

25. *Arizona Republic*, May 29, 1966; Peter L. Sandberg, "Phoenix Through the Eyes of a Yugoslavian Poet," *Phoenix Point West*, 6 (November 1965), 43.

26. Peter L. Sandberg, "The Phoenix Theatre Center, 1966: Snatching Defeat from the Jaws of Victory," *Reveille*, 1 (July–August, 1966), 4–7; Anita Welch, "Phoenix Little Theatre: Looking Forward to the Second Fifty Years," *Phoenix*, 6 (May 1971), 24–25; Michael Dixon, "The Year in Theatre: A Mixed Bag," *Phoenix* 15 (August 1980), D13–D14.

27. Tim Kelly, "The Phoenix Art Museum," *Arizona Highways*, 42 (March 1966), 4–27; Patricia Hartwell, "The Phoenix Art Museum: Ten Years Old and 54 Years Young," *Phoenix*, 4 (November 1969), 31–35, 63–64; Barbara Cortright, "The Arts: Past and Future Highlights," *Phoenix*, 15 (August 1980), D7–D8.

28. Donna Lederman, "Will the Orchestra Survive?" *Reveille*, 2 (January 1967), 8–11; Helen Backer, "The Symphony Story," *Phoenix*, 10 (October 1970), 41–42, 90, 112; Bryan Carol Stoneburner, "The Phoenix Symphony Orchestra, 1947–1978" (M.A. thesis, Arizona State University, 1981), 33–78; Nan Birmingham, "Phoenix: The Place in the Sun," *Town & Country*, 130 (January 1976), 108–09.

29. *Boston Globe*, May 18, 1980; Simington, *Metro Phoenix*, 38–40; Ardelle Coleman, "Arizona's Lifestyle," *Phoenix*, 9 (March 1974), 34–53; Diane Thomas, "Their Kind of Town," *Phoenix*, 9 (August 1974), 74–77; Anita Welch, "The Phoenix Mystique," *Phoenix*, 11 (March 1976), 44–45, 69; Birmingham, "Phoenix," 36–38, 90–99, 108–09.

30. Bill Lewis, "The Phoenix Suns: Basketball Comes to Town," *Phoenix*, 3 (October 1968), 22–23, 70–71; Leo Moore, "Phoenix: Big League Sports Town," *Phoenix*, 5 (October 1970), 60–62; Wayne Amos, "The Year of the Coliseum," *Arizona* (October 23, 1966), 22–29; Doug MacEachern, "The Score on Sports," *Phoenix*, 15 (August 1980), E1–E2.

31. Bud De Wald, "They Built the Zoo in '62," *Arizona* (November 18, 1962), 21–26; Edward H. Peplow, Jr., "The Phoenix Zoo," *Arizona Highways*, 44 (March 1968), 10–27; Nora Burba, "What's Gnu at the Phoenix Zoo," *Phoenix*, 15 (August 1980), D1–D2.

32. Dan Lee, "Parks, Preserves and All the Problems," *Arizona* (May 2, 1976), 57–62; Pam Hait, "A Conversation with Mayor Driggs," *Phoenix*, 9 (April 1974), 42–45; "Phoenix Mountain Preserve," *Phoenix*, 13 (August 1978), 49; Doug MacEachern, "Mountain Preserves: A Battle for Survival," *Phoenix*, 15 (August 1980), F8–F11.

33. *Arizona Republic*, September 5, 1974; *Phoenix Gazette*, June 20, 1977; Kenneth Welch, "Publisher's Letter," *Phoenix*, 15 (August 1980), 8; Sandy Gale,

"A Problem That Won't Vanish into Thin Air," *Phoenix*, 16 (August 1981), 130–31; Altheide and Hall, "Crime and Politics," 225–28, *passim*.

34. *Arizona Republic*, August 18 and December 24, 1974, August 28, 1975, June 3, September 26, October 17, and November 14, 1976, February 17, March 13, May 28, and November 10, 1977, June 25 and 26, 1978, December 13, 1981, June 25, 1986; *New Times*, March 23 and 30, 1977, June 3, 1986; Altheide and Hall, "Crime and Politics," 225–28, *passim*; Patricia A. Simko, "Arizona: The Land of Laissez-Faire," in Jean M. Halloran, ed., *Promised Lands* (New York: Praeger, 1978), 140–80; Robert Lindsay Sherman, "Public Officials and Land Fraud in Arizona" (M.A. thesis, Arizona State University, 1978), 65–82, *passim*; Martin Tallberg, *Don Bolles: An Investigation into His Murder* (New York: Popular Library, 1977), 25–52, 60–62, 145–200, 219–53, *passim*; Michael F. Wendland, *The Arizona Project: How a Team of Investigative Reporters Got Revenge on Deadline* (Kansas City: Sheed, Andrews & McNeel, 1977), 81–209, 220–21, 238, *passim*.

35. Luckingham, *The Urban Southwest*, 124–25, 138–39.

36. Luckingham, *The Urban Southwest*, 117–18, 124; Richard E. Harris, *The First 100 Years: A History of Arizona's Blacks* (Apache Junction: Relmo, 1983), 94–115; *Hearings Before the United States Commission on Civil Rights, Phoenix, Arizona, February 3, 1962* (Washington, D.C.: U.S. Government Printing Office, 1962), *passim*; Andrew Kopkind, "Modern Times in Phoenix," *The New Republic* (November 6, 1965), 14–16; John E. Crow, *Discrimination, Poverty, and the Negro: Arizona in the National Context* (Tucson: University of Arizona Press, 1968), 1–49.

37. Harris, *The First 100 Years*, 94–115; Crow, *Negro*, 1–49.

38. Richard Newhall, "The Negro in Phoenix," *Phoenix Point West*, 6 (September 1965), 15–18; Lois Boyles, "A Look at the Problem Through the Eyes of the Negro," *Arizona* (June 2, 1968), 5–10; Gary A. Stallings, "Phoenix and the National Press: A Cracked Image," *Phoenix Point West*, 7 (March 1966), 14–77.

39. *Arizona Republic*, October 27, 1965, July 18 and 26–31, 1967; Crow, *Negro*, 1–17; Altheide and Hall, "Crime and Politics," 217–18; National Urban League, *Economic and Cultural Progress of the Negro: Phoenix, Arizona* (New York: National Urban League, 1965), *passim*; The University of Arizona, *Civil Disorders, Lawlessness, and Their Roots* (Tucson: University of Arizona Press, 1969), 50–74; City of Phoenix, *Chronological History of LEAP* (Phoenix: City of Phoenix, 1967), 1–16; John Preston, "Look Who's Fighting 'Police Harassment,'" *Arizona* (May 3, 1970), 7–9.

40. Crow, *Negro, passim*; Harris, *The First 100 Years*, 102–38; Shirley J. Roberts, "Minority Group Poverty in Phoenix," *Journal of Arizona History*, 14 (Winter 1973), 360–61; "A Brief History of Urban League in Phoenix" (typescript, Phoenix Urban League, 1981), 10–11; Franklin J. James *et al.*, *Minorities in the Sunbelt* (New York: Oxford University Press, 1984), 135–39, *passim*; Charles N. Glaab and A. Theodore Brown, *A History of Urban America*, 3rd ed. (New York: Macmillan, 1983), 349–50.

41. Harris, *The First 100 Years*, 77–78, *passim*; *Hearings, passim*; James E. Officer, *Arizona's Hispanic Perspective* (Phoenix: Arizona Academy, 1981), 143–61, *passim*; Patricia A. Adank, "Chicano Activism in Maricopa County—Two

Incidents in Retrospect," in Manuel P. Servin, ed., *An Awakened Minority: The Mexican-Americans* (Beverly Hills: Sage, 1974), 246–65.

42. *Arizona Republic*, October 9–December 2, 1970; *Phoenix Gazette*, October 7–December 3, 1970, January 13 and 16, February 2, 1971; "Furors on a High School Campus," *Arizona* (November 20, 1970), 6–11; Adank, "Chicano Activism," 246–65.

43. Jose A. Hernandez, *Mutual Aid for Survival* (Malabar, Fla.: Krieger, 1983), 56–59; Mary R. Titcomb, "Americanization and Mexicans in the Southwest: A History of Phoenix's Friendly House" (M.A. thesis, University of California, Santa Barbara, 1983), 73–95, 102–04; Officer, *Arizona's Historical Perspective*, 153–61; Arabella Martinez and David B. Carlson, "Developing Leadership in Minority Communities" (typescript, Chicanos por la Causa, Phoenix, 1983), 81–87.

44. Officer, *Arizona's Hispanic Perspective*, 113–61; James *et al.*, *Minorities in the Sunbelt*, 135–39; Pam Hait, "South Phoenix," *Phoenix*, 9 (August 1974), 54, 129; Joe Kullman, "The Youth Gang Controversy," *Phoenix*, 14 (August 1979), 152–57; Susan Shultz, "Illegal Aliens: Today's Underground Railroad," *Phoenix*, 14 (September 1979), 71–75, 112–13, 129.

45. *Hearings*, 96–98; Joyotpaul Chaudhuri, *Urban Indians of Arizona* (Tucson: University of Arizona Press, 1973), 22–33; Phoenix Indian Center, "Center Development" (typescript, Phoenix Indian Center, 1980), 2–6; Edward B. Liebow, "A Sense of Place: Urban Indians and the History of Pan-Tribal Institutions in Phoenix, Arizona" (Ph.D. dissertation, Arizona State University, 1986), 119–308, *passim*; Sister Mary Rose Christy, "American Urban Indians: A Political Enigma. A Case Study: The Relationship Between Phoenix Urban Indians and Phoenix City Government" (Ph.D. dissertation, Arizona State University, 1979), 155–91.

Chapter 8. Southwest Metropolis, The 1980s

1. *Phoenix Gazette*, November 7, 1979; *Arizona Republic*, May 24 and November 29, 1980, October 25 and November 4, 1981; John Stuart Hall, "Retrenchment in Phoenix, Arizona," in George E. Peterson and Carol W. Lewis, eds., *Reagan and the Cities* (Washington, D.C.: The Urban Institute Press, 1986), 185–207.

2. *Arizona Republic*, August 19, 1979, January 7, May 22, and November 4, 1981; *Phoenix Gazette*, October 9 and November 4, 1981; *New Times*, October 23–November 3 and November 10–16, 1981.

3. *Phoenix Gazette*, October 7 and 22, 1981, February 25, June 30, November 29, and December 2, 1982; *Arizona Republic*, January 25, November 28, and December 2, 1982; *New Times*, November 10–16, 17–23, and 24–30, 1982.

4. *Phoenix Gazette*, November 29, December 21 and 22, 1982; *Arizona Republic*, November 28 and December 2, 1982; *New Times*, November 17–23, 1982; Richard M. Bernard and Bradley R. Rice, eds., *Sunbelt Cities* (Austin: University of Texas Press, 1983), 23–26, *passim*; Carl Abbott, *The New Urban America* (Chapel Hill: University of North Carolina Press, 1981), 244–56, *passim*.

5. *Phoenix Gazette*, November 28 and 29, December 2 and 22, 1982; *Arizona*

Republic, November 28, December 2 and 9, 1982; *New Times*, October 19–25, November 17–23 and 24–30, December 8–14, 1982.

6. *Phoenix Gazette*, April 27, May 20, June 24, July 21, 1983; *Arizona Republic*, June 9, October 2 and 3, 1983; Doug MacEachern, "What Is Terry Goddard Really up to?" *Phoenix*, 18 (May 1983), 67–75, 133.

7. *Phoenix Gazette*, October 10, 19, and 20, 1983; *Arizona Republic*, October 10, 15, and 26, 1983; *New Times*, October 19–25, 1983; Terry Goddard, "Now What?" *Phoenix*, 18 (December 1983), 143–44; Catrien Ross Laetz, "Charles Keating, a Business Legend in His Own Time," *Phoenix*, 21 (September 1986), 55–56, 146–48.

8. *Arizona Republic*, October 29 and 30, November 2, 3, and 6, December 14, 1983; *Phoenix Gazette*, November 2 and 3, December 14, 1983; *New Times*, October 26–November 1, December 7–13, 1983.

9. *Phoenix Gazette*, May 12 and December 11, 1983, January 2, 6, and 9, 1984; *Arizona Republic*, January 4, 1984.

10. *Arizona Republic*, April 21, June 21, July 8, September 9 and 19, 1985; *Phoenix Gazette*, June 13 and 21, September 9 and 19, 1985; Ted Rushton, "District System: Ward Politics or Open Government," *Phoenix*, 20 (May 1985), 63–67.

11. *Arizona Republic*, February 1, March 18, May 19, June 5, 1986; *Phoenix Gazette*, March 27, April 3 and 7, September 1, November 20, December 26, 1986; Terry Goddard, *State of the City and Budget Message, 1986* (Phoenix: City of Phoenix, 1986), 1–7, *passim*.

12. *Phoenix Gazette*, June 3, 1987; *Arizona Republic*, June 4, 1987; Bradford Luckingham, *The Urban Southwest* (El Paso: Texas Western Press, 1982), 125–27; Bernard and Rice, *Sunbelt Cities*, 20–26, *passim*; Abbott, *The New Urban America*, 13–14, 245–50, *passim*; John Naisbitt, *Megatrends: Ten New Directions Transforming Our Lives* (New York: Warner Books, 1982), 112–13.

13. *Arizona Republic*, May 3, 1981, April 25, 1985, January 8, 1987; *Greater Phoenix Business Journal*, December 22, 1986; Tom R. Rex, "On Guard: Taking Valley's Property for Granted Is Dangerous," *Phoenix*, 21 (August 1986), 109–10; "Dynamic Growth Pattern Persists in the Phoenix Metro Area," *Arizona Progress*, 41 (February 1986), 1–3; Tom R. Rex, "87 Likely to Be Fifth Year of Expansion," *Arizona Business*, 34 (January 1987), 1–5.

14. *Arizona Republic*, May 3, 1981, April 25, 1985; *Phoenix Gazette*, January 9, 1987; Showalter, "Diversified Economy," 4; Rex, "On Guard," 109–10; Marshall Vest, "Arizona Remains Fastest Growing State," *Arizona's Economy* (April 1986), 1–4; Tom R. Rex, "Record Population Gains Continue," *Arizona Business*, 33 (July/August 1986), 1–4; Phoenix Metropolitan Chamber of Commerce, *Business Formation and Employment Growth in Metro Phoenix: 1980–1985* (Phoenix: Metropolitan Chamber of Commerce, 1986), 3–7; "Maricopa County," *Arizona Labor Market Information Newsletter*, 10 (September 1986), 4–7.

15. *Arizona Republic*, May 19, 1987; *Phoenix Gazette*, May 20, 1987; "Arizona's Changing Labor Force," *Arizona Labor Market Information Newsletter*, 6 (January 1982), 1–3; Nat de Gennaro, "Arizona's Service Industry: An Analysis," *Arizona Labor Market Information Newsletter*, 9 (May 1985), 1–4; Don

Anderson, "Service Employment Growth," *Arizona Labor Market Information Newsletter*, 10 (January 1986), 1–5; Phoenix Metropolitan Chamber of Commerce, *Business Formation and Employment Growth*, 3–7; Douglas Kukino, "Arizona's Growing Service Sector," in Bernard Rowan, ed., *Arizona's Changing Economy: Trends and Prospects* (Phoenix: Commerce Press, 1986), 107–30; Rex, "Fifth Year of Expansion," 1–5.

16. *Phoenix Gazette*, January 5, 1981, January 8 and February 4, 1987; *Arizona Republic*, March 16, 1986; Timothy S. Mescom and Sheila A. Adams, "Arizona: An Incubator Economy," *Arizona Business*, 28 (September 1980), 3–11; Robert Berg, "Manufacturing in Arizona," in Rowan, ed., *Arizona's Changing Economy*, 131–48; Phoenix Metropolitan Chamber of Commerce, *Business Formation and Employment Growth*, 3–7; Ron Simon, "Jobs in the High Tech Industries," *Arizona Labor Market Information Newsletter*, 7 (June 1983), 1–3; "High Technology: Growth Industry for Arizona," *Arizona Progress*, 40 (May 1985), 1–5; Lee R. McPheters, *High Technology Manufacturing: The Economic Impact in Maricopa County* (Tempe: Arizona State University, 1987), 1–10; Philip L. Harrison, "High Tech Gambling," *Arizona Living*, 16 (July 1985), 28–31; Phoenix Economic Growth Corporation and the Fantus Company, *Phoenix: A Blueprint for Growth* (Phoenix: City of Phoenix, 1986), 16–19, 31–33, *passim*.

17. *Phoenix Gazette*, October 7, 1980, April 15, 1984, October 2, 1986, January 8, 1987; *Arizona Republic*, January 15, 1987; "Metro Tourist Boom Continues," *Arizona Progress*, 39 (August 1984), 1–3; "Tourism Activity Accelerates," *Arizona Progress*, 40 (August 1985), 1–3; Stephen K. Happel, Timothy D. Hogan, and Deborah Sullivan, "The Social and Economic Impact of Phoenix Area Winter Residents," *Arizona Business*, 30 (First Quarter 1983), 3–10; Jacqueline Fifield, Stephen K. Happel, and Timothy D. Hogan, "Valley's Winter Residents Spend $381 Million," *Arizona Business*, 33 (June 1986), 1–4.

18. *Arizona Republic*, November 23, 1980, September 23, 1986; "The Future of Crop Agriculture in Arizona," *Arizona Progress*, 36 (April 1981), 1–4; Luke Air Force Base, *Luke AFB Economic Resource Impact Statement* (Luke AFB, 1984), iii, 29–30; Jeffrey D. Bowman, "Agribusiness—an Industry in Transition," *Arizona Labor Market Information Newsletter*, 9 (December 1985), 1–5; James E. Walters, "The Changing Fields: Agriculture's Future Tied to Diversification," *Phoenix*, 21 (August 1986), 118–21.

19. *Arizona Republic*, March 7, 1984, February 2 and 9, 1987; *Phoenix Gazette*, June 19, 1986; *Greater Phoenix Business Journal*, August 11, 1986.

20. *Arizona Republic*, February 25, 1982, January 1, 1987; *Phoenix Gazette*, June 14, 1986; *Greater Phoenix Business Journal*, February 16, 1987; Margaret T. Hance, "Phoenix—My Kinda Town," *PSA Magazine* (April 1982), 74, 76; Richard Louv, *America II: The Book That Captures Americans in the Act of Creating the Future* (New York: Penguin Books, 1983), 47–64; Edward Abbey, *The Journey Home: Some Words in Defense of the American West* (New York: Dutton, 1977), 146–57.

21. *Arizona Republic*, November 19, 1985, June 11, 1986, January 25, 1987.

22. *Phoenix Gazette*, August 6, 1980, October 25, 1985, November 14, 1986; *Arizona Republic*, December 19, 1984; City of Phoenix, *Phoenix Planning Issues* (Phoenix: City of Phoenix, 1982), *passim*; *Phoenix Concept Plan 2000* (Phoenix:

City of Phoenix, 1979), *passim*; City of Phoenix, *Phoenix General Plan, 1985–2000* (Phoenix: City of Phoenix, 1985), *passim*; Robert J. Early, "Phoenix," *Phoenix*, 21 (November 1986), 224–28.

23. *Arizona Republic*, June 7, 1984, March 8, 1985, April 7, 1986; *Phoenix Gazette*, November 1, 1986, March 21, 1987; *New Times*, March 28–April 3, 1984; Terry Goddard, *State of the City and Budget Message, 1985* (Phoenix: City of Phoenix, 1985), 7–18; Goddard, *State of the City and Budget Message, 1986*, 5–6, 18–20; Peter Russell, "Downtown's Downturn: A Historical Geography of the Phoenix Central Business District, 1890–1986" (M.A. thesis, Arizona State University, 1986), 117–30; Central Phoenix Redevelopment Agency, *Downtown Phoenix: A Vision of the Valley Center* (Phoenix: The Agency, 1980), 4–39; Nora Burba, "Camelback Corridor," *Phoenix*, 15 (May 1980), 112–18; Vicky Hay, "Dome, Sweet Dome?" *Phoenix*, 21 (July 1986), 51–55, 59.

24. *Arizona Republic*, October 2, 1983, February 19, 1984, February 20, July 14 and 29, October 9 and 29, November 13, 1985; *New Times*, May 22–28, October 3–8, 1985; Doug MacEachern, "Papago Lost? The Story of the Battle for a Freeway," *Phoenix*, 17 (February 1982), 95–99; Carole Novick, "Is Relief Finally in Sight?" *Phoenix*, 20 (August 1985), 137–38; Maricopa County Board of Supervisors, *Special Election, October 8, 1985* (Phoenix: Maricopa County, 1985), 1, 4–10.

25. *Arizona Republic*, October 6, 1984, March 28, 1986; *Phoenix Gazette*, October 11, 1985, March 29, May 27, September 8 and 15, November 5, 1986; *Greater Phoenix Business Journal*, December 1, 1986; *New Times*, May 14–20, 1986.

26. *Los Angeles Times*, January 3, 1982; *San Francisco Chronicle*, January 31, 1982; *Arizona Republic*, March 1, 1985, November 18, 1986, June 8, 1987; *Phoenix Gazette*, December 1, 1984, December 4, 1985, September 8, 1986, February 12 and March 5, 1987; *Arizona Business Gazette*, August 4, 1986; *Special Election*, 4–10; Michael Derr, "Powder Keg of Impurities," *Phoenix*, 20 (August 1985), 127–29.

27. *Arizona Republic*, November 9, 1982, October 26, 1983, July 14, 1985, January 1, 1987; *Phoenix Gazette*, May 25, 1984, January 7, 1987; Sharon M. Thomas, "Perception of Airport Hazards by Land Users in the Vicinity of Phoenix Sky Harbor International Airport" (Ph.D. dissertation, Arizona State University, 1980), 3–11, *passim*.

28. *Phoenix Gazette*, June 23, 1982, October 1, 1985, April 7 and October 13, 1986, March 6, 1987; *Arizona Republic*, October 10, 1985, May 3 and 23–26, 1986, March 6, 1987; Paul Bracken and Herman Kahn, *A Summary of Arizona Tomorrow* (New York: Arizona Tomorrow, 1979), 15–17; Frank Welsh, *How to Create a Water Crisis* (Boulder, Colo.: Johnson Books, 1985), 13–17, *passim*; Marsha Carter and Roseanne Carter, "The Ups and Downs of Arizona's Water Supply," *Phoenix*, 16 (August 1981), 146–47; Joe Kullman, "On the Waterfront," *Arizona*, 16 (July 1985), 32–35; Ted Schwarz, "Water! Water?" *Phoenix*, 20 (August 1985), 87–89; City of Phoenix, *Phoenix Water Resources Plan, 1985* (Phoenix: City of Phoenix, 1985), 23–82.

29. *Arizona Republic*, December 17, 1986, March 1, 1987; City of Phoenix, *Water Resources Plan*, 23–82; Kullman, "On the Waterfront," 32–35; Candice St. Jacques Miles, "Husbanding Desert Water," *Phoenix*, 17 (August 1982), 100–04.

30. *Phoenix Gazette*, March 28, 1984, July 22, 1985, September 19, 1986; *Arizona Republic*, January 18, June 3 and 5, 1985; *New Times*, February 12–18, 1986; Miles, "Desert Water," 100–04; Carrie Sears Bell, "Trouble in the Tap," *Phoenix*, 19 (August 1984), 88–89, 228.

31. *Arizona Republic*, October 13, 1984, December 6, 1986; *Phoenix Gazette*, January 1 and July 20, 1985.

32. *Phoenix Gazette*, November 23, 1981, March 7, 1984, September 30, 1985, February 27 and March 7, 1987; *Arizona Republic*, November 5, 1982, October 8, 1983, December 19, 1984, August 8, 1985, December 3, 1986, January 28, 1987; *New Times*, August 21–27, 1985; Candice St. Jacques Miles, "Education: Facing Tough Issues," *Phoenix*, 17 (August 1982), 109–12; J. Russell Nelson, *Arizona State University: A Centennial Commitment to Excellence for a New Century* (Princeton: The Newcomen Society, 1985), 20–24; Helene Feger, "What Business Still Has to Learn About Education," *Arizona Trend*, 1 (March 1987), 39–43.

33. *Arizona Republic*, May 28, 1981, July 24, 1983, November 24, 1985, May 4 and August 14, 1986, January 1, March 12 and 21, 1987; *Phoenix Gazette*, November 7, 1984, May 11, 1985, May 30 and August 23, 1986, January 23 and March 7, 1987; *New Times*, June 7–13, 1982, March 4–10, 1987; Michael Dixon, "State of the Arts," *Phoenix*, 21 (March 1986), A3–A6; Anne Stephenson, "Craving for Culture," *Phoenix*, 21 (September 1986), A3–A4.

34. *Phoenix Gazette*, November 5, 1984, December 10, 1986; *Arizona Republic*, August 7, 1982, December 16, 1984, December 7, 1985, December 3, 8, and 19, 1986, January 18 and 23, 1987; *New Times*, March 7–13, 1984, February 27–March 5, 1985, December 3–9, 1986, February 18–24, 1987; Doug MacEachern, "Preserving the Preserves," *Phoenix*, 18 (November 1983), 66–70; Vicky Hay, "Dome, Sweet Dome?" *Phoenix*, 19 (September 1984), 87–89, 142–43.

35. *Phoenix Gazette*, November 18, 1981, June 30, 1982, January 1, 1983, June 24, 1984, November 26, 1986, January 9 and March 21, 1987; *Arizona Republic*, July 26 and August 7, 1982, July 11, 1983, September 6, 1984, December 12, 1985, January 27 and December 28, 1986, February 22, 1987; *New Times*, February 11–17, 1987; Michael Higgins, "Tent City," *Commonweal*, 110 (September 23, 1983), 494–96; The Consortium for the Homeless, *The Homeless of Phoenix* (Phoenix: The Consortium for the Homeless, 1983), 114–17, *passim*; Phoenix South Community Mental Health Center, *Alcohol, Drugs and Mental Health in Arizona* (Phoenix: Phoenix South Community Mental Health Center, 1983), 1–21; Phoenix South Community Mental Health Center, *Arizona's Quality of Life* (Phoenix: Phoenix South Community Mental Health Center, 1986), 1–6; Phoenix South Community Mental Health Center, *Alarming Trends —1986* (Phoenix: Phoenix South Community Mental Health Center, 1987), 1–11.

36. *Arizona Republic*, June 13, 1982, October 16, 1983, October 31, 1986, January 8 and May 16, 1987; *Phoenix Gazette*, December 18, 1984, September 30, 1985, April 8, 1986, January 8 and 26, 1987; *New Times*, December 19–25, 1984, May 1–7, 1985; Vicki Hay, "Calvin Goode: South Phoenix Survivor," *Phoenix*, 19 (April 1984), 57–58.

37. *Arizona Republic*, March 1, 1984, June 16, 1985; *Phoenix Gazette*, January 19, 1983, March 9, 1984, March 16, 1986, April 6, 1987; *New Times*, Decem-

ber 31, 1986–January 6, 1987; Ad Hoc Committee on Human Relations, "The Phoenix Commission on Human Relations: A Promise Unfulfilled" (typescript, City of Phoenix, September 12, 1984), 1–5, 47–58, *passim*; "Partnership in Fair Housing Conference" (typescript, City of Phoenix, May 21, 1986), 8–9; Franklin J. James *et al.*, *Minorities in the Sunbelt* (New York: Oxford University Press, 1984), 62–81, 135–39, *passim*.

38. *Phoenix Gazette*, March 30 and 31, 1983, April 1, 1984, March 13, 1986, March 24, 1987; *Arizona Republic*, February 22 and 27, 1985, March 24 and May 31, 1987; *New Times*, December 19–25, 1984; "Housing Discrimination in Phoenix" (typescript, City of Phoenix, 1986), 1–2; Boye De Mente, "Living Black in Phoenix," *Phoenix*, 17 (September 1982), 102–05, 125–26; Joseph Stocker, "Are Blacks Losing Hard-Won Ground?" *Phoenix*, 20 (May 1985), 24.

39. *Phoenix Gazette*, May 4, 1983, June 14, 1984, January 21, 1985, November 7, 1986, January 1 and 12, February 3, March 9 and 26, 1987; *Arizona Republic*, May 17, 1986, January 4, 17, and 25, March 27, 1987; *New Times*, January 30–February 5, May 4–10, 1985; *Greater Phoenix Business Journal*, March 30, 1987; Mary R. Titcomb, "Americanization and Mexicans in the Southwest: A History of Phoenix's Friendly House" (M.A. thesis, University of California, Santa Barbara, 1983), 95–97; Kris Aaron, "Chicanos por la Causa: Developing Leadership for the Future," *Phoenix*, 19 (December 1984), 101–02, 130–35.

40. *Phoenix Gazette*, May 30 and June 15, 1986, February 23 and March 23, 1987; *Arizona Republic*, February 10 and 17, March 6 and 7, May 23, 1986, January 1, February 4 and 23, March 14 and 24, 1987; *New Times*, November 28–December 4, 1985; Phoenix Indian Center, Inc., *1985 Annual Report* (Phoenix: Phoenix Indian Center, 1985), 1–10; Liebow, "A Sense of Place," 78–93, *passim*.

41. *Phoenix Gazette*, July 30, 1986, January 7, 1987; *Arizona Republic*, March 13 and June 9, 1986, January 8 and March 29, 1987; *Greater Phoenix Business Journal*, December 1, 1986; Patricia Myers, "United They Stand: Partnership Propels East Valley to Powerbroker Status," *Phoenix*, 21 (September 1986), 50–52; Jon Kamman, "Metro Phoenix Soars Toward the Big Time," *Arizona Trend*, 1 (April 1987), 53–59.

42. *Arizona Republic*, December 26, 1984, February 8, 1985, November 2, 1986, January 3 and 27, February 8, April 24 and 29, 1987; *Phoenix Gazette*, February 10, 1983, October 10, 1984, January 23, June 5, October 18, 1985, December 10, 1986, January 1, 7, and 27, 1987; *Arizona Business Gazette*, August 29, 1986; *Greater Phoenix Business Journal*, May 4, 1987; *New Times*, March 19–25, 1986; Myers, "United They Stand," 50–52; Catrien Ross Laetz, "Mesa," *Phoenix*, 21 (November 1986), 229–31.

43. *Phoenix Gazette*, August 14, 1985, June 2, 1986; *Arizona Business Gazette*, November 19, 1986; *New Times*, March 19–25, 1986; Candice St. Jacques Miles, "Tempe: A College Town Grown Up," *Phoenix*, 17 (December 1982), 66–70; Rebecca Mong, "Tempe," *Phoenix*, 21 (November 1986), 234–35.

44. *Arizona Republic*, January 13, 1985, August 9, 1986; *Phoenix Gazette*, August 24, 1982, April 15, 1983, June 2, 1986, January 14 and 27, February 24, March 13, 1987; *Arizona Business Gazette*, October 27, 1986; *New Times*, March 11–17, 1987; Tom Miller, ed., *Arizona: The Land and the People* (Tucson: University of Arizona Press, 1985), 265–69.

45. *Arizona Republic*, December 18, 1983, January 22, 1984, July 9, 1986, January 18, 1987; *Phoenix Gazette*, August 8, 1985, August 27 and December 13, 1986; *Greater Phoenix Business Journal*, August 25, 1986; *New Times*, March 11–17, 1987; Karen Monson, "Scottsdale and the Arts," *Phoenix*, 19 (March 1984), 75–80; Patricia Myers McElfresh, *Scottsdale: Jewel in the Desert* (Woodland Hills, Calif.: Continental Heritage Press, 1984), 57–97; City of Scottsdale, *IBW: Indian Bend Wash* (Scottsdale: City of Scottsdale, 1985), xi–xv, *passim*.

46. *Arizona Republic*, February 6 and November 11, 1985, August 10, 1986, February 15, 1987; *Phoenix Gazette*, June 22, 1984, January 1, 1986, January 23 and March 13, 1987; *Arizona Business Gazette*, December 8, 1986; *Greater Phoenix Business Journal*, February 16, 1987; *New Times*, August 7–13, 1985; Miller, *Arizona: The Land and the People*, 264–65; Dean Smith, "Phoenix's Family of Suburbs," *Arizona Highways*, 60 (October 1984), 60–65; Karen Auge, "Glendale," *Phoenix*, 21 (November 1986), 248–49; City of Peoria, Arizona, *Profile 1985* (Peoria: City of Peoria, 1986), 12–16, *passim*.

47. *Arizona Republic*, January 19, 1985, October 15, 1986, February 11, April 25, May 11 and 17, June 8, 1987; *Phoenix Gazette*, February 28, 1983, October 8, 1984, February 1, 1985, June 25 and July 5, 1986, January 24, February 20, April 25, May 30, June 10, 1987; *Greater Phoenix Business Journal*, February 2 and 23, 1987; *New Times*, January 30–February 5, 1985; Patricia Myers, "Downtown," *Phoenix*, 22 (April 1987), 79–85; John R. Alba, "Maricopa County," *Phoenix*, 21 (November 1986), 239–42; Abbott, *The New Urban America*, 241–56; Zane Miller and Patricia Melvin, *The Urbanization of Modern America* (New York: Harcourt Brace Jovanovich, 1987), 249–50.

ACKNOWLEDGMENTS

I wish to thank all the historians, librarians, and students who have helped me in my work. Special appreciation is due several institutions and the able people who staff them: the Arizona Historical Society, the Arizona State Department of Library, Archives, and Public Records, the Phoenix Public Library, the Tempe Public Library, and the Hayden Library, Arizona State University. The Arizona Collection and the Arizona Historical Foundation, both located in the Hayden Library, proved indispensable.

I am deeply indebted to Michael Konig, Michael Kotlanger, S. J., and the late Geoffrey Mawn, whose Ph.D. dissertations are cited time and again throughout the chapter notes; their spadework helped make this book possible. Also of assistance were Blaine Lamb, Larry Schweikart, Margaret Finnerty, Richard Lynch, Susie Sato, Jim McMillan, Evelyn Cooper, Maria Hernandez, David Introcaso, Christine Marin, Edward Oetting, and Dennis Preisler.

Special thanks go to Evelyn Cooper, Herb and Dorothy McLaughlin, Bob Rink, and Bob Wallace for helping me assemble the photographs. Eventually, the Herb and Dorothy McLaughlin Photographic Collection will be housed in the Arizona Collection, Hayden Library, Arizona State University.

I wish to acknowledge the support of the Arizona State University Faculty Research Grants Program. To the Arizona State University Data/Text Conversion section, Computing Services, I am also indebted.

Finally, I wish to express my gratitude to my wife, Barbara, for her aid and encouragement.

BRAD LUCKINGHAM

INDEX

ABOUT THE AUTHOR

Bradford Luckingham, professor of history at Arizona State University, Tempe, holds a B.S. degree from Northern Arizona University in Flagstaff; an M.A. degree from the University of Missouri, Columbia; and a Ph.D. from the University of California at Davis. Professor Luckingham is the author of *The Urban Southwest: A Profile History of Albuquerque, El Paso, Phoenix and Tucson* (1982) and *Epidemic in the Southwest, 1918–1919* (1984). He also has published articles in numerous journals, among them *Southern California Quarterly*, *Journal of the West*, *Journal of Arizona History*, *Western Historical Quarterly*, and *Journal of Urban History*.